THE GIOVANNI SCHIAVO SERIES 1

THE GIOVANNI SCHIAVO SERIES is, to echo its namesake, "an attempt to rescue from oblivion," the work of the founders of Italian American and Italian Diaspora studies as an academic discipline. The field has expanded greatly, especially during the last twenty-five years of the twentieth century; as a result, a plethora of contemporary works fill the shelves of scholars, readers, and university libraries. However, many of the classics remain out of print. Hence, in the spirit of Giovanni Schiavo, who sought to highlight the experience of Italian Americans' forgotten past, we seek to do the same but with scholarly works on Italian American subjects.

Our mission is to re-shed light on works that are no longer easily accessible or widely read. Plans include the creation of "readers" for some of the field's founders and, hopefully, a collection from contemporary scholars analyzing the founders of the field. We hope you enjoy the current reprint and continue to support our endeavor.

The Italians in America Before the Revolution is the first reprint for this collection. We plan to reproduce two other monographs by Schiavo as part of this collection. Once the key texts of Schiavo are released, the works of other founders of the field will be republished. An abundance of out-of-print materials is on our proverbial radar. Though the field of Italian American studies formalized in the 1960s and 1970s, scholarly material on Italian Americans or Italians in America stretches back to the late 19th century.

The Italians in America
Before the Revolution

THE ITALIANS IN AMERICA BEFORE THE REVOLUTION

Giovanni Schiavo

Introduction by Stephen J. Cerulli

BORDIGHERA PRESS

Philadelphia-based Italian American artist Samantha Pinto designed the portrait of Francis Vigo featured on this book's cover. Giovani Schiavo named his press Vigo Press in honor of Francis Vigo. Schiavo fought to highlight Vigo's role in the American Revolutionary War and to integrate him into Italian American history. In this spirit, we honor Vigo's legacy with his portrait on the covers of the Giovanni Schiavo Collection.

Bordighera Press would like to thank Giovanni Schiavo's granddaughter, Catherine Leonard Ellis, and family for their generosity and permission to reprint this important contribution to Italian American Studies.

Library of Congress Control Number: 2023931718

Published by
BORDIGHERA PRESS
John D. Calandra Italian American Institute
25 W. 43rd Street, 17th Floor
New York, NY 10036

The Giovanni Schiavo Series 1
ISBN 978-1-59954-204-1

GIOVANNI SCHIAVO, THE GREAT CHRONICLER OF ITALIAN AMERICA

A Critical Re-Introduction

While creating a list of monographs for scholars of Italian diasporas and cataloging the bulk of the works listed on *The Calandra Italian American and Italian Diaspora Studies Bibliography*, I learned about Giovanni Schiavo, an author of numerous volumes on Italians in the United States decades before the dawn of the "white ethnic revival."[1] Impressed by the breadth and quantity of his work, I suggested to the dean of the John D. Calandra Italian American Institute, Anthony J. Tamburri, that *The Italians in America Before the Revolution* necessitated a reprint. It is a primer of Schiavo's career and his final published book. The volume supports contemporary students in their study of Italian diasporic history and is a much-needed re-introduction to the great chronicler of Italian America.[2]

In 1898, Giovanni Schiavo was born in Castellammare del Golfo, Trapani, Sicily, to a family of tailors. He attended *liceo classico,* where he learned Latin, Greek, and French. In 1915, his father immigrated to the United States. In 1916, Schiavo followed his father to Baltimore with the rest of his family and, a few weeks after immigrating began teaching Italian at the Berlitz School of

---

1 A period of "awakening" for hyphenated European Americans as a social group with a history. For a primary source on this see, *Rise of the Unmeltable Ethnics: The New Political Force of the Seventies* by Michael Novak. For a critical historical analysis see, *Creating the New Right Ethnic in 1970s America: The Intersection of Anger and Nostalgia* by Richard Moss.

2 The crux of Schiavo's career is several fold: cataloguing and documenting primary sources related to Italian Americans, scholarship on the historical presence of Italians in North America, criticism of Italian Americans and Americans for their lack of knowledge of this history, and ethno-cultural critiques of Italian American institutions and leaders.

Languages. In 1917, he attended Baltimore City College, a high school, to master his English, and subsequently enrolled at John Hopkins University, where he completed a B.A. in 1919. While there, Schiavo was a part of the Student Army Training Corps, which granted him US citizenship. Even though he graduated in 1919, Schiavo continued to attend various university courses into the 1930s.[3]

Schiavo's early career saw him oscillate between different jobs. In 1920, he took a job as a reporter for *The Baltimore Sun*. He would return to journalism many times over the years. However, in the early 1920s, he came across an opportunity on Wall Street as a clerk. During this time, Schiavo enrolled in several graduate courses at New York University and published his writings in various outlets. Between 1923 and 1926, Schiavo worked for American Express. Part of his responsibilities included visiting Italian communities across the country and encouraging them to send remittances home through American Express. In 1927, he went on to work for an importer in Chicago. While there, he became the publisher and editor of *Il Corriere di Wisconsin*.

In 1928, Schiavo published his first book on Italian America, *The Italians in Chicago*, with a preface penned by social reformer and co-founder of Hull House Jane Addams. In 1929, he continued his localized studies of Italian Americans with *The Italians in Missouri*. His academic merits landed him a fellowship at New York University, where he was part of a team that studied the New York Boys Club of East Harlem. His intellectual pursuits continued into 1930 when Schiavo enrolled as a Ph.D. candidate in International Law and Foreign Relations at Columbia

---

3 For more detailed biographical information on Schiavo see: Belfiglio, Valentino J. "The Christopher Columbus of Italian-American Studies." *Italian Americana*, FALL/WINTER 1979, Vol. 5, No. 1 (FALL/WINTER 1979), pp. 37-45; Pane, Remigio U. 1985. "In Memoriam: Giovanni Schiavo (1898-1983)" In *Italians and Irish in America*, by Francis X. Femminella, 1-11. Staten Island: The American Italian Historical Association; Cavaioli, Frank J. 2011. "Giovanni Schiavo, the pioneer of Italian American Studies." *CiaoAmerica*. October 11. http://www.ciaoamerica.net/news/2011/giovanni-schiavo-by-frank-cavaioli.html.

University. Passing his orals in 1931, he was awarded a fellowship to study Italian International Law and wrote his thesis on Benito Mussolini's foreign policy. However, Schiavo never completed the program due to a lack of funding. Unable to publish his thesis, a requirement for the degree at the time, he was unable to complete the doctorate. He attributed this failure to the financial fallout of the Great Depression.[4]

Nevertheless, Schiavo continued chronicling and writing about Italian Americans, in major outlets such as *Il Progresso Italo-Americano*. Schiavo arguably became the first historian of Italian America with *The Italians in America Before the Civil War*, self-published by his publishing house, The Vigo Press, in 1934.[5] It was a massive 399-page historical monograph on Italians in America, at a time, when the bulk of the scholarship, on Italian Americans, was analyzing behaviors of recent immigrants and their offspring. Many assumed, at the time, that there was no Italian American history before the 1870s. Schiavo disproved the notion by establishing an Italian American historical canon. As he noted, his book was "an attempt to rescue from oblivion the names of the Italians who helped to build the Republic," which he did by providing biographical information on figures such as the so-called "Great Navigators," the Tonti brothers, Francesco Vigo, and Filippo Mazzei, among others.[6] This was the first of many books published by The Vigo Press.[7] This

---

4   Belfiglio, Valentino J. "The Christopher Columbus of Italian-American Studies." I could not find more information on this manuscript or its title.

5   Cavaioli, Frank J. 2011. "Giovanni Schiavo, the pioneer of Italian American Studies." *CiaoAmerica*. October 11. http://www.ciaoamerica.net/news/2011/giovanni-schiavo-by-frank-cavaioli.html.

6   Schiavo, Giovanni. 1934. *The Italians in America Before The Civil War*. New York: The Vigo Press. 1

7   For notes on his contemporaries, see Schiavo's multivolume series *Italian-America Who's Who: A Biographical Dictionary of Italian-American Leaders*. For larger histories, see *Italian-American History: Volume 1: Italian-American History* & *Volume II: The Italian Contribution to the Catholic Church in America* (1947), and *Four Centuries of Italian-American history* (1952). For biographies *see Philip Mazzei: One of America's Founding Fathers* (1951) and *Antonio Meucci: Inventor of the Telephone* (1958).

moment ignited Schiavo's transformation into the great chronicler of Italian America.[8]

Towards the end of his life, and posthumously, Schiavo received much praise. Peter Sammartino, one of the founders of Fairleigh Dickerson University and its first president, wrote in the *Italian-American Digest*, "Giovanni Schiavo was a combination of a historian and investigative reporter . . . No one has approached him in the sheer quality of his investigations into the role of Italians in America, in the United States or anywhere in the world."[9] Valentine J. Belfiglio, a professor at the Texas Woman's University, bestowed Schiavo with the title "The Columbus of Italian American Studies," describing him as one who "has done more than any other person to uncover and explore the contributions of Italians to America. He is the founder of Italian-American history."[10] In a letter to historian Dominic Candeloro, Rudolph Vecoli, one of the founders of what is now the Italian Americans Studies Association [IASA] and its first president, described Schiavo as "a true pioneer of Italian American historiography when there was no field and (when) it had no academic standing."[11] In a paper delivered to the American Italian Historical Association [now IASA], Frank J. Cavaioli called Schiavo "the pioneer of Italian American Studies," who "provided a major thrust in the battle to overcome stereotypical images of this large ethnic

---

8   I choose the noun *chronicler* for a few specific reasons. As historian, a scholar who analyzes primary sources through a methodology and reaches a synthesis or original argument, Schiavo is rather lacking. As a chronicler of the Italian American experience, however, no single individual has documented as much in terms of temporal or geographical scope. He is arguably still the first historian of Italian Americans, despite the limits of his scholarship.

9   Gesualdi, Louis J. 2012. *The Italian/American Experience: A Collection of Writings*. Lanham: University Press of America. 37

10   Belfiglio, Valentino J. "The Christopher Columbus of Italian-American Studies."

11   The ANNOTICO Report, and Dominic Candeloro. 2005. "Giovanni Schiavo and Professor Rudolph Vecoli: Their Legacies: Pride vs Anti-Filiopietism." ItaliaUSA.com. May 14. http://www.italiausa.com/ra/2137.html. Brackets mine.

group," and that "contemporary scholars owe a debt of appreciation . . . for his pioneering work in Italian American Studies."[12]

Conversely, according to some scholars, Schiavo is not without criticism. Despite merited praise, his scholarship has notable limits. In 1935, in a review of *The Italians in America Before the Civil War*, Carl Wittke, a prominent historian of US immigration, criticized Schiavo, arguing that he "never quite succeeds in arranging . . . [his chapters] in anything like a logical narrative pattern, which might present something of a synthesis of Italian influences upon America. There is too much about individual immigrants and hardly anything about the life of Italian groups."[13] This lack of social history, scholarly synthesis, and hyper-focus on individuals was a pattern that continues into this book – his final publication. According to historian Stefano Luconi, Schiavo's "filiopietistic approach has long bulked large in the examination of the early stages of the Italian experience in North America."[14] This filiopietistic methodology is especially noticeable when Schiavo hones in on colonial leaders and explorers, such as Filippo Mazzei and Christopher Columbus. Luconi extends this assessment further when he notes that scholarship included in *"the Italians in America Before the Civil War* . . . has engaged itself almost exclusively in a hagiographic defense of Italian immigrants . . . to counter negative stereotypes of Italians as foreigners incapable of assimilation into their adoptive country."[15] With that in mind, it is evident that Schiavo's contributions are paradoxical. Where on the one hand, he examines the unappreciated history of the Italian American contribution to the United States, thus lifting a veil off a buried ethnic history; on the other, said history lacks a critical

---

12   Cavaioli, Frank J. "Giovanni Schiavo, the pioneer of Italian American Studies."

13   Wittke, Carl. 1935. "Reviewed Work: The Italians in America before the Civil War by Giovanni Schiavo." *The Mississippi Valley Historical Review* Vol. 21, No. 4 (March 1935) 560-562.

14   Luconi, Stefano. "Reviewed Work(s): Building Little Italy: Philadelphia's Italians before Mass Migration by Richard N. Juliani." *Italica*, Vol. 76, No. 1 (Spring, 1999) 121-122.

15   Ibid.

examination, and in most cases, is a wholesale celebration, instead of a scholarly analysis, of those contributions.

While the importance and watershed of Schiavo's work is undeniable, his biases towards *italianità* and rose-colored sentiments of North American history require acknowledgment and reckoning. In a public debate, with journalist Luigi Barzani Jr., Schiavo outright denied the existence of the Mafia.[16] A great irony, considering, at that time, Carmine Gallante was one of the most prominent *Mafiosi* in America, whose family also hailed from Castellammare del Golfo.[17] He also uncritically celebrated the United States and European colonization of North America and fought to inject Italian Americans, *en masse,* into this history. In the 1930s and 1940s, this notion is debatably defensible due to the lack of common understanding and scholastic knowledge of Indigenous American history and the brutal processes of colonization. However, by 1976, with the rise of the American Indian Movement [founded in 1968] and its literature, awareness of the brutality of North American colonization was well documented, easily available, and known among academia and the American public.[18] Another example of his bias towards *italianità* is apparent in Schiavo's repudiation of pre-Columbian Viking presence in North America as "purely academic" since it decenters the Italian-born Christopher Columbus in history.[19]

Despite the limits of his scholarship, Schiavo made many persuasive points on the inadequacies of Italian America. Much of Schiavo's ethno-cultural commentary remains applicable today. Observing the lack of histories on Italian Americans, in 1934, Schiavo argued, "The writing of American History for a long time was monopolized by Eastern college professor of Teutonic descent

---

16   Barzani, Luigi, and Giovanni Schiavo. 1969. "Sicilians and Others." *The New York Review.* September 04. https://www.nybooks.com/articles/1969/12/04/sicilians-and-others-2/.

17   Sullivan, Kevin B. 2014. "When Bushwick Was Bonanno." Narratively.com. November 11. https://narratively.com/when-bushwick-was-bonanno/

18   See *The Italians in America Before The Revolution* and Chapters II through XI in *The Italians in America Before The Revolution.*

19   Schiavo. *The Italians in America Before the Revolution.* 43

who . . . were more . . . interested in the doings of Anglo-Saxon settlers than in those other immigrant groups."[20] In mainstream academia, the issue somewhat remains, in part due to the lack of Italian American studies programs at the doctoral level, where the creation of such historical scholarship could bloom.

In this volume, Schiavo also lamented that Italian Americans have an "inferiority complex."[21] He contends, "Such inferiority complex could have been eradicated a long time ago if the Italians had had the benefits of an enlightened leadership like that of the Jews in America, plus their splendid philanthropy and spirit of co-operation."[22] This argument resonates today. For instance, not a single major Italian American organization or group is pushing to sponsor a doctoral-level Italian American studies program.[23] In an interview, when asked for advice on how to conduct research in Italian American studies, Schiavo exclaimed, "If you want to write anything about the Italians the first thing you have to do is to study the language. Learn Italian history and Italian geography. Go to Italy and see things for yourself."[24] One would imagine that this is a prerequisite for "enlightened leadership" as well.

Along with being a primer of Schiavo's opus, this reprinting is one of utility and re-introduction. John Viola, former president of the National Italian American Foundation [NIAF] and co-host of the

---

20   Schiavo. *The Italians in America Before the Civil War.* 1

21   Schiavo. *The Italians in America Before the* Revolution. 3. The introduction is debatably the most important section of the book, because it contains suggestions and critiques that remain relevant in 2022.

22   Ibid.

23   For more on this see: Tamburri, Anthony Julian. 2021. "More Graduate Italian-American Studies to Bridge the Gap of Our Cultural Knowledge." *La Voce Di New York.* March 04. https://www.lavocedinewyork.com/en/arts/2022/03/04/more-graduate-italian-american-studies-to-bridge-the-gap-of-our-cultural-knowledge/ and Tamburri. 2022. "Where Ignorance Reigns, Life Is Lost: The Dangers of Neglecting History." Anthony's News Letter. https://anthonyjuliantamburri.substack.com/p/where-ignorance-reigns-life-is-lost. August 01.

24   Belfiglio. 256

Italian American Podcast, demonstrates an example of this utility in a piece he wrote on Salvatore Catalano, noting, "it was one of these rare texts, long ago purchased at a collectible bookstore . . . which . . . lead me to the answers I sought. Giovanni Schiavo's . . . '*The Italians in America Before the Civil War*' provided two whole chapters of clarification and expansive new details."[25] May this book, too, provide such illumination and launch greater research worthy of graduate dissertations.

The necessity of re-introduction is two-fold. There has not been any republication of Schiavo's volumes, in almost a quarter of a century, since the reprint of *Four centuries of Italian-American History* in 2000. However, perhaps more importantly, much of Schiavo's critical commentary on Italian America remains pertinent. For these reasons, we believe that Giovani Schiavo deserves a critical re-introduction. From here, scholars of the Italian diaspora can continue Schiavo's endeavors and dig deeper into the figures, facts, and events presented in this book. *The Italians in America Before the Revolution* is the optimal initial re-introduction to the work of Giovani Schiavo, the great chronicler of Italian America.

Stephen J. Cerulli

The John D. Calandra Italian American Institute
Queens College, City University of New York
New York, NY
January 2023

---

25   Viola, John M. "The Curious Case of Salvatore Catalano." *Ambassador* Vol. 27, Iss. 3. (Spring 2016) 44-48.

BIBLIOGRAPHY

Barzani, Luigi, and Giovanni Schiavo. 1969. "Sicilians and Others." *The New York Review*. September 04. https://www.nybooks. com/articles/1969/12/04/sicilians-and-others-2/.

Belfiglio, Valentino J. "Reviewed Work: The Italians in America before the Revolution by Giovanni Schiavo." *Italian Americana* Vol. 3, No. 2 (SPRING/SUMMER 1977) 265-266.

_____. "The Christopher Columbus of Italian-American Studies." *Italian Americana*, FALL/WINTER 1979, Vol. 5, No. 1 (FALL/ WINTER 1979), pp. 37-45

Capozzola, Richard A. 2003. *Five Centuries of Italian American History*. Altamonte Springs: Five Centuries Books.

Cavaioli, Frank J. 2011. "Giovanni Schiavo, the pioneer of Italian American Studies." *CiaoAmerica*. October 11. http://www. ciaoamerica.net/news/2011/giovanni-schiavo-by-frank-cavaioli. html.

Cerulli, Stephen and Paolo Giordano. 2021. "The Calandra Italian American and Italian Diaspora Studies Bibliography." *Calandra Institute*. https://calandrainstitute.org/research-and-education/ the-calandra-italian-american-and-italian-diaspora-studies-bibliography/

Del Giudice, Richard. 1988. *Giovanni E. Schiavo Papers, 1874-1983*. New York: Center for Migration Studies.

Gesualdi, Louis J. 2012. *The Italian/American Experience: A Collection of Writings*. Lanham: University Press of America.

Luconi, Stefano. "Reviewed Work(s): Building Little Italy: Philadelphia's Italians before Mass Migration by Richard N. Juliani." *Italica,* Spring, 1999, Vol. 76, No. 1 (Spring, 1999) 121-122.

Moss, Richard. 2017. *Creating the New Right Ethnic in 1970s America: The Intersection of Anger and Nostalgia.* Madison: Fairleigh Dickinson University Press

Novak, Michael. 1972. *Rise of the Unmeltable Ethnics: The New Political Force of the Seventies.* New York: Macmillan

Pane, Remigio U. 2000. "Schiavo, Giovanni Ermengildo." In *The Italian American Experience: An Encyclopedia,* by Salvatore J LaGumina, Frank J Cavaioli, Salvatore Primeggia and Joseph A. Varacalli, 150. New York: Garland Publishing Inc.

_____. 1985. "In Memoriam: Giovanni Schiavo (1898-1983)" In *Italians and Irish in America,* by Francis X. Femminella, 1-11. Staten Island: The American Italian Historical Association.

Schiavo, Giovanni. 1934. *The Italians in America Before the Civil War.* New York: The Vigo Press.

_____. 1976. *The Italians in America Before the Revolution.* New York: The Vigo Press.

_____. 1949. "Illiteracy." The New York Times, December 18: 171.

Sullivan, Kevin B. 2014. "When Bushwick Was Bonanno." Narratively.com. November 11. https://narratively.com/when-bushwick-was-bonanno/

The ANNOTICO Report, and Dominic Candeloro. 2005. "Giovanni Schiavo and Professor Rudolph Vecoli: Their Legacies: Pride vs Anti-Filiopietism." ItaliaUSA.com. May 14. http://www.italiausa.com/ra/2137.htm

Tamburri, Anthony Julian. 2021. "More Graduate Italian-American Studies to Bridge the Gap of Our Cultural Knowledge." *La Voce*

Di New York. March 04. https://www.lavocedinewyork.com/
en/arts/2022/03/04/more-graduate-italian-american-studies-to-
bridge-the-gap-of-our-cultural-knowledge/

_____. 2022. "Where Ignorance Reigns, Life Is Lost: The Dangers
of Neglecting History." Anthony's News Letter. https://
anthonyjuliantamburri.substack.com/p/where-ignorance-
reigns-life-is-lost. August 01.

Viola, John M. "The Curious Case of Salvatore Catalano." *Ambassador*
Vol. 27, Iss. 3. (Spring 2016) 44-48.

Wittke, Carl. 1935. "Reviewed Work: The Italians in America
before the Civil War by Giovanni Schiavo." *The Mississippi Valley
Historical Review* Vol. 21, No. 4 (March 1935) 560-562.

FOREWORD

Although this volume includes a few pioneers who came between 1783 and 1800, the word "REVOLUTION" is used because the reader would more easily identify that period.

Some of the chapters, furthermore, are reprinted from my previous works, especially *Italian-American History*, Vol. I, 1947, Vol. II, 1949, and *Four Centuries of Italian-American History*, 1952. Most of them are revised and updated, particularly the bibliography. In some cases, as in the chapters about Vigo, Mazzei, Niza, Vespucci, I have re-evaluated their place in American history, or at least modified it or clarified it. Nevertheless, my study on Mazzei published in 1951 (54 large pages, with three photographs, 44 facsimiles, and 244 footnotes — not to be confused with my 7-page chapter in my book, *Four Centuries* published a year later) still remains the only scholarly work on Mazzei to this day — until a copy of the first article by Mazzei, as translated by Jefferson, signed "Furioso" and inserted as a supplement in the *Virginia Gazette* is found, here or abroad. But I have my doubts, as explained in Chapter 21.

I have added three Appendices because I am fed up with the raids on my books by a pack of petty thieves who have been ransacking them for over thirty years, palming off as the fruit of their own research what has taken me over forty years of hard labor in many parts of the world, untold sacrifices and God only knows how many thousands of dollars. A little fortune which, if invested in buying and selling potatoes, would have made me rich.

The fact is, as I have shown in Appendix C, that practically nothing about the Italian pioneers in America was known before I came along with my 1934 book and, even before that, with my 1930 articles in *Atlantica* magazine. And that is true not just of the names, but especially of the illustrations which took me years and years to locate and thousands of dollars to have photographed. Thus, thanks to my intellectual honesty, whereby I gave full credit to the institutions and organizations that provided me the copies, anybody today can obtain the same copies with only a few dollars, giving the same credit I have given in my *Four Centuries*. But where would the indefatigable researcher have known where to look for those documents and illustrations, if I had not made those sources known to the world?

As for my work, I don't have anyone to thank. Not one Italian-American society, civic organization, fraternal association, foundation, individual, has given me a plugged nickel.

Finally, I want to pay tribute to my late wife, Anne Maher Schiavo, the most patient woman in the world, without whose enduring understanding and love my books could not and would not have been written.

GIOVANNI SCHIAVO

February 12, 1976.

INTRODUCTION

Some writers, including at least two of Italian origin, are inclined to believe that Italian immigrants were too few to have played a significant role in American history or civilization before the mass immigration of 1880, which in itself is a faulty premise because brawn can hardly be compared with brains. As, for instance, in the case of Professor Alexander De Conde, the author of a lopsided book, *Half-Bitter, Half-Sweet* (1972) which is not, by any stretch of the imagination, a solid history of Italian-Americans as people, as proclaimed by *The New York Times Book Review* in supreme ignorance of the subject. It is, instead, primarily a history of the diplomatic relations between Italy and the United States, with a cursory survey of immigrant life in America, a field beyond his specialization. But this is not the place to dissect that work. At any rate, according to Professor De Conde, the Italians in Colonial America did not amount to anything simply because Professor Marraro noted in "several articles" that the influence of the Italians or of Italian culture in early America did not amount to much. Which, of course, is nonsense, as the present volume amply demonstrates. Anyway, Professor Marraro wrote only two brief articles on early America (that is, before 1800), one on the Italians in New York and the other on the Italians in Philadelphia, both following what I had written in my 1934 book, *The Italians in America Before the Civil War*, repeating much of what I had written, but mentioning my book, as the chief source, only in his Philadelphia article, as indicated in his footnotes. Enough to say that as late as 1942, according to Professor Marraro, Mazzei's role was principally that of Virginia's envoy to Europe. Professor Richard Garlick, likewise, held that Mazzei's influence was local, limited to what is today Albemarle County, Virginia. But on this point see Chapter 21 in the present volume.

Thus, Professor De Conde ignored such gigantic figures as Father Chino, Tonti, Vigo and Mazzei, with fleeting reference to Ceracchi, Traetta and a few other Italians, all of whom I first revealed in my 1934 book and further illustrated with several facsimiles in my *Four Centuries of Italian-American History* (1952). Professor De Conde, to be sure, does mention both Vigo and Mazzei, but in both cases he has simply missed the bus. Vigo, for instance, was not an explorer and as for Mazzei the Professor simply does not know what it is all about. But see Chapters 21 and 22 in the presente volume.

1

Be that as it may, according to Professor De Conde, unless I am mistaken, and other professors (I am sure about them) the real contribution to America was made by the 5,000,000 immigrants who came over after 1800, another mistake, because no five million Italians ever came to America, if we have to start from 1492 and end with the present year, 1976. Five million Italians were admitted, that is true, but from 15 to 20 percent of those who were admitted had been in the country before and in some cases were counted six or seven times, depending on the number of times they had left the country and re-entered.

On the other hand, some writers are inclined to believe that the immigrants who came after 1880 were to a very large extent little more than beasts of burden. As Professor-journalist Giuseppe Prezzolini put it in his book, *I Trapiantati,* it is true that the Italians built thousands of miles of railroad track, that they dug sewers, paved street, swept them, collected garbage, built highways and buildings of all types, mined coal and copper and iron, worked in steel mills, loaded and unloaded ships and railroad cars, that they made shoes and clothes, pianos and ice boxes; in a word, it is true that they produced billions and billions of dollars of goods of all kinds, as Professor Commons pointed out in one of his books after he had seen Italian and Jewish workers plying at their trades. All that is true, says Giuseppe Prezzolini, but what would the millions of Italians have done without the engineers, the managers, the entrepreneurs, the capitalists, who provided the brains and the capital necessary to keep the ball rolling?

Thus, if Professor De Conde and author Prezzolini were right, Americans of Italian extraction would have nothing to celebrate in 1976. I should mention here that Signor Prezzolini tried in 1933 to get together a book on *Italy and the Italians in Washington's Time* (a collection of five essays — 132 pages in all) which bombed out with the result that he got on his hind legs when my book came out a year later and was welcomed with raving reviews which he ignored and even denied. But see Appendix C in the present volume.

Sixty years of continuous contact with the Italians in America to this very day, January 6, 1976 (I landed at Ellis Island on January 6, 1916) have convinced me that, without belittling the contribution of labor, what counts in the long run is quality and not quantity. Thus, as I see it, just four men, Fr. Chino, Tonti, Mazzei and Vigo, exerted greater influence on American history and civilization than hundreds of thousands of indentured servants or inarticulate people, just as one hundred men, from Adams to Washington, did more to mould America's destiny than three million white Americans at the start of the Revolution.

The hard fact is that per capita, that is, in proportion to their number in the country at any time, whether during the Revolution or since 1900, the Italians have contributed as much as any other ethnic group, including the Anglo-Saxons. Yet, that is not the point.

As I see it, the chief problem of the Italians in America has always been and still is their fathomless inferiority complex, due in part to discrimination and prejudice (for which the Italians have been and still are largely responsible) which has kept them in no small measure from the mainstream of American life. Such inferiority complex could have been eradicated long time ago if the Italians had had the benefit of an enlightened leadership like that of the Jews in America, plus their splendid philanthropy and spirit of co-operation, which are still absent among the Americans of Italian extraction of today. What is more discouraging is my belief that there will be no change in the near or distant future. Pleading with the mass media to abandon their scurrilous and nauseating campaign of hatred and prejudice is useless, because the only way would be to do what the Jews have been doing for years, but even then I have my doubts. I see only three ways of changing for the better the image of the Italians in America:

1) Personal contact with Americans of non-Italian extraction, because only through personal contact Americans of Italian extraction can show that they have no horns, like the devil, and not in the sense of the Italian word, *corna* (cuckold); that they are decent, law-abiding, God-fearing citizens. That is, unquestionably the best remedy.

2) Publication of a first class magazine like *Commentary* which would expose the ignorance or bad faith of the mass media, not by ranting, but by correcting facts and demonstrating the falsity of some allegations.

3) Publication of books by serious students, scholars, that is, showing the contributions of Americans of Italian extraction to America's greatness, not only economic but also moral—especially moral. Since the second remedy is rather visionary, this third alternative is quite possible because I am convinced that there are in America today numerous young men and women of Italian origin who are proud of their heritage, not in the sense of those hoodlums who scream about Italian power, or "Italian is beautiful" and similar imbecilities, but in the sense of awareness of one's hereditary values. This can be done, provided one is willing to spend years and years digging and digging, without expectation of any reward, except the feeling of doing some good. As the Blessed De Andreis once wrote to Mother Duchesne of the Sacred Heart in New Orleans, if throughout his many years of labor in the vineyard of our Lord he had succeeded in saving just one soul, he would have considered his life well spent.

What good can those books or articles do? Let me give two illustrations:

Recently, an Italian-American told in a brief piece on the Op-Ed page of The New York Times how his American-born mother used to refer to her own people as "Italians" and to the others as "Americans." That, of course, is not quite correct, because the Italians have always referred to the Jews as Jews and to the Blacks as blacks, not Negroes. Anyway, the Italians always felt that they were strangers in the land, that they did not belong, as one president of the American Historical Association (I think it was Professor Bridenbaugh) put it. And he was right, because for years I felt the same way.

Actually, for years after I became naturalized (3 years after my arrival, because of my service in the American Army—a volunteer, by the way) I hesitated to refer to our founding fathers as "our," because I felt that the Italians had done nothing to create the American republic. It was only later, when I began to dig into that unexplored mine that still is the story of the Italians in America before the Civil War, that I acquired confidence in myself as an American, not only by conviction and devotion, but also because I had learned that I belonged, and, as an American of Italian origin or birth, I had as much right as anybody else, historically or otherwise.

One more illustration:

Shortly after World War Two, when I had an office at 120 Liberty Street, in New York City, where the World Trade towers now are (incidentally, a century before the first Italian newspaper in America, *Eco d'Italia*, had its office only a few doors away), a young man dropped in to sell me some service or publication of the U.S. Chamber of Commerce. He was a college graduate, as I learned later, clean-cut, of striking personality. During our conversation he asked me my name and when I told him he stopped in his tracks. "Are you," he asked me, "the author of that book on the Italians in America before the civil war?" When I answered in the affirmative, he continued, "You don't know how much good you did us, that is, me and my fellow-students of Italian descent at Villanova. The Irish students there were picking on us on every possible occasion, good-naturedly, of course, but we still felt like strangers in our own land. Then your book came along and all we had to do after that was to wave your book under their noses. The teasing stopped then and there."

To conclude, I wrote this book to give all Americans of Italian descent the knowledge that their ancestors, too, helped to build America, so that they can say "I am an American" holding their heads high.

4

1

NO ITALIANS IN AMERICA IN 1776?

At the time of the Declaration of Independence in 1776, there were in the Thirteen Colonies, as well as in the French and Spanish possessions that are now part of the United States, many families of Italian birth or descent. How many, we can't even estimate because of the change of Italian names, such as Martino in Martin (French or Spanish), or Martineau (French), or Sapri into Sapry. Yosti of St. Louis, for instance, was a native of Piedmont, but I haven't figured out yet what his name was in Italy. I know, however, that the name Yost, Yohst, Yoest, Youst, was one those represented by more than 100 heads of families in the 1790 census, especially in Pennsylvania, New York, Maryland, and other southern states. Since the Missouri Yosti (later Yost) was born in Italy, it must be assumed that he Anglicized his name. I mention these facts because of the difficulty of the problem. When we get to the English, as we shall presently see, the question is beyond any speculation.

Of course, my theory regarding the relatively large number of Italians (that is, people of Italian ancestry) in the Thirteen Colonies is disputed by the so-called "experts" of the Bureau of Census and other institutions, who have examined the returns of the 1790 census and reached the conclusion that in 1790 the population was largely of English-Scotch origin (69.2%) followed by the Irish (9.7%), the Germans (8.7%), the Dutch (3.4), the French (1.7%), the Swedes (0.7%), leaving 6.6 percent unassigned. Figuring the white population of 1790 at about 3,200,000, that would leave about 211,000 white residents unaccounted for. A trifle, of course.

What is regrettable about those 1790 estimates, notwithstanding the fact that they have been discredited time and again, is the fact that they are being quoted by people who should know better, simply because they were later studied and approved and published by the American Council of Learned Societies, published in the *Annual Report of the American Historical Association* for the years 1931-1932, which Maldwyn Allen Jones, the author of a so-so book on American immigration, published in 1960 by the University of Chicago Press, calls authoritative (*American Immigration*, p. 327). The fact that Mr. Jones' book is one of the volumes in *The Chicago History of Amer-*

ican Civilization edited by Daniel J. Boorstin, now Librarian of [the Library of] Congress does not impress me in the least. Professor Boorstin is the same professor who said in his book, *The Americans: The Democratic Experience*, New York, 1973, that both Mont Tennes and Al Capone were born in Italy. One might even overlook Capone, but Mont Tennes, the top gambler in America for many and many years! And to say that Prof. Boorstin had spent 25 years at the University of Chicago, where he could easily have found out all about Al Capone (he was born in Brooklyn) and especially Mont Tennes. Prof. Boorstin's book includes other ridiculous and equally erroneous statements about the Italians, which a scholar or a high school girl could have checked without any trouble, but that's another story, which I explain in my bibliography on the Mafia.

Getting back to that 1790 census, the report of the Council of Learned Societies was taken seriously because of the word "learned" which covers a multitude of sins, and has led other people with little time to check the facts to repeat the same garbage, as for instance, in *The World Almanac & Book of Facts* for 1976, page 271, and by other irresponsible people, like Mr. David Brinkley in the first of his three-part N.B.C. program "Life, Liberty and the Pursuit of Happiness" (I almost wrote, "stupidity'") late in October, 1975. Of course, no knowledgeable person takes Mr. Brinkley seriously. But the *World Almanac* and Professor Jones could have noted that those figures have been disputed by scholars who are far more authoritative than Mr. Rossiter, the author of *A Century of Population Growth* (1909), reprinted by the Baltimore Genealogical Society in 1967. The least Professor Jones should have done (and Professor Boorstin should have noted, as editor of the books) was to cite also the report by President Coolidge's Commission which investigated the 1790 eensus reports by Rossiter and Trevor and others, and took exception to their conclusions.

That Commission was headed by Secretaries Hoover (later President), Kellogg, and Davis who, after examining all that had been written on the subject, reached the conclusion that 'the statistical and historical information available raises grave doubts as to the whole value of these computations as a basis for the purpose intended. We therefore cannot assume responsibility for such conclusions under these circumstances." But the American Council of Learned Societies surely did, adding other material, equally worthless, as Prof. Hansen's report. I did not expect Professor Jones to cite my study of the 1790 census in my book, *The Italians in America Before The Civil War*, pp. 338-345. So far as he is concerned, there were no Italians in America before 1790. I should add that the notorious Immigration Quota Act of 1924 was based on those misleading reports.

But how did the "experts" reach their conclusions?

To start with, the enumerators or census takers did not ask anybody their place of birth or national origin, which, at any rate, would have been useless, as few people knew anything about their origins. The enumerators simply put down a name, as it sounded to their ears, ordinarily phonetically, without regard to actual spelling. And that's the only information the "experts", such as Mr. Rossiter and Captain Trevor, had at their disposal. Then they went about trying to determine whether a name looked English or German or Swedish or Dutch, as if the Germans and the Swedes and the Dutch did not often Anglicize their names, as one can learn from H. L. Mencken's masterpiece, *The American Language*.

Here I must refer to two documents which I reproduced in facsimile on page 13 of my book, *Four Centuries of Italian-American History* (1952). The first, at the top, is a facsimile of two pages from a partial list of aliens in London in 1567 in Vol. 82 of the *Publications of the Camden Society*, and the second of two pages from Volume X of the *Huguenot Society Publications* (but see also Vol. XXIII).

The first, lists a number of names, with their nationality at the left (that is, Italians, Dutchmen, Frenchmen, etc.) and whether or not they were "Denizens" or 'Nodenizens", also spelled "Nodenisens", on the same page. Here are some of the names of persons who were listed as Italians, both citizens and aliens:

Jacobina wife to Fraunces de la Fares
Francisco [not Francesco] Lucatello [obviously the well-known Lombard family Locatelli]
Baptiste Fortune marchante
Laurence Gualterott
James Maryan
Bartholmewe Talefere [the well-known Taliaferro who later moved to Virginia — then still an alien in London.]
Gabrielle Brangier
Marke Bos miliner (denizen)
Raphaell Gettye Tailor [an ancestor of the billionaire Getty?] (in those days Italian fashions were popular in London).
Gaspyn Sonhall Physician
Anthony Brusquett Broker
Peter and Jerome sonnes of Fraunces Rose or Ross [name blurred]
Peter Frangilder
John from Canchurche
Jone Delegge [a well-known name in the United States at the present time]

John Regallz, his servaunte
Katheren Osmatrach maid servaunt
Anthonny Counties, the queene man servaunt
Reginald his sonne
Lucas, wif to Anthony Conties [one "n", but two in the preceding listing]
Francis Tissie a poste
Nicholas Degotes merchant
Jacome Van Hust, Androwe Boxe, — his servauntes
Widow Woder
Jasper and Balthasar sojourners
Stephan Jon, broker
Dyno Pickering, broker
John Jones, his servaunt
Jacob Frauncis surgeon
Jane wif to Gales Corner
Aserbo Vilutell merchaunt
Epolito [Ippolito] Lyamount
Askano [Ascanio] Lyamount
Petro Deasidock (?)
Alexander Mynutelie [Minutoli?] broker
Ragustine merchaunt
Jerome Volpe
John Gochmego
Bastian Rise merchaunt
Lyon Sampson
Evangelst [Evangelista]
Domynico
Vincent Gosslgerden merchaunt
Loise Gade
Christian Deshorto.

ALL ITALIANS, strange as it may seem!

From the other list we learn that Grady was born at "Raygusa in in Dolmasio" [Ragusa, now Dubrovnick, in Dalmatia, now Yugoslavia]; that Cornelius Canmore was born at "Luca, a free state in Italy", in England about 42 years, and that "Raphiell Furetti [was] merchant lodgeing with Sr Stephen Gradye, aged about 20 years.b. at Raousa in Dalmatia, a free statt" [note the different spelling as Grady, Raygusa and Dolmasio, of the same name, above]. On another page, also in facsimile on page 13 of my *Four Centuries*, we find the names of three Venetian glassmakers, Barcaluso, Barnarden, Bosse and Frauncis Booteso. In another volume we find the names of other Italians, like

Lambert Garrett, Arnold Giles, Godfey Sokes, Peter Fox [Volpe?] James Flotrye, John Gillam, Giles Corner and many other apparently English names, but actually Italian.

Such being the case, it is hard to understand how the 1790 Census "experts" could classify such names, if found in the 1790 census, as anything but English, although they were unquestionably Italian, as indicated in the reports or returns.

But how could one say whether some names in the same census were Italian or Spanish or Portuguese or French? Oh, I forgot, when the experts were in doubt, they allocated a given name according to the majority of people living in a community. But suppose they came across such names as Revel, or Cavour, or Robilant, would one say that they were French or Italian? What about the Italians who served in Canada and in French regiments in Canada and during the Revolution? How would we know, for instance, that Phinizy was Italian, if I had not found out from one of his descendants?

Thus it is impossible to say how many Italians who came with the French or had settled in Canada and later moved to the Great Lakes region, or to Ohio and Indiana, or came with the Spaniards, and later moved to St. Louis and nearby communities, were counted as French. Did not George Rogers Clark spell Vigo's name as Vague and did not other historians call him a Spanish merchant?

Over and above everything else, since the "experts" left out those names which did not represent at least 100 heads of family, that is, about 225,000 people, as already noted, and supposing that there were 10,000 Italians with not one single name representing at least 100 families, such as Paca, or Bellini, or Taliaferro, none of which is in the printed list, how can one tell whether there were more Italians than Swedes in the thirteen colonies, aside from those in the French and Spanish possessions?

It is therefore preposterous to assume that there were no persons of Italian origin in America before 1790. Personally, I am convinced that there must have been literally thousands.

See also Chapter 6.

In connection with the Immigration Quota Act see the article by Fiorello H. LaGuardia in *Current History Magazine* for November 1928, pp. 228-229. For the full title of the Hansen report, see Chapter 4, in this volume.

2

IN THE THIRTEEN COLONIES

As noted in the preceding chapter, during the second half of the sixteenth century, or about 50 years before Jamestown or Plymouth Rock, there were in England Italians with such names as Fox, Pickering, Gillam, Moore, Fortune, Kennythe, Rise, Pitcher, Benson, and so on. That they were Italians there is no doubt. We do not know, of course, if any of those Italians with strictly English names, or their children, ever came to America. But, if they did, is there an expert in the world who could single out their descendants in the 1790 census? Who, for instance, would have been able to identify one Symn, who died at Warwick River, near Jamestown, in 1623, as an Italian, if we did not find his nationality next to his name? (Hotten, J. C., *The Original List of Persons of Quality*, London, 1874, p. 235.)

By the same token, who can tell us whether the Symn who died in 1623 was related to one Benjamin Symnes, who before 1648 endowed a free school in Virginia "With two hundred acres of land, a good house, forty milch cows and other appurtenances"? (Winsor, *Narrative and Critical History of America*, Vol. III, p. 147.) Another Symnes, incidentally, was a member of the Continental Congress and Chief Justice of New Jersey a century later; his daughter was the wife of President W. H. Harrison. Of course, I am not claiming any relationship between Chief Justice Symnes and the Italian Symn, but, on the other hand, who can deny that there was one? I mention it only as a further proof of how hard it is to tell one's nationality by one's name.

One thing, however, we know; namely, that before and after the Reformation numerous Italians had settled or lived temporarily in England, where some of them married into English families. Some of them were connected with the Catholic Church (before the Reformation); others were artists, musicians, merchants, writers, educators. Men like Cornelio Vitelli, the earliest teacher of Greek at Oxford, or Polydore Virgil, the author of *Historia Anglica*, which he wrote at Henry VII's behest. Others were religious refugees, like Michael Angelo Florio, the father of Montaigne's translator, who was a minister of the Italian church in London in 1550. Other outstanding Italians in England shortly before or during Elizabeth's reign were Acontius, Alberico Gentili (regius professor of civil law, 1587), Petruccio Ubaldini, Sir

Horatio Pallavicino, Cesare Adelmare (the father of Sir Julius Caesar), Thomas Lupo, all men of renown, whose biographical sketches can be found in the British *Dictionary of National Biography*. Another immigrant was one Champanti, the great-grandfather of John Champante, who was appointed Agent of the Province of New York in 1699.

Both the Pallavicino and Caesar families were connected, directly or indirectly, with the establishment of the Virginia Company of London. As shown in the facsimiles in my book, *Four Centuries*, p. 98, Edward Palavicine and Toby Palavicine were shareholders, or "adventurers," in the company. (Toby, in 1606, incidentally, married the daughter of Oliver Cromwell, the Protector's uncle.) Edward Palavicine was one of the commissioners appointed by James I to create a new form of government for Virginia in 1624. Sir Julius Caesar also was appointed a commissioner at the same time. He was a member of the Privy Council, chancellor of the exchequer in 1606, and master of the rolls from 1614 to 1636. He "married Dorcas Martin, sister of Captain John Martin, one of the first councillors at Jamestown and the owner of 'Brandon' on James River. A John Caesar obtained a grant of land in King and Queen County in Virginia in 1690." (*Tyler's Quarterly*, Vol. 8, p. 273.) (On Sir Julius Caesar, the son of Cesare Adelmare, physician to Queen Mary and Elizabeth, and other noted Italians in England in those days, see my book, *The Italians in America Before the Civil War*, Chapter II, pp. 12-28.)

Albino, or Albiano, Lupo, another shareholder of Italian birth or extraction, owned two and a half shares in 1620. At one time he and his wife owned 400 acres of land in Virginia. Lieutenant Lupo, one of the earliest English officers in the Colonies, arrived on the *Swan* in 1610. He was then 40 years old. His wife, Elizabeth, aged 28, came in the *George* in 1616. Their daughter, Temperance Lupo, was born in Virginia in 1620/21. The records show two more Lupos, Philip, aged 42, who arrived in the *George* in 1621, and William who died in Virginia in 1623. (Hotten, *op. cit.*, p. 185 ff.) Incidentally, in the early 1930's a Jewish woman named Lupo, a native of London, had an apartment in the same Brooklyn apartment house in which I was then living.

It should not be necessary here to dwell at length on the Taliaferro family, the Italian origins of which seem to be well established. As early, or as late, as 1786, members of that family knew little about their ancestors, for in that year, George Wythe, the signer of the Declaration of Independence, who had married Elizabeth Taliaferro, asked Thomas Jefferson to trace her ancestors in Italy. Jefferson was at that time in Europe and did all he could to find the right information but, in my opinion, he failed. According to Mr. William B. Mc

11

Groarty (*William and Mary Quarterly*, April 1924, pp. 191, ff.), the family goes back to one Bartolomeo Tagliaferro, a native of Venice who settled in London in the reign of Elizabeth, whom he served as a musician. He died in London in 1602. Most likely he was the same Bartholmewe Talefere whose name I found in the *Return of Aliens in London in 1567*. (See facsimile on page 12 of *Four Centuries*.) His grandson, or great-grandson, was born in 1635 and came to Virginia in 1655. According to Major Lawrence Taliaferro, however, the first Taliaferros to come to America were four brothers, John, Lawrence, James and Francis, who came to Jamestown from Genoa by way of England in 1637. (*Minnesota Historical Society Collection*, Vol. VI, p. 190.) The name was also spelled Taillefer, Toliferro and, especially, Toliver, as in the case of that "Miss Tolliver (Taliaferro) who sang some airs, the words of which were English, but the music was Italian" mentioned by Chastellux in his *Travels*, Vol. II, 384 and 577 (the latter about her sister, Mrs. William Nelson).

Also well known is the Fonda family which is said to have hailed originally from Genoa, by way of Holland, coming to America in 1642. They settled near Albany. (W. A. Williams, *Early American Families*, Philadelphia, 1916, p. 24.) The family soon became so numerous that during the Revolution at least 49 persons named Fonda, Fondas, Fondey, and exclusive of Fonna and Funday, were listed. (*New York in the Revolution*, Office of the State Comptroller, Albany, 1941, Vol. I.)

Another famous pioneer family of Italian extraction was that of the Danas. Francis Dana, a member of the Continental Congress from 1776 to 1778, America's first minister to Russia, and Chief Justice of Massachusetts, did not know much about his Italian origin. Philip Mazzei called his attention to it, as we learn from a letter from Mazzei to Thomas Adams, dated June 10, 1780, now in the archives of the Virginia Historical Society. But Dana, as he noted in a postcript in his own handwriting to Mazzei's letter, did not care. All he was proud of was to be an American. As for his alleged French ancestry (See Spooner, W. F., *Historic Families of America*, Vol. III, p. 47), the name clearly is not of French origin. D'Anna, however, is common in Italy.

The same thing may be said of the name Rossi, which in America occasionally became Ross. Mr. Howard F. Barker, however, is mistaken in considering Rossi a French name, possibly because he found it in some list of French soldiers during the last century. (*Annual Report of the American Historical Association*, 1931, p. 149.) Rossi is nothing but Italian. (Pellegrino Rossi, the dean of the law school of the College de France, was born at Carrara, Italy.)

Were one to look for names that seem of Italian origin, and probably they were, one will find plenty of them in the early records of America. Names like Basse (Jeremiah Basse was governor of New Jersey in the 17th century); Amory; Benzio, a resident of New Haven in 1654; Carrico, in Maryland; Polentine, a burgess at Jamestown in 1624; Claude Ghiselin, who petitioned the King of England in 1621 for a concession in the Virginia Company; et cetera, et cetera.

There are, furthermore, three facts which may account for the immigration of some Italians before the Revolution:

The first, is the trade between Italy and the Colonies, as allowed by Britain; the second, is the number of Italian Protestants who came over either directly from Italy or through France, Britain or other countries; the third, is the law which allowed Catholics to settle in Maryland.

As I have noted in *Four Centuries*, p. 107, Italy imported tobacco and other products and, naturally, there must have been some Italians who jumped ship. They may not have been many at a time, or in a given year, but in a century the number may not have been negligble.

As it is also well-known, Italy had its share of Protestants, as far back as the 11th century, as described in Gioacchino Volpe's book, *Movimenti religiosi e sette ereticali nella società medievale italiana*, Florence, 1922, but there are many books by other authors, before and since Volpe. As I have noted on page 106 of my *Four Centuries*, quite a few Italian Protestants sought refuge in France, later coming to America as Huguenots, such as the Prioleaus of South Carolina, including Elias Priolcau, the grandson of Doge Priuli of Venice, who founded and was first pastor of the Huguenot Church at Charleston in 1687. Other Italian Protestants moved to other colonies, including William Diodati, the grandson of the famous Italian translator of the Bible. He lived in New Haven from 1717 to 1757, where he worked as banker and broker. His daughter married the son of the first Governor Griswold of Connecticut (*op. cit.* p. 107). Of course, there were also the Waldenses, as told in Chapter 6 of the present volume.

Maryland opened her doors to Catholics in 1649, specifically mentioning persons of "French, Dutch or Italian descent," who "either are already planted or shall hereafter come and plant in our said province (*op. cit.* p. 103). See also the following chapters. It is, however, in the parish registers that we find numerous instances of children of Italian extraction, as in the registers of St. Joseph's Church in Philadelphia from 1763 to 1783, where I found such names as Mignati, Cangemy (Cangemi), Orlandy (Orlandi), Orlandino, Palumbo, Morelli, and many more (*op. cit.*, p. 107).

3

THE ITALIANS IN NEW SPAIN

I need not repeat here what I have already said in my books, from *The Italians in Missouri*, 1929, to *The Italians in America Before the Civil War*, 1934, to *Italian-American History*, Vol. II, 1949, to *Four Centuries*, 1952. From the days of Diego Columbus, the son of the Discoverer, to Fra Marco, Father Chino, all the way to Vigo (the Spanish merchant, as he was known), the Italians played a leading role, especially if compared to their number, in Mexico and the West Indies (Cuba, Puerto Rico, etc.) as noted for the early days by Ruth Pike in her book, *Enterprise and Adventure: The Genoese in Seville and the Opening of the New World* (Cornell University Press, Ithaca, N. Y., 1966). See especially Chapters V and VI and the excellent bibliography. I shall recall two of the Italian viceroys in Mexico, Bucareli, of Florentine extraction, the greatest of all viceroys, and Branciforte, Sicilian, who founded the city of Branciforte in California, renamed Santa Cruz in 1845. But then there was Malaspina, and probably Costanso (Costanzo) and Father Crespi, who were in all likelihood Italian, especially Costanso, in part because there is no such name in Spanish, but also because he was an engineer, at a time when Spain's leading engineers and architects, such as Antonelli, were Italian, like her navigators.

It seems well established, thus, that the Italians were among the first colonizers and settlers in the West Indies. For that matter, not long ago, I found an item from Madrid, Spain, in the *Virginia Gazette* for November 21, 1751, dated July 23, according to which the Spanish government was willing to grant special privileges and financial assistance to Europeans, especially Italians, who wanted to emigrate to the Antilles (Cuba, Porto Rico, etc.) to offset the natives who were planning to "shake off the yoke and set up for themselves as the Word is." The government offer specifically mentioned an "offer of Priviliges, Immunities and Pecuniary Assistance to any Italian families who will enter themselves to settle in the King's American Dominions and there follow the same Trades and Occupations by which they maintained themselves at home." The *Virginia Gazette* has no further reference to the plan.

It is well-known, however, that many Italians moved to the West

Indies in the 18th century and from there they moved to New Orleans and later St. Louis and other southern states. That was during the period in which Louisiana belonged to Spain, that is, from 1762 to 1800. In 1803 the United States took over. A number of Italians, it is likewise well-known, joined the Spanish Army and served in New Orleans, like Francis Vigo. That explains why there were so many Italian business and professional men around St. Louis before and shortly after the Revolution, as I have shown in my book on Missouri, but there were many more in New Orleans whose names are not known to this day.

According to Prof. Marcus Hansen (Annex B, p. 360 ff. of the report of the Council of Learned Societies—see page 18), in 1790 there were 25,625 people in the Spanish possessions which are now part of the United States, with 23,000 in the Southwest and 125 in East Florida — but Prof. Hansen does not explain what happened to the immigrants from Minorca (Spain), Greece and Italy who were brought over to Florida by Dr. Turnbull (see Chapter 7). Anyway, neither Professor Hansen nor anybody else could estimate even approximately the population of the Southwest because of the open border along the Rio Grande, with people coming in or going out at all times. Has it not been said that in 1975 there were probably one million illegal aliens in the United States, mostly from Mexico?

For a general overview of the problem see, besides Pike's book, I. F. Bannon (ed.), *Bolton and the Spanish Borderlands*, Norman, Okla., 1964; Eric William, *From Columbus to Castro*, N. Y., 1970, with a comprehensive and excellent bibliography; Troy S. Floy, *The Columbus Dynasty in the Caribbean*, Albuquerque, 1973; J. F. McDermott (ed.), *The Spanish in the Mississippi Valley*, Urbana, Ill., 1974 (has roster of Militia with quite a few Italian names, like Vigo, Sanguinet, etc.)

4

IN NEW FRANCE

What I have said about the Italians in Spain and New Spain in the preceding chapter applies as well to the Italians in France and in New France, even more so because of the much closer relations between Italy and France. Accordingly, the reader is referred to my books, especially *Four Centuries.*

Leaving out Verrazzano or the Italians who came with the French in 1565, or the Huguenots, or the two Tonti brothers, we might start with the members of the De Lieto family (in French Desliettes) who were related to Enrico Tonti. One of them seems to have been the first white man to settle in what is now the city of Chicago, where he lived from 1698 to 1702. He served as commandant at Fort Illinois and was of great assistance to Bienville in Louisiana. Another Desliette was commandant at Fort Chartres, near the present city of St. Louis, from 1726 to 1730. Still another Desliettes was second in command at Green Bay, Wis. Daniel Greysollon Duluth, after whom the city of Duluth is named, was a cousin of Enrico Tonti, but I have not looked too closely in the matter, as I don't believe that he was of Italian origin.

Then there were Antonio and Tomaso Crisafi, political exiles from Messina, both of whom were captains. Antonio was governor at Three Rivers from 1703 to the time of his death in 1709. Previously he had been in charge of the fort at Onondaga, near the present city of Syracuse, N. Y. (*op. cit.* pp. 83 and 81).

The largest groups of Italian immigrants under the French Flag must have been either soldiers or political exiles, especially the former, many of whom served in such regiments as the *Royal Italien* (See *Historique des Corps de Troupe de l'Armée Francaise,* 1569-1900, Paris, 1900) and in the Carignan Regiment (See Benjamin Sulte, *Le Régiment de Carignan,* Montreal, 1922, and Regis Roy et Gerard Malchelosse, *Le Régiment de Carignan,* Montreal, 1925). To distinguish the nationality of the members of the Carignan Regiment is next to impossible. Take the name, for instance, of Pierre Salvage, equerry Sieur de Fromont. How could one ever tell that he was an Italian, except for a note in the records according to which he was born in the parish of "Saint-Donnat, Ville de Peginerolle, Diocese de Genes, Italie"? (Sulte, *op. cit.*, p. 126.) He was granted one of the large islands of St. Ignace and is remembered by "La Riviere Salvaye." He died in 1689. Or again, take the case of Ensign Jean Nicalis de Brandis, a native of Turin, who served in Canada between 1665 and 1667. (Malcheloss, *op. cit.*, p. 113.) The Regiment was raised by the Prince of Carignan in 1644 and was the first body of regular troops sent to Canada. It was made up of 20 companies. Most of the soldiers remained in America and settled in various parts of the present territory of the United States, primarily Indiana, Ohio and Missouri. Lest one should be misled by the "French" name of Carignan, let us remind the reader that Carignano is a city near Turin, in Italy, and that the name denotes the House of Savoy.

A notable, and possibly large, group of Italians settled in Louisiana in the 18th century, but when and how we do not know. Certainly there must have been quite a few of them at the beginning of the last century, if Col. Nichols of the British Artillery in the appeal that he issued to the population of New Orleans on August 29, 1814, addressed himself to the local "Spaniards, Frenchmen, Italians and Britons."

A prominent Italian to settle in that city was one Giovanni Gradenigo, a member of the famous Venetian family by that name, who settled there before the Revolution. For a time he lived in Mobile, Ala., but later he moved to Louisiana. Another prominent, but earlier family, was that of François Reggio, who was a member of the first Cabildo, or Council, in 1796. His granddaughter was the mother of the famous Civil War General, Pierre Gustave Toutant Beauregard. (See Hamilton Basso's Life of Beauregard.) We do not know whether the Louisiana Reggio was related to the Admiral Reggio who was commander of the Spanish Squadron which fought Admiral Knowles in the West Indies in 1748. (See Stone, W. L., *Life and Times of Sir W. J. Johnson*, 2 vols., Albany, 1865, Vol I, p. 369.) Two other pioneer Italians in Louisiana were the Rev. Lupiano, who settled there in 1773, and one Mr. Istaffi, who was first in command. (*Georgia Gazette*, February 28, 1765.)

Our most intriguing and mysterious find regarding the emigration of Italians to New France is in connection with the proposed transportation of 400 Italian families to Louisiana in 1720.

As we know, John Law sought immigrants for his Mississippi Company in France, Switzerland, Germany and Italy. (Lavisse, E., *Histoire de France*, Vol. 8, pp. 35-36.) In Italy a small group of men headed by one Chevalier de Fontana advanced and risked large sums of money for the transportation. Actually some 250 persons left Genoa in May, 1790, on the 300-ton ship "Our Lady of the Conception," Captain Vincent Blanc, master, directed to Agden, France. Whether the ship proceeded to Louisiana have not been able to ascertain. (Extrait des Registres de la Chancellerie du Consulat de France à Gennes, (sic) Fol. 242. *MS, Bibliotèque Nationale,* Paris.) On this planned emigration to Louisiana there are in the National Library of Paris two other documents of which I have been able to obtain photographic copies. They are a six-page complaint by Fontana and a letter from Cardinal Gualterio, reproduced in facsimile in my *Four Centuries.* The matter certainly deserves further investigation. (See also Chapters 8, 9, 10 and 25 for some of the pioneers under the French such as craftsmen, artisans, artists and musicians. *France in America,* a book by W. J. Eccles, New York, 1972, deals with the Carignan-Salières regiment, over one thousand strong, which arrived in 1665, and tells how 400 of them were given land and financial grants if they settled in Canada at the end of their military service. Four hundred of them did. Later, some or many of them (we do not have precise data), moved over to the United States, or what later became part of the United States.

It is, therefore, impossible to estimate how many of the "French" settlers in either the Northeast or in the Midwest or later in Louisiana were really French or Italians. One estimate, I am confident, *is* way off, and that is the number of residents in what is now the United States, outside of the Thirteen Colonies in 1790, which was estimated at about 18,500. (*Surnames in the United States Census of 1790. An analysis of National Origins of the Population. American Council of Learned Societies—Annex B, The Minor Stocks* by Marcus L. Hansen, p. 360.) Originally published in the Annual Report of the American Historical Association for the year 1931, Vol. I, pp. 103-441, Washington, 1932. Reprinted in 1971 (1968) by the Baltimore Genealogical Publishing Company.

As any student of census statistics knows, even recent population statistics are far from accurate. As for 1790, one's guess was as good as another, especially if we consider the occupations of the frontiersmen, of the fur traders, and other individuals without a permanent address, as noted in the preceding chapter.

See also, N. E. Dionne, *Origines des familles émigrées de France. d'Espagne, De Suisse, etc., pour venir se fixer au Canada.* Originally published in 1914, reprinted in 1969 by the Baltimore Genealogical Publishing Co.

5

CESARE ALBERTI

Not even ten years had elapsed from the day the Dutch purchased Manhattan Island from the Indians, when a Venetian sailor, named Cesare Alberti, or Alberto, deserted his ship and settled in the rising New Amsterdam.

Where and when Alberti joined the Dutch crew we do not know, nor is it important. For centuries past, commercial relations between Italy and Holland had been close, both by land and by sea. Just before Alberti's arrival in 1635, Alvise Contarini, the Venetian ambassador in England, reporting to the Doge and Senate in 1628, wrote that "good treatment and pay are given all along the coast of Flanders to mariners of any race whatever, and at Lubeck they reckon that more than 400 builders of ships and galleys from Provence and Italy have passed through that place." (*Calendar of State Papers, Venetian*, Vol. 20, p. 575.)

At that time, we might add, the Dutch fleet that used to visit Leghorn regularly every year, included two ships for Venice. (*op. cit.*, Vol. 21, pp. 36-39.) Possibly it was on one of those voyages that Alberti joined the Dutch vessel.

Alberti's life in America is of no historical importance, except for its implications regarding other Italian immigrants who may have come over the same way he did. One has indeed but to go through the *Records of the Reformed Dutch Church in New Amsterdam and New York,* to find numerous names which may have been of Italian origin.

Alberti married a Dutch woman in 1642 and became the father of seven children, six of whom were still living at the time of his death in 1655, apparently the victim of an Indian onslaught. His children moved to the interior of Long Island and, later, to the other colonies. One of them, William Alburtus, the son of Pietro (d. 1652) moved to Lawrenceville, near Princeton, N.J., served in the Hunterdon County, N.J. Grand Jury in 1714, and as a constable from 1722 to 1726. Thus he was, in all probability, the first Italian-American to fill a public office. In 1729 he owned 175 acres of land in New Jersey (*Genealogical Magazine of New Jersey*, October 1938). The other sons also scattered throughout the colony. At any rate, it has been estimated that at the normal rates of prolification there should be in the United States upwards of 3,000 descendants, directly or indirectly, of the Venetian pioneer.

Alberti was probably the first producer of tobacco at Wallabout, within the present city limits of Brooklyn, where his name is perpetuated by Alburtis Avenue. He also owned large tracts of land in various parts of Long Island and a house and garden along the canal, or graft, which used to run through what is now Broad Street, in Manhattan's financial district.

As related in Chapter 2, a physician by the name of Alberti was active in New York and Philadelphia between 1791 and 1837, but we have not been able to ascertain whether he was a descendant of the Venetian immigrant of 1635.

6

WALDENSES AND OTHER ITALIAN PROTESTANTS IN COLONIAL AMERICA

The first emigration from Italy to North America took place in 1656 when 300 Waldenses landed in New Amsterdam, eight years before it was taken by the British who, thereupon, christened it New York. All of them had French names, spoke a French dialect, and the few who could read and write did so in French. But so did the Piedmontese, among whom they lived. But like the Piedmontese they were Italians and not French, even though centuries before the ancestors of most of them came from France. Two hundred and thirty-seven years later another strong group of Waldenses also came to America, settling in North Carolina, where they founded an agricultural settlement which they called Valdese (Italian for Waldensian) instead of its French equivalent, Vaudois. And when they organized a bank, they called it The Piedmont Bank (of Morganton, N. C.).

The Waldenses are the followers of Peter Waldo, a rich merchant of Lyons, France, who gave his wealth to the poor and embraced poverty in 1170. Many years later the Pope pronounced him and his followers heretics. Persecution followed persecution, with the Waldenses fleeing to Holland, Switzerland, Germany, England and other countries, including other parts of Italy, as far south as Sicily, where they were persecuted by the French in 1280, or two years before the French were put to death and chased out of the island (with the exception of a handful in two towns) during the famous Sicilian Vespers. Thus, as the years went by, the Waldenses included people from all over Italy, founding even towns, as Guardia Piemontese in the province of Cosenza in Calabria, in the 13th century. According to the Italian Touring Club guidebook, *Italia Meridionale e Insulare* (1951) the people of that town still speak the Provencal-French dialect and they still wear their original costumes, just as in some towns in Sicily, in which the Lombard dialect is still spoken. In Guardia Piemontese, it is interesting to note that the gate to the town is still called "Porta del Sangue" (the gate of the blood, or bloodshed) so named because of the slaughter of centuries before. No less interesting is the Waldensian

21

church of Grotte, a town in the province of Agrigento, in Sicily, a hotbed of the Mafia in the 1890's and the former home of the Reverend Enrico Vinay, the first pastor of Valdese, N. C. who married a local woman, did not get along with her and came to America. Apparently there were many converts in Grotte, for many of them emigrated to Rochester, N. Y. where they organized the local Italian Presbyterian Church. (Watts, George B., *The Waldenses in the New World*, Durham, N. C., 1941, p. 178.) Therefore, when dealing with Italian protestants in America one must bear in mind that those who came over in the 17th and 18th centuries seldom had Italian names because of their residence as religious refugees in such countries as France and Switzerland and Holland, where their names underwent a transformation, as in the case of the Italian Huguenot Priuli which became Prioleau in France, or Quaglia, that became Quigley, and later Quiggle, to avoid any confusion with an Irish Catholic name. Once here, however, the Italian Protestants joined the nearest Protestant Church, regardless of denomination. Thus, when we read that John Wesley, the founder of Methodism, read prayers in Italian to a group of Italians in Savannah, Georgia, at least on one occasion in 1737, we must not jump to the conclusion that they were Waldensians, although they may well have been, as noted by Woods, *op. cit.*, p. 30.

Getting back to the 1656 Waldensians, their history in America is far from clear, although there is no doubt that several hundreds of them came over between 1656 and 1776. Many more came later, after the North Carolina settlement. Personally, I knew at least two pastors of Waldensian churches in America in the 1930's. In an event, I have told all there is to be told about them in my two books, *The Italians in America Before the Civil War* (1934, pp. 137-142) and *Four Centuries* (p. 105). Woods adds practically nothing on this point, except for his conviction that the Waldenses did really settle on Staten Island, which is exactly what I wrote.

7

A FLORIDA TRAGEDY

The cession of Florida to Britain in 1763 fired the imagination of a number of people, who dreamed up get-rich-quick schemss. One of them, a wealthy Scottish doctor married to a Greek woman born in Smyrna, now Izmir, in Turkey, had visions of an agricultural empire in Florida, and, after securing over 100,000 acres of land from the British Government, transported over 1,200 natives of Minorca (Spain), Corsica, Greece and Italy, to a settlement, near present Daytona Beach, which he called New Smyrna, in honor of his wife's birthplace. Getting the men over was not hard, for they were recruited from among the indigent people of those countries; besides, he promised them, so it seems, fifty acres of land at the end of a specified term of labor (indenture), but with the condition that if the settlers were not satisfied with their life in the settlement, the doctor would return them to their native countries within six months. At least, that's what they understood. This point, however, is not clear, but it is quite possible that the men, who could not understand English and most likely were all, or in the greatest number, illiterate, were made to believe that such was the case. The settlement, however, turned out to be a veritable inferno, a point on which everybody agrees.

Everything seemed indeed so hopeless, since the good doctor refused to send the settlers back, that a small group of them, quickly grown to about 300, planned to flee to Cuba in a boat which they stole, and with blankets, foodstuff and other goods which they also stole. Unfortunately for them, the tide was low and while waiting for the tide to rise, they were apprehended, jailed, tried and released (they were needed for the work to be done), with the exception of three men, two Italians and a Greek, all of whom were sentenced to death. The leader, so we learn from one of the early historians, a Dutch surveyor named Bernard Romans, was an Italian named Forni, a man of more than average ability, because he had been serving as an overseer. And it was to him that the court offered to have his life spared on condition that he execute his two companions. This he rejected with contempt. The offer was then made to the Greek, who accepted although after an agonizing indecision.

To make a long story short, the men returned to work, and the settlement kept on growing, but amidst all sorts of handicaps and under such horrible conditions that 300 men and women and 150 children died within a few months of their arrival, in 1768. Twenty-eight died during the crossing, or while picking up the various groups. The trip lasted four months.

This arrangement, or life of desperation, lasted about ten years until, following a long quarrel between Doctor Turnbull and the new British governor, the men were set free and offered some land in New Smyrna. But they were so afraid of being returned into servitude, that they moved, all of them, to St. Augustine, Florida, where their descendants now represent a solid community, what with their intermarriage and other events.

The failure of New Smyrna is just a comma in the annals of history, but in the story of the Italians in the United States it has a particular significance, first, because it shows that the Italians were not totally absent, as the interpreters of the 1790 census had concluded, and second, because it may have deterred thousands of Italians in coming to America in greater numbers during the following century.

There is, however, a footnote to the New Smyrna incident, and that is Professor De Conde's reference to a recent book by E. P. Panagopoulos, *New Smyrna: An Eighteenth Century Greek Odyssey*, as providing "data on Italian settlers." If De Conde had read my account of the Florida settlement in my *Italians in America Before the Civil War*, instead of tossing around irresponsible opinions without even examining the entire field, he would have learned that my account is still the most concise and the most accurate about Dr. Turnbull's experiment, with the only possible error that I have been able to note in my recent re-examination, and that is, the nationality of Bernard Romans, who was not English, but a native of the Netherlands. Furthermore, Mr. Panagopoulos deals primarily with the Greeks, as the title of his book indicates, and has only brief references to the Italians. According to him, he tried to get some information about the 110 Italians who left Leghorn with Dr. Turnbull, but notwithstanding the assistance of two Leghorn officials, he was unable to obtain any extra data. Yet, he tells us that Carlo Sforza told Carita Daggett Corse, the author of the book, *Dr. Andrew Turnbull and the New Smyrna Colony*, 1919, that he had read in the records of Leghorn that the Granduke of Tuscany had let the Italians in Leghorn emigrate because they were strangers in the city. That granduke, by the way, was the friend of Mazzei, and the same man who later became Emperor of Germany in 1790 — he was also the brother of Marie Antoinette. Now is it possible that in a city like Florence, the capital of Tuscany, its well-known newspaper, "Notizie Del Mondo," would not have heard of the rebellion of the Leghorn Italians in New Smyrna, when a full account had appeared in the Boston Chronicle of September 26, 1768, which I quote at the beginning of my chapter in my Civil War book? And if Count Sforza had seen those documents, or whatever, about the Leghorn "strangers" most likely in the early 1920's, one must conclude that the men who tried to help Mr. Panagopoulos did not know how to go about in their search.

In any event, Mr. Panagopoulos says that there is no agreement as to the length of time the indenture was to last, whereas John Lee Williams, who must have interviewed some of the survivors of the New Smyrna rebellion, clearly states on page 188 of his 1837 book, *The Territory of Florida* (reprinted in 1962) that Dr. Turnbull had promised the Minorcans, Greeks and Italians that 'if they were dissatisfied, in six months, he agreed to send them back."

One more thing: it is true that the man who executed his two companions in return for his own life was the Greek, one of the three sentenced to death, but, according to Romans, the offer had been made to Forni who preferred to die rather than kill his two friends. I don't have a copy of Romans's book and I am unable to check. However, in my book I quote the passage regarding Forni, who, accordin- to Mr. Panagopoulos, was "An accused rapist and probably one of the basest of men." My quotation from Romans refers to Forni as "an Italian of very bad principles but of so much note that he had formerly been admitted to the overseers's table." However, since there were two editions of Romans's book, it is possible that the edition consulted by men is different from that consulted by Panagopoulos. Therefore, if Professor De Conde had cited more than one authority on the New Smyrna settlement, the readers would have learned two, and not just one, sides of the story. And that goes also for Carita Doggett Corse's book, which Panagopoulos criticizes, simply because she defends Dr. Turnbull. But does he not show mostly the other side?

8

ARTISANS, MERCHANTS AND
PROFESSIONAL MEN

The Italians who came to the American Colonies before the Revolution were not indentured servants or unskilled workers. Actually, in the *Virginia Gazette Index*, 1736-1778, by Cappon and Duff, 2 vols., 1950, I have found only one entry which seemed to indicate the presence of an Italian indentured servant in 1775 ("Italian language spoken by convict servant," Purdie's *Virginia Gazette*, July 21, 1775), but it turned out to be a Swiss convict with a German name. In all my years of research, the only Italian names I have come across have been those of skilled workers, merchants, skilled farmers, artisans, restaurant owners and professional men, except for the Florida colonists.

The first records about the Italians in Virginia deal with Italian glassworkers, some years before the landing of the Pilgrim Fathers at Jamestown. At any rate, we have definite proof of the arrival of some of them about 1621 or 1622.

According to John Strype's *Annals of the Reformation*, the first man to set up a glasshouse in London about 1580 was a Venetian named Verselyn, as the English spelled his name (I suppose the 1790 Census experts would have taken that name for purely Anglo-Saxon since there is no letter "y" in the Italian alphabet). Forty years later the English had not made much progress and were compelled to lure Venetian glassmakers to establish factories in England. A few came to Virginia, as we learn from a report of the Venetian ambassador in London. "The Republic," he sadly commented referring to Venice, "has no more bitter enemies here than some of her subjects" (see facsimiles in my book, *Four Centuries*, p. 99).

By 1622 some 16 glassworkers "Italians and others" (some of the early ones were Poles) arrived in Virginia where they soon erected and operated a glasshouse. The Italians, apparently, did not get along with the English, who called them disorderly. One of them, named Vincenzio (Vincenzo), is said to have cracked the furnace with an iron bar. But that's one side of the story. What became of those Venetians we do not know, except that in February, 1625, five of them were still working in Jamestown, and that one of them, Bernardo, had wife and child there. At any rate, it would seem that the Italians established the first manufacturing plant in the Colonies.

Another century had to elapse before we hear of other Italian skilled workers in one of the Colonies, and that was in connection with Oglethorpe's plan to make Georgia a silk-growing center. The plan did not succeed, but the Italians came.

The most proficient silk-throwers in the world in those days were the Piedmontese, many of whom had emigrated to Lyons, France. It was only logical, therefore, that Oglethorpe should have turned to Piedmont to engage the necessary men to start the industry in the new colony and to provide teachers for the apprentices he expected to recruit among the colonists. Oglethorpe, it should be recalled, was well acquainted with Italy and with the Italians, having served under Prince Eugene of Savoy. His servant, too, was an Italian named Charles Grimaldi, a man without many scruples, for during the crossing to Georgia he drank all of the several dozen bottles of Cyprus wine which Oglethorpe had ordered especially for himself. The general became so furious when he found that out, that he had ordered the rascal to be bound hand and foot, but the celebrated Rev. John Wesley, who was on board, reminded Oglethorpe that he also was liable to sin. Whereupon all was forgiven. Grimaldi settled in the new colony and became a prosperous citizen.

The first Italian to come to Georgia was one Paul Amatis. He landed with the first colonists at Charleston, South Carolina, on January 13, 1733, proceeding south, with Oglethorpe, a few days later. Paul Amatis soon called for his brother, Nicholas Amatis, then a resident of Lyons. He came over with another group of seven Italian silk experts in April, 1733. The party included one Giacomo Luigi Camuso, his wife and three children. Others came in later years, including one Joseph Ottolenghi, superintendent of silk culture in 1764. A pamphlet entitled "Directions for breeding silk-worms, extracted from a letter of Joseph Ottolenghi, Esq., later superintendent of the Public Filature in Georgia" was published at Philadelphia in 1771. In 1786, when Count Castiglioni of Milan visited Ebenezer, he was presented with some silk by one Mrs. Postell, whose name suggests its Italian origin.

Notwithstanding its initial success, however, the silk industry at Savannah was not fated to last long. Silk was last produced there in 1790. The filature was later used as city hall and public house, but was destroyed by fire in 1839.

Philip Mazzei's large scale agricultural plan in 1773, when he brought over more than a dozen skilled workers, is well known and need not be repeated here (see Chapter 21), but it seems that another Italian, one Col. Tasco (Tasker) was making good wine before 1760 in Maryland, when the Rev. Andrew Burnaby drank some of it. (*Travels Though the Middle Settlements in North America*, 1759-1760, London, 1798, reprinted 1970, p. 55. Notice that his name was sometimes spelled Tasker, which reminds me of the spelling of Paca's name as Peaker or Packer.)

IN THE RESTAURANT BUSINESS

One business in which the Italians did well in Colonial days or shortly after was the restaurant business. After all, the teachers of the French in this delectable art were the chefs Catherine De Medici brought with her to France, and to this day the best restaurants in Soho in London are still Italian and French (I must add, however, that once I had an excellent dinner in a Chinese restaurant not far from Piccadilly). Of course, there are other fine foreign restaurants in London today.

One of the first successful Italian restaurateurs or innkeepers in the Colonies (there may have been others before him) was Serafino Formicola, a Neapolitan who had been in Russia but later came with Lord Dunmore, the Governor of Virginia. At first he owned a hotel in Williamsburg, but later he moved to Richmond, where he owned the famous Eagle Tavern which was patronized by Washington and other leaders. It was at his inn that Aaron Burr was arraigned before Chief Justice Marshall in 1807.

Formicola married one Mathilda Newman in 1774. Their only daughter, Evelyn, who is said to have been one of the leading belles of Williamsburg, married Stewart Bankhead, one of whose descendants, a leading motion picture actress, died in 1968. Formicola's grandson was killed at the Battle of Chancellorsville during the Civil War. He became a man of consequence, just as the Marquis of Chatellux had foreseen when he stopped at his Richmond inn in 1781. Five years later, Formicola subscribed the sum of $500 towards the erection of Quesnay's *Academy of Science and Fine Arts*. For more details see *Four Centuries*, pp. 307-309.

In Philadelphia, the musician Vincent M. Pelosi owned for a time the Pennsylvania Coffee House in Market Street but in 1788 he moved to Camden, N. J., where he opened a new coffee house "being provided with all sorts of the best Wines, Liquors, Preserves, Tea, Coffee, &c." &c."

Another prominent merchant of those days was Ferdinand Phinizy who, as noted in the following chapter, came with Rochambeau and saw action at Yorktown. During the war with the Indians (1792-1796) he equipped a company of soldiers and served as captain and later as major. His son was the first Italian-American I know of to serve as mayor of an American city, Augusta, Ga. When he died he left an estate of $120,000. His descendants have been bankers, prominent lawyers, planters, publishers of newspapers, railroad directors, civic leaders, etc., etc. (See *Four Centuries*, p. 309.)

The men who came over with Mazzei also did well. One of them, we learn from a letter that Jefferson wrote to Bellini in 1799, "has got rich as a grocer in Richmond . . . is in flourishing circumstances." In 1802 he resigned as captain after having served for 17 years in the militia. Also from Jefferson we learn that Anthony Giannini, another of Mazzei's men, "has raised a large family, married several of them, & after thriving for a while has become embarrassed . . . Francis, his brother in law & and Anthony Molina have done terribly well." One of Giannini's sons became a Baptist minister in 1807.

The Italians who did very well were those who settled in St. Louis and became prosperous merchants, especially in the fur trade, like Francis Vigo (see Chapter 22), Yosti, Bouis and Berthold (Bertoldi).

Emilien Yosti was born at Novara about 1740 and died at St. Louis in 1818. He was one of the earliest real estate operators in the city, a member of the first grand jury in 1804, and the owner of an inn in which was held the first court of justice as soon as St. Louis became a part of the United States. He was a partner of Francis Vigo and was prominent in the organization of the civil government in Missouri. His son, Francis, who was born in St. Louis in 1798, lived an eventful life. In 1830 he started for Santa Fe, New Mexico, where he arrived after 90 days, and where he operated a store for two years. In 1834 he settled in St. Charles, Mo., where he served as a judge of the County Court for four years and became president of the First National Bank of St. Charles. He was a Catholic and a Democrat. In Missouri and other parts of the country one finds today several prominent men named Yost, but whether they are descendants of the immigrant Piedmontese we cannot say.

Antoine Bouis was born in Genoa in 1752, emigrated to New Orleans in 1780 and settled in St. Louis in 1782. He was the father of ten children, one of whom, André V. Bouis, became a school teacher, and another, Pascal V. Bouis, graduated from West Point as a second lieutenant in the artillery in 1806 and was killed in a duel about 1811. Thus he seems to have been the first Italian-American to have graduated from the United States Military Academy. Antoine Bouis was also the grandfather of Alexander Leseur, who became secretary of state of Missouri and was for many years editor of the Lexington (Mo.) *Intelligencer*. The elder Bouis must have been active in the fur business, according to a *Map of the Trans-Mississippi Territory*, 1807-

1843, in which we find Fort Defiance, or Fort Bouis on the White River, just south of the present city of Bismarck, N. D.

Bartholomew Berthold, a partner in the American Fur Company, one of the largest firms of its kind in the history of that industry, was born at Trento, Italy, in 1780, the son of Alessandro Bertoldi and Maddalena Beltrami. In 1809 he settled in St. Louis, where in 1811 he married Pelagie Chouteau, a member of the famous family that founded the city half a century before. Shortly after his marriage he formed a partnership with Auguste Chouteau, which lasted until Berthold's death on April 20, 1831. He had four sons and two daughters. Fort Berthold in the Upper Missouri region was named after him. He, Chouteau and others are said to have been connected with John Jacob Astor as partners, according to an item in the *St. Louis Republican* for May 26, 1875, but we have found no reference to it in any of the biographical accounts of Astor or in Chittenden's *The American Fur Trade of the Far West*.

In the East, worthy of notice would be a banker, Diodati, already mentioned in Chapter 2, one Dr. Borgella, who received a doctorate in medicine from the University of Pennsylvania (as mentioned by Chastellux), one Dr. Batacchi who arrived in Philadelphia in 1765 and one Dr. Magra (Magrath? — see facsimiles in *Four Centuries*, p. 108); also one Dr. Bertody, a graduate of the University of Padua, who married Ursula Plimpton of Wrentham, Mass. in 1785, a dentist, one Mr. Ruspini in 1786, one Dr. De Angelis from Naples who came over in 1798 and died in New York in 1841 at the age of 83.

But then there were other merchants, art dealers, teachers of languages, craftsmen, and, last but not least, one Anthony Trapani, a native of Meta, not far from Naples, an importer of Italian citrus fruits, as well as figs (his name was also spelled Trepan) "the last but one of those that assisted in erecting the first Catholic Church in this city and state, namely St. Peter's, to which church he was a very constant hearer until the period of his decease. His remains were interred in St. Patrick's Cathedral" [on Prince and Mott Streets], in one of the best known Little Italies in New York City.

9

PIONEER MUSICIANS, ARTISTS
AND ENTERTAINERS

Although America could afford few inducements to musicians before 1800, we find some Italian teachers of music in the Colonies as early as 1757, when one John Palma gave a concert in Philadelphia. Palma may have been in America long before 1757. His music, at least, was played here, for we find a "large Book of Songs" by Palma, priced at five shillings, in the inventory of the estate of Cuthbert Ogle, who died in 1755. Three compositions by Palma were included in *Hopkinson's Book*, a manuscript volume of music copied by Francis Hopkinson, the Signer of the Declaration of Independence. It is now in the Library of Congress.

Next in order of time we find Francis Alberti, a native of Faenza, Italy, who came to America not later than 1759. He may have been the same Alberti who gave a concert on April 10, 1757, which was attended by Washington, and another at Hanoverstown, near Williamsburg, Va., on May 19, 1769. According to Thomas Jefferson, "Alberti came over with a troop of players and afterwards taught at Williamsburg. Subsequently I got him to come up here (Monticello) and took lessons for several years." (Randall, H. S., *Life of Jefferson*, Vol. I, p. 131.) Alberti gave vocal and musical lessons, his pupils including Martha Skelton, who later became Jefferson's wife. He taught the violin, the harpsichord and other instruments. In 1774 he signed the pledge not to do business with England, known as *The Association*. After 1778 he was in Paris, where Jefferson wrote to him following Burgoyne"s surrender. (Parton, *Life of Jefferson*, pp. 133 and 221.) On his 1769 concert see *Rind's Virginia Gazette*, May 11, 1769.

Giovanni Gualdo, probably the best known musician in Colonial America, arrived in Philadelphia in 1767, and lived there until he died in the insane asylum four years later. The facsimiles dealing with Gualdo's concerts in my book, *Four Centuries of Italian-American History*, pp. 114-115 tell more about this unfortunate man who initiated the people of Philadelphia to the appreciation of fine music.

That music conditions in the Colonies were not very promising, we may presume from the fleeting appearance of one Tioli at Provi-

31

dence in 1768, or by the little success which Nicholas Biferi found in New York in 1774. Biferi, together with two other Italians, Pietro Sodi, a dancing master, and Joseph Cozani, a teacher of languages, had planned the establishment of a conservatory of music in New York, where vocal and instrumental music, dancing, and both French and Italian were to be taught. The minimum of twelve pupils they depended on to start, however, did not materialize and their dreams of a conservatory vanished in thin air. They remained in America at least for some time, as we learn from the newspaper advertisements of the day.

Still another violinist and orchestra leader who appeared in Charleston, Philadelphia and New York between 1774 and 1783 was Gaetano Franceschini. A trio Sonata of his for two violins, cello and continuo (harpsichord) was recorded by "New Records" of New York in 1951.

More interesting from the historical point of view is the appearance of "Signiora" Mazzanti, probably the first Italian woman to sing before an American audience. She appeared in New York on April 24, 1774, and rendered English and Italian songs.

Nor should we forget a lone dancing master, one Peter Vianey (Viani), who was active in New York as early as 1768.

PAINTERS AND SCULPTORS

Americans had neither time nor inclination for art before 1800 and for many years after that. That is why, with the exception of the sculptor Ceracchi and possibly the painter Perovani, no Italian artist of any distinction came to America before 1800, as I have shown in *Four Centuries,* pp. 214-222. Cornè arrived in 1797 or 1794, he was active mostly after 1800, and as such he does not belong to the Revolutionary period.

Joseph Perovani, however, is said to have arrived in 1795 and to have left in 1801, when he moved to Cuba where he is said to have distinguished himself (*op cit.,* p. 219). He was at first associated with one Giacinto Cocchi, but possibly because of their precarious financial circumstances, they may have been forced to accept work below their skill. In any event, Perovani was commissioned by the Spanish minister in Philadelphia to do a full-length portrait of Washington which later was presented to Godoy, the Prince of Peace, and Spain's prime minister, which later was transferred to the Academy of San Fernando in Madrid, where I may have seen it in the 1950's. I only remember that the Academy is near the Puerta del Sol.

Other Italian painters, all noted in *Four Centuries,* p. 220, were

John B. Bossetti, J. Bartoli and Lewis Pise, all minor artists. Pise, however, is remembered as the father of Charles Constantine Pise, a well-known Catholic priest, and possibly the first Catholic priest of Italian parentage born in the United States.

Another Italian artist, Charles Ciceri, a Milanese, found life in America a little more comfortable than the others, for he made a living painting scenes for Philadelphia and New York theaters. Even that, apparently, did not pay well, and he turned to the importation of French goods, amassed a small fortune and returned to Italy (*op. city.*, p. 230). Then there were the art dealers, but on them see Chapter 8.

VAUDEVILLE ARTISTS

A few vaudeville artists, conjurers, magicians, necromancers, pyrotechnists, tightrope walkers, circus men and women, came over before the Revolution or shortly after, not many to judge by their ads in the local newspapers, but see *Four Centuries*, pp. 203-206, for facsimiles of their advertisements and illustrations.

10

FIGHTERS FOR AMERICAN INDEPENDENCE

To judge by the names that are Italian or appear to be Italian, the number of the "Italians" who served in the armed forces of the Colonies or 13 States during the Revolution is rather insignificant. Then again, if we consider that usually it is almost impossible to tell one's national origins by the way a name is spelled; that for each name that is singled out there must be two or three or ten which remain buried; that the names that stand out are in most cases those of officers and not of enlisted men; that, according to the 1790 census, there were no Italians to speak of in the United States, etc., etc.; then, we must conclude that during the Revolution the people of Italian stock either must have been more numerous than it is generally assumed, or that the Italians contributed a much larger share than other ethnic groups in proportion to their total number in the total population. In any event, no matter how we look at it, there seems to be no doubt that the Italians did more than their share, qualitatively speaking.

Yet, to judge by the total absence of a mention of the Italian contribution to the American Revolution in American history books, whereas historians never fail to balloon 20-year-old Kosciusko, Pulaski, the bogus baron De Kalb and some inconsequential French officers, they continue to ignore men of the caliber of Mazzei and Vigo. To my mind, Major Cosmo De Medici alone displayed more bravery and distinguished himself more in battle than the two Poles and the German combined. Von Steuben was something else. I could mention numerous other discriminatory instances, some ludicrous, some asinine, ending with the latest listing in a "Who's Who in the American Revolution" in the 1976 edition of *The World Almanac & Book of Facts* [and fiction], pages 275 and 276, in which we find one Haym Salomon and one Salem Poor," American black soldier cited for his leadership and bravery at Bunker Hill." Presently I shall tell who Salomon was. But first let me point out how the *World Almanac* editors don't check their facts, because the black soldier, one of 1,500 at Bunker Hill, is listed as "Poor, Salem" on page 276, and "Peter Salem" on page 507. *The World Almanac* has no list of noted Italian-Americans, even though I called their attention to this omission a couple of years ago, but continues to include insignificant facts and persons.

Getting on to more solid ground, no historian would question the fact that without the help in men, equipment, and money, as well as leadership, of the French (for whatever reason of their own), the war would have lasted much longer. By the same token, I am convinced that Washington would never have given up and that a ragged army that did not disintegrate at Valley Forge, arousing the immense admiration of the French officers and of the entire world, would have been able to endure anything and was bound to win, sooner or later. Geographical factors and Britain's difficulties with the French and the Spanish in Europe and the West Indies would still have been a factor, but without stamina and incomparable leadership the army would have crumbled. And the Americans had plenty of that, plus George Washington.

While at it, I fail to understand why our eminent historians continue to belittle or ignore the contribution of the Spaniards, which was far from inconsequential, as in the case of Lieutenant Colonel Miranda of the Spanish Army who raised 1,200,000 livres in Cuba shortly before Yorktown when Robert Morris could not even raise $30,000 and had to borrow $20,000 from Rochambeau. (See A. Whitridge, *Rochambeau*, 1965, p. 182.)

Now a few words about Haym Salomon.

According to the *Dictionary of American Biography*, Salomon helped to finance the American Revolution, advancing hundred of thousands of dollars, loaning money to Madison and other members of Congress without charging a penny of interest, and so on. Salomon was alleged to have done so much for America that the United States Post Office issued a commemorative stamp with a summary of Salomon's alleged achievements printed on the back of the stamp, the first time, to the best of my knowledge, any such printing ever took place. Anyway, some coreligionists of his, without examining the facts, erected two monuments in his honor, one in Chicago and one in Los Angeles that I know of, the latter representing Washington in the middle, flanked by Robert Morris to his right and Haym Salomon to his left.

Those two monuments are frauds, and let me tell you why.

To start with, Salomon did not advance any money. He was named assistant to Morris only a few months before Yorktown, when the war came to an end, for all practical purposes (let us remember that Morris was unable to raise $30,000 and had to borrow $20,000 from Rochambeau, as already noted). Salomon was chosen at the suggestion of the French and other allies because of his knowledge of foreign languages. The money that Salomon advanced the Americans was money advanced by France, Spain and Holland. Salomon put the money in the bank, to his own name, kept his commission, and turned the rest over to the Americans. As for his loans without interest, that was a form of bribery, so as to keep influential congressmen on his side, as he was doing business with the government. Just in case I should be suspected of distorting the facts, there is the brief article about Salomon in the *Encyclopaedia Judaica*, New York, 1971, and the book, *Early American Jewry* by Jacob R. Marcus, 2 volumes in one, New York, 1975, Chapter VIII. Needless to say, the article on Salomon in the *Dictionary of American Biography* (1935) is now worthless. And that goes also for the statement "some Jews like Haym Solomon (sic) helped finance the American war effort" in the volume *American Immigration* by A. M. Jones, a lecturer at the University of Manchester, England. It should be added that the Jones volume is one of several in the series, *The Chicago History of American Civilization*, edited by Daniel J. Boorstin, now Librarian of Congress, whose asininities about the Italians in one of his history books I expose in my forthcoming book, *The History of the Mafia*. See page 6.

Before going further, let me note that recently on a flight to New York I read an article by Professor Richard B. Morris of Columbia University in *American Way*, the magazine of American Airlines, for January 1976 in which the professor tells us how it was Kosciusko who, back in Poland," spread the word about the happy results of a successful revolution in the New World." That's incredible! As if Mazzei's *Recherches* had had no effect all over Europe and as if Mazzei's skillful work as diplomatic agent of the King of Poland had been a waste of time! May I suggest to Professor Morris to read Mazzei's four volumes, as well as his letters to the King of Poland, plus a few more books in Polish and Italian about Poland during the reign of Stanislaus II (Poniatowski) from 1785 to the end of his reign, when he abdicated, in 1793?

Enough of that.

Getting down to a few simple facts, the "Italian" military participation in the Revolution may be divided into four parts:

1) Americans (more accurately colonists) of Italian descent;
2) Italian volunteers;
3) Italians who came with Rochambeau and De Grasse;
4) Italian privateersmen.

1) An even approximate survey is impossible. Even if we go through the thousands and thousands of names, as of those who applied for pensions, it is next to impossible to tell whether some of the

veterans were of Italian birth or descent. In some cases there is no serious doubt, as in the case of Captain Taliaferro, who was killed at the Battle of Guilford Hall, or of Captain, later Brigadier General, Christopher Baldy (Baldi) of the Continental Army, or Lieutenant Bracco who was killed at White Plains in October, 1776, or of Captain, later Colonel, Isaac Corsa, or of 13-year-old De Angelis, the son of Neapolitan father and French mother, or of Joseph Carlo Mauran, of Villafranca (after 1859 turned over to France, like Nice), or of Baldeschi (Pulaski's paymaster), or of Peter Gully (Gulli). The latter, probably from Calabria, was "born in Italy, labourer," enlisted under Major James Moore on October 7, 1783, just a month before Washington demobilized his army, but we do not know whether he had served before. I could mention numerous similar instances, but they would not mean much, except for the fact that the Continental Army never had more than a few thousand men at any time, out of a population of close to 3,000,000. (According to the *World Almanac* the participants in the Revolution were 290,000, a meaningless figure and one more proof of the unreliability of that almanac, even if the source is the Veterans Administration. See the contradictory figures, 184,000 to 250,000 on page 364.)

MAJOR DE MEDICI

The highest-ranking officer of Italian birth we know of for sure, is Major Cosmo or Cosimo De (or de') Medici who served through the Revolution. Except for his war record, we know very little about his life except that he was a painter of little value, as noted in my book, *Four Centuries*, (pp. 214-215). According to an irresponsible so-called art historian, Medici's record as a soldier is cloudy, a charge unsupported by any evidence; on the contrary, there is ample evidence, from beginning to end, that Medici's record was excellent, so much so that at the end of the war the State of North Carolina granted him 1872 acres of land for 41 months of service. Medici saw action at the Battle of Trenton, at Brandywine and Germantown. He was in charge of four corps of cavalrymen when he was wounded and made prisoner. If that's not a better record than Kosciusko's I let the reader decide. But no historian ever mentions the Italian volunteer. For further details see *Four Centuries*, pp. 140-141.

Another native of Italy (Florence) who volunteered and served very honorably in America (he fortified Charleston, etc.), was Lieutenant Colonel Luigi Antonio De'Cambray-Digny, one of the two foreigners who received two of the eight medals struck by Congress during the war. See *Four Centuries*, p. 139; H. V. Rankin's, *The North*

Carolina Continentals, 1971, pp. 220-234; B. A. Uhlendorf, *The Siege of Charleston*, Ann Arbor, 1938; David Stick's, *The Outer Banks of North Carolina*, 1958, pp. 56-59, 62-63 notes. Du Portail, mentioned by Samuel Morison in his *Oxford History* had nothing on Cambray. Incidentally, a member of the family, Guglielmo Cambray-Digny, was Italian minister of finance, and senator of the Kingdom from 1860 to his death in 1906.

Other Italians may have volunteered and served in the Continental Army, but it would be quite a task to flush them out. I leave that detective work to the researchers of the Anti-Defamation League of B'nai B'rith who are supposed to be so skillful at the work, although I have yet to see one of their nuggets. Anyway, according to D. Visconti (*Le Origini degli Stati Uniti d'America e l'Italia*, Rome, 1940, p. 122), a few Italians tried, but we have sure data about only one, Luigi Giovannetti Pellion (Giovannetti is the surname), an officer in the Piedmontese army who in 1777 requested to be sent to America and serve in the American army so as to acquire more experience. Other Italians saw action on both French and English warships, where they were training as cadets, and some of them took part in the Battle of Long Island (under the British flag). Those on French ships saw action against the English in various battles.

WITH ROCHAMBEAU AND DE GRASSE

The largest number of Italians to fight during the Revolution but under the French flag, were in at least four regimnts that I know of. Three regiments were made up exclusively of Italians, or just about, as the soldiers were recruited in Italy (the officers were, of course, also Italian). They were, the "30th Du Perche" with 1064 men, the "Third Piemont" (Piedmont, in northern Italy) with 473 men and the "Royal Italien." The other regiment in which I have found some Italians was "Le Gatinais," which saw action at Yorktown, and was chosen to storm one of the first two redoubts put up by the British, the 9th, the other, the 10th, having been reserved for the Americans who had no trouble in winning it. (Wm. De Deux Ponts, *My Campaign in America*, 1868 translation, pp. 54-56.)

Among the Italians who fought at Yorktown we know that there were Philip Phinizy, Paly Bonaventure, who was killed in action, and Antonio Sylvester Bilisoly, who came with De Grasse in 1777. Vincent Cussel, another Italian who served in the "Gatinais" regiment, was killed at Savannah in 1779. Still another Italian, Biny Francois, was shipwrecked in 1782. Jean Francois of Villefranche (Gian Francesco da Villafranca) was a chaplain with De Grasse's fleet. There must have been many more, as those mentioned either rose to success in America, like Phinizy and Bilisoly (a Corsican named Buonisola), or were identified as natives of Italy in some records. (See *Four Centuries*, pp. 138-139.)

The most interesting group of Italians in the Revolution I have come across were five brothers named Scalvini, from Brescia (I was there a few months ago and somehow it did not cross my mind to look up the family). They joined the French Army as cadets, for training purposes, in a regiment recruited in Italy and accordingly named "Le Royal Italien," but then the regiment was shipped to America and the Scalvini brothers had no choice but to come. Alessandro, one of the brothers, was put in charge of the unit, with the rank of lieutenant (uually a captain is put in command of a regiment). The regiment, as we know, saw action at Yorktown and in other battles, finally in a sea battle against the British, commanded by Admiral Rodney, who defeated De Grasse soundly, but the ship on which the "Royal Italien" was on, "Le Pluton," escaped to the West Indies and none of the Italians was made prisoner.

The interesting part about Scalvini is his lack of interest in America when he came over, but became a fervent admirer of this country once he was here, especially after he met Washington whom he idolized as the greatest man on earth, never stopping to talk about him to his children and grandchildren, repeating word for word, time and time again, what Washington had told him. His son, Giovita, was active in the revolutionary movement of Lombardy in 1821 and had to seek refuge first in Switzerland and then in London. Obviously, his father's words had not fallen on deaf ears. (On Scalvini, already mentioned by Amy Bernardy, as noted by me in *Four Centuries*, see Visconti, *op. cit.*, p. 123, with a note about Scalvini's writings.)

NICOLA, BELLI, AND RIVARDI

Lewis Nicola, a brigadier general in 1783, is best remembered because of his suggestion to Washington himself that he be named king. His birthplace is not clear. According to one source, he was born in Dublin, according to another, he was born in France and was a Huguenot. In his youth he went to Ireland, where he was educated, but that seems strange, because a Huguenot would not go to Ireland and would not marry an Irish Catholic woman, as it seems to have been the case. What seems more absurd is that an Irishman, if he was born in Dublin, or a Frenchman, if he was born in France, would change the name of Nicholas, which is the same in both French and English, into an Italian name. The name in Italy usually is De Nicola.

39

Some graduate student or professor should look into the matter, beginning with the birth certificates of his children in Irish parishes. Incidentally, he started a monthly periodical, *The American Magazine* but only 9 issues were published. See both the *Dictionary of American Biography* and the *Pennsylvania Magazine of History and Geography* for July 1922, pp. 269-270.

Major John Belli was deputy quartermaster general in 1792, and Major J. J. Rivardi was appointed by Washington to fortify Baltimore, Alexandria and Norfolk. Later he fortified Detroit and other cities. Washington said that he was a Swiss, obviously an Italian-Swiss. On both of them see *Four Centuries*, pp. 141-142.

THE PRIVATEERS

A field of investigation I had not thought of until I read the paper, "The Ethnic Factor in the Episode of the Prison Ships Martyrs of the American Revolution," by Dr. Joseph J. Palisi, Borough Historian of Brooklyn, is that of the privateers who played havoc with British shipping not only along the Atlantic Coast but also in the Caribbean and in Europe. Dr. Palisi was able to identify from 43 to 50 prisoners with Italian names, but even if all the 50 prisoners were not of Italian birth or descent, it is safe to assume that many more names were so distorted that they could not be identified as Italian by any stretch of the imagination.

The field is so vast and the data available so scanty, that it would be idle to speculate on the number of Italians who joined the French and the Spaniards and applied for American letters of marque, both in Europe and in the Caribbean. That type of buccaneering was not new to the Italians who had been masters at it for a long time.

MAZZEI AND YORKTOWN

Finally, the greatest contribution to the Revolution by Italians would have been made by Mazzei, aside from his preaching and writing in Virginia as well as in Europe, if it could be proved that his plan to use the navy to win the war was really adopted by Washington, Rochambeau and De Grasse. But on this point see Chapter 21.

Part Two

FROM COLUMBUS TO BUSTI

Columbus

By Joaquin Miller

They sailed. They sailed. Then spake the mate:
"This mad sea shows his teeth tonight,
He lifts his lip, he lies in wait
With lifted teeth, as if to bite!
Brave Admiral, say but one good word:
What shall we do when hope is gone?"
The word leapt like a leaping sword:
"Sail on! sail on! sail on! and on!"

Then pail and worn he kept his deck,
And peered through darkness, Ah, that night
Of all dark nights! And then a speck —
A light! a light! a light! a light!
It grew, a starlit flag unfurled!
He gained a world; he gave that world
Its grandest lesson: On! sail on!"

The Reason

By M. Lucille Ford

In Fourteen hundred and ninety-two
Columbus crossed the ocean blue
He found America and then
He sailed right back to Spain again
But when the good news got around
That this great country had been found,
A lot of people came to stay —
And that's why we're here today!

The Instructor, October, 1925, reprinted in *Columbus* by H. Paulmier and R. H. Schauffler

11

COLUMBUS

Any historian will agree that a discovery of new land or the exploration of the interior of a land, has value only if

1) it becomes incorporated (as one writer put it) into the geographical knowledge of the world;

2) if it starts a chain of events which will lead sooner or later to colonization, settlement, trade, and finally political independence.

We may therefore dismiss as purely academic pastime the voyages of the Vikings, of Leif Eiriksson and his friends, and all the stories about Markland and Vinland.

All empty talk aside, the fact remains, as John Bartlet Brebner put it in his book, *The Explorers of North America* 1492-1806, in 1933, page 3 (reprinted by The World Publishing Company in 1955 and 1968) that "the whole train of North American events runs in a continuous line from the work of Columbus." And that should be enough, so far as the American people are concerned, as it would be idle to go into the change that Columbus's voyage made in the course of world history.

We may likewise dismiss with a shrug and a sneer all the attempts made by countless individuals who have questioned Columbus's origins, his place of birth, his geographical and cosmographical knowledge, and even his motives, especially since all doubting thomases or inquisitive boys and girls will find all the answers in the two volumes by Samuel Morison, *Admiral of the Ocean Sea,* and in the more recent (1975) two volumes (660 pages) *Cristoforo Colombo — La genesi della grande scoperta* by Paolo Emilio Taviani, published by the Istituto Geografico De Agostini (38,000 lire — about $60). We may likewise ignore the infantile argument that Columbus did not discover America because he did not set foot on the American continent (to most people, the present United States of America). Honduras, where Columbus landed in 1502, is not, of course, a part of the continent.

As for the alleged Jewish origins of Columbus (I have written a book on that subject which I have not published because economically it is not profitable), that's a figment of the imagination of Salvador De Madariaga. In this connection, I may reveal that in 1950, while doing some research in Mexico City (I suppose the researchers of the

Anti-Defamation League of B'nai B'rith who conducted "extensive research" on the Italians in America went there, too), I had the opportunity to meet the curator of the rare book section of the National Library in that capital, a former professor of history at the University of Madrid, and a political refugee. While discussing with him some aspects of American history, I happened to say that De Madariaga was a first class writer, in both Spanish and English, but he was no historian. The professor's answer was: "Lo sè, es mi primo." (I know it, he is my cousin.)

12

AMERIGO VESPUCCI

A voice alta e noi soltanto
Possiamo dire con nostro vanto:
"Se ti chiami americano
Tu lo devi a un italiano."

—MONSIGNOR SCIOCCHETTI

We all know that America was named after the Florentine Amerigo Vespucci; at least most of us do. Quite a few well-informed persons know that Vespucci had nothing to do with the naming of America after him. Few people, on the other hand, know that Vespucci has been abused, maligned, calumnied, called an impostor, a liar, a thief and other epithets.

The story is too complicated to be told in a couple of pages; accordingly, I will limit myself to the references to Vespucci in three books by Professor Samuel E. Morison of Harvard, one of America's eminent historians, a leading authority on Columbus and on the discoverers and explorers of the New World. The three books are: *Admiral Of The Ocean Sea*, 2 vols., Boston, 1942 (also one volume edition, at the same time); *The Oxford History Of The American People*, New York, 1965 — also in three volumes of the New American Library, New York, 1972; *The European Discovery of America, The Northern Voyage*, New York, 1971. My references are to the one volume edition of the first book, to the American Library edition of the second, and the regular edition of the third.

On page 568 of *Admiral Of The Ocean Sea* we are told that Vespucci joined the Hojeda expedition to America of 1499, that he wrote the account of the voyage "predated by two years and not mentioning his commander" and that it was this account which "led to the continent being given his name." On page 666 we learn how Columbus, who had called Vespucci "a very honourable man and always desirous of pleasing me," "little suspected that Vespucci's predated account of his voyage with Hojeda, just published as a news letter, would cause the Florentine to be hailed as the discoverer of the New World, or

45

that in consequence of this faked-up narrative the world of Columbus's discovery would be named America." Professor Morison does not say who faked the narrative and leaves the impression that it was faked by Vespucci.

In Volume I of his *Oxford History*, page 65, Professor Morison tells how "by a strange comedy of errors" America got the name of a man who never commanded a voyage of discovery," how Vespucci made a voyage with Hojeda in 1499, and how later he made three more voyages, "again as a passenger or junior officer, along the coast of Brazil." Then he tells how some of Vespucci's letters about those voyages were printed in Florence in 1504-05, that with the exception of some spicy stories they could just as well have been lifted from the voyages by Columbus and Hojeda. Then he adds: "Whoever did write or compile these letters intimated that Vespucci was the captain of all four voyages" and put in Vespucci's mouth the statement, "These regions we may rightly call *Mundus Novus*, a New World, because our ancestors had no knowledge of them."

Professor Morison has nothing to say about Vespucci in his *European Discovery*, except that although Vespucci got the credit for calling South America *Mundus Novus*, his concept was not different from that of Columbus's *Otro Mundo*. Both meant that South America was a continent "which was at the bottom of Asia, just like Vietnam" (p. 324.) In this book, however, he refers to Professor Giuseppe Caraci as "the eminent Roman geographer" and to his "scathing attack" on the Vinland map, which was exposed as a fake by the late Justice Michael Angelo Musmanno in 1966. But Musmanno's work was just "an amusing, emotional assault on what he calls Scandikna very'" (pp. 71-72). Anyway, I wonder why Professor Morison did not bother to mention what Professor Caraci had to say about Vespucci, way back in 1956, as we shall presently see.

Thus, according to Professor Morison, Vespucci predated the account of the voyage he made with Hojeda by two years, giving the impression that it was done deliberately. Actually, nobody knows how that voyage was said to have taken place in 1497 rather than in 1499, unless the 1497 voyage is the first voyage during which Vespucci went as far north as Chesapeake Bay, in the present city of Washington area. But there is no proof whatever that such a voyage took place, as charged by Las Casas, who could not find any document in its support.

In his *Oxford History*, Professor Morison says that Vespucci never commanded a voyage of discovery, and that after the voyage of 1499 with Hojeda he made three more voyages, "again, as passenger or junior officer." That is not correct, first of all because, according to

Las Casas, who examined the original documents on which he wrote his famous *Historia de las Indias,* which was well known in manuscript form long before it was printed three centuries after his death, in 1875, Vespucci may have contributed to the fitting of the expedition and may have had the command of one or two ships. On this point see the article by Alberto Magnaghi on Vespucci in the *Enciclopedia Italiana Treccani* (1937). Magnaghi, I should add, wrote two volumes on Vespucci (1926).

Vespucci, as confirmed by Hojeda, joined his 1498-99 voyage as navigator. Furthermore, it seems (Magnaghi is certain) that when the expedition reached the present Guiana, Vespucci left Hojeda and went forth on his own, discovering on the way the mouth of the Amazon River, six months before Pinzon, as noted by Magnaghi. After exploring that river for quite a few miles, thus actually discovering Brazil a few months before Cabral, he turned north, saw the mouth of the Orinoco River in Venezuela, and then proceeded toward Haiti to rejoin Hojeda.

Professor Morison does not mention that back in Spain Vespucci planned a new voyage, but the Spanish government turned him down and he offered his services to Portugal. It was thus that at the head of a well-equipped expedition Vespucci sailed on May 13, 1501 on a voyage that Magnaghi describes as having been after that of Columbus, "the most glorious of all expeditions preceding that of Magellan." Almagià also calls this voyage "of fundamental importance in the history of geographical discovery in that Vespucci himself, and scholars as well, became convinced that the newly discovered lands were not part of Asia, but a New World." (Almagià, article on Vespucci in *Enciclopaedia Britannica,* 14th edition, 1973 reprint, when Almagià was already dead.) It was during that voyage that Vespucci explored the entire Atlantic coast of South America, from Venezuela to the Strait of Magellan. No small feat, indeed, aside from the fact that in March 1508 Spain named him *piloto mayor,* an office created expressly for him, which he held until his death. That alone should be proof enough not only of his "outstanding knowledge of the theory and practice of nautical science" as noted by Almagià, but also of his integrity and trustworthiness, especially if we take into account the jealousy of Spanish navigators who did not relish the idea that a foreigner, even though naturalized, had been named chief navigator of their country. Magnaghi calls Vespucci the greatest cosmographer of his time, a most audacious navigator, and the forerunner of Magellan. To quote Almagià once more, "As a seaman and navigator he may be said to stand comparison with Columbus, though the latter became more famous."

As for the naming of America after him, Vespucci had absolutely nothing to do with it, for it was the German mapmaker Waldseemüller who felt that the name of America, like Europa, Asia and Africa, should be given to the New World (actually South America at first) because it was Amerigo Vespucci that realized that it was a new world. But on that point, the "new world" was not much different from that of Columbus.

But why Vespucci? Why not Columbus? Was not Columbus a Nordic, whose ancestors, as Professor Morison puts it, "doubtless belonged to other races than Italian?" Doubtless, of course! Other Nordics had been saying the same thing about other famous Italians from Dante and Leonardo to Garibaldi. By the same token, I could say that I, too, am a Nordic, because I have blue eyes, a light complexion, and other Norman features. As a matter of fact, Amari in his *Storia dei Musulmani di Sicilia* mentions one Norman count named Schiavo. But I was born in Sicily, of Sicilian parents, my grandparents were born in Sicily (my grandfather and my father were born in the same house I was born in). Et cetera, et cetera. But what does that prove?

13

JOHN CABOT

Giovanni Caboto, or John Cabot, as he was known in England, is one of the major discoverers and explorers about whom we know very little, possibly because, as told by Alberto Magnaghi in the *Enciclopedia Italiana Treccani*, of the secrecy with which England wanted to surround her rights (actually claim) to North America. His son, so it seems, may have added to the paucity of the information allegedly to give more importance to his own voyages of exploration, more than discovery. But this point is still open to question.

Giovanni Caboto, briefly, was born in Genoa, like Columbus, but in his youth he moved to Venice where he married a Venetian and thereby became a Venetian citizen. Shortly before the discovery of America, so it seems, he settled in England, at Bristol, but soon after that came Columbus and he decided to follow on his track, or more appropriately, on his wake.

To make a long story short, Henry VII, the King of England, gave Cabot a commission for a voyage of discovery, provided it was done at his expense (more likely of his backers), and in May, 1497, he sailed, together with his three sons, on a voyage of discovery during which he explored the coast of North America, planting the English flag for the first time on American soil. His boat was even smaller than that of Columbus's Niña, or about 50 tons, a frail little thing compared to the 65,000 tons of the Queen Elizabeth II. With the possible exception of his three sons, he had a crew of 18 men, one of them a Frenchman, and the other an Italian, a barber, so that he could be clean-shaven and would not frighten the natives (whom he never met), as humorously noted by Prof. Morison in his recent book, *The European Discovery of America*.

Cabot, however, did not get to see anybody, except schools or shoals of fish, the famous cod, which was to change the diet of Europeans because it could be dried in the sun and thus exported to Europe as stockfish. So, after planting the English flag and, next to it, the standard of St. Mark (Venice's flag) on June 24, Saint John's Day (his own saint's day), he returned to England, where he was welcomed with great joy. The King, as a reward gave him a pension of 20 English pounds (one hundred dollars) and authorized him to start a new voyage with five ships. He sailed a year later, but only one ship ever came back to England. The other four, including Cabot's ship, were never heard of.

Thus, an Italian gave a world to Spain, another Italian, Cabot, gave an empire to Britain, and still another Italian, Verrazzano, gave another world to France. Briefly, it was Cabot who gave England her claim to North America.

Years later, Benjamin Franklin tried to argue that England had no claim or right to America because the King did not pay a pence for the expedition, as Franklin stated in his famous address on "Vindication for the Colonies" on June 15, 1775. The King, said Franklin, "granted a commission to Sebastian Cabot [it was John and not his son Sebastian, as erroneously stated by Franklin], a Venetian, and his sons to sail into western seas for the discovery of new countries; but it was to be 'suis corum propriis sumptibus et expensis,' at their own cost and charges," thus flatly contradicting the allegation made in 1622 that Virginia "being the rightful inheritance of his Majesty, as being first discoured at the costs and charges of that most prudent Prince of famous memory, *King Henry the Seventh*."

The exact words of the patent are:

"The King, to all of whom, etc. . . . . Greetings: Be it known and made manifest that we have given and granted as by these presents we give and grant, for us and our heirs, to our well-beloved John Cabot, citizen of Venice, and to Lewis, Sebastian and Sancio, sons of the said John, and to the heirs and deputies of them . . ." (for the full text in Latin in facsimile and its English translation, see my *Four Centuries*, p. 52.)

No less interesting is the report that a Venetian residing in London sent to his brothers in Venice (also reprinted in my book, on page 54) in which he tells that

"These English run after him like made people, so that he can enlist as many of them as he pleases, and a number of our own rogues besides. [The Venetians called rogues any citizens of Venice who joined foreign service.]

"The discoverer of these places planted on his new-found land a large cross, with one flag of England and another of St. Mark, by reason of his being a Venetian so that our banner has floated very far afield."

It is clear that the English flag was planted by Cabot and not by the Englishmen, as assumed by Professor Samuel Morison in his *Oxford History of the American People*, New American Library edition, 1972, Vol. I, page 62.

14

GIOVANNI DA VERRAZZANO

"1524 — Giovanni da Verrazano [with one "z"], Italian, explored New England coast for French, probably New York Bay."

That's what the *World Almanac & Book Of Facts* [including quite a few tall stories] for 1976 says on page 711, at 1524. But the *Almanac,* one of the best of its kind in the world, is not always reliable, especially so far as the Italians are concerned. It does not even include Vespucci among the early explorers of the Western Hemisphere (p. 567), or Francis Vigo, or Mazzei, but it does include "Haym Salomon, American merchant, banker, raised money to help finance the American army," a claim which has no leg to stand on as noted in Chapter 10.

Anyway, Verrazzano discovered New York Bay in 1524, and that was 85 years before the arrival of Henry Hudson, as I emphasized in a 24-point type in my book, *Four Centuries of Italian-American History* in 1952. Eighteen years before, however, I had devoted 5 pages (plus the bibliography) to Verrazzano in my book, *The Italians in America Before the Civil War.* Since then very little has been written to change what I wrote in 1952 and in 1934, with the exception of two fine books, a scholarly booklet and an authoritative chapter by Professor Samuel Morison in 1971 (see notes).

The knowledge of Verrazzano's epochal voyage, however, might have been limited to a few scholars or students of geography and the such, had it not been for the ballyhooed celebration of the 300th anniversary of the arrival of Henry Hudson in 1909. Actually, the plans for the celebration were announced three years before, in 1906, enough time for the New York Italians to erect their monument to Verrazzano which was dedicated with great fanfare on October 6, 1909. Whether or not the projected monument and celebration had anything to do with it, an unknown copy of the report which Verrazzano had written for King Francis I, his patron, on his return from America, was found in 1908 in the library of Giulio Macchi di Céllere (accent on the first "e" and not in the second, as in Morison's *European Discovery*), a relative of Ambassador Vincenzo Macchi di Céllere who served in Washington after 1914.

The copy proved to be an Italian duplicate dictated by Verraz-zano, in Italian, with some marginal notes by himself, and as such a document of the utmost importance, because the known copies con-tained so many errors made by the copyists that experts doubted the veracity of the great navigator. The document was so important that it was acquired for a large sum by the Pierpont Library in New York where it remains. It was printed originally in Italian in the *Bollettino della Società Geografica Italiana*, Rome, 1909, by Professor Alessandro Bacchiani of Rome. An English translation by E. H. Hall was printed in 1910 in the *15th Annual Report* of the American Scenic and His-toric Preservation Society of Albany, New York. The translation in Wroth's book, however, is more accurate. See notes.

The passage regarding the landing on what is probably Staten Island is still interesting and so, worth quoting. The translation is Hall's:

"At the end of a hundred leagues," says Verrazzano, "we found a very agreeable situation located within two small prominent hills [un sito molto ameno posto fra due piccoli colli eminenti], in the midst of which flowed to the sea a very big river [riviera], which was deep within the mouth; and from the sea to the hills of that [place] with the rising of the tides, which we found eight feet, any laden ship might have passed. On account of being anchored off the coast in good shelter, we did not wish to adventure in without knowledge of the entrances. We were with the small boat, entering the said river to the land, which we found much populated. The people, almost like the others, clothed with the feathers of birds of various colors, came to-ward us joyfully, uttering very great exclamations of admiration, show-ing us where we could land with the boat more safely. We entered said river about half a league [little less than two miles] where we saw it made a very beautiful lake with a circuit of about three leagues [about 11 miles] through which they [the Indians] went, going from one and another part to the number of their little barges, with in-numerable people, who passed from one shore and the other in order to see us. In an instant, as is wont to happen in navigation, a gale of unfavorable wind blowing in from the sea, we were forced to return to the ship, leaving the said land with much regret because of its com-modiousness and beauty, thinking it was not without some properties of value . . . The anchor raised . . ." That gale spoiled a beautiful day of great historical importance, because had it not been for the gale Verrazzano might have ventured north into either the Hudson River or East River of today. Needless to say, the whole account is of the utmost interest and should be read by those devotees of nakedeness, because even the Indian savages (?) had a sense of shame and pro-

52

priety, as they covered their "private parts with some skins of little animals like martens, a girdle of fine grass woven with various tails of other animals which hang around the body as far as the knees; the rest nude; the head likewise. Some wear certain garlands of feathers of birds."

After his return to France, Verrazzano sailed out again on another voyage to America in 1528, from which he was not to return, either dead or alive. Because of his past experience during the 1524 voyage, Verrazzano believed that all Indians were friendly and so, near Panama, in the Gulf of Darien, he got down to his barge with six of his men, only to be attacked by local cannibals who killed him and his companions and devoured them while Verrazzano's brother, Girolamo, and the other members of cthe crew, were looking on helplessly. If he was born in 1485, Verrazzano was only 43 years old when he came to his end.

What did Verrazzano's two voyages accomplish? For one thing, they kept alive the interest of the French into further expansion in America, to offset the Spanish and English pretensions. More important was the fact that Verrazzano confirmed, once and for all, that the lands discovered by Columbus and the other navigators after him were not a continuation of Asia, but indeed a new world, as Columbus had become convinced that it was, although as a continuation of Asia.

And why did King Francis I choose an Italian, just as the Spaniards and the English kings had done?

Partly because the Italians were the leading navigators of their day — at least not in the service of their own countries — but also because of the close connections of the King, the son of Louise of Savoy, with Italian artists, generals, men of letters and bankers. It was in his arms that Leonardo Da Vinci died at Amboise, and it was at Pavia that he was made prisoner in 1525, returning to freedom a year later. It was after Pavia that the King is supposed to have written to his mother, "Tout est perdu, for l'honneur" (all is lost save honor), which actually is a short form of what he wrote to his mother, condensed by contemporary historians.

15

MARCOS DE NIZA

There is not one book on exploration that does not deal with Coronado's famous wild-goose chase in 1540-1542 and with Marcos De Niza, to use his Spanish name.

The story is well known. A year before, in 1539, Marcos, who was a humble Franciscan friar, had been sent by the Spanish viceroy to try and locate the famous Seven Cities of Cibola which were said to be full of gold, emeralds and other fabulous jewels. Marcos went, together with another Italian friar named Onorato, a Negro survivor of the famous settlement of Narvaez in Florida eight years before, and a number of Indians. The Negro, named Estevan or Estevanico in Spanish (Stephen in English), was sent ahead, sending back some reports in the guise of crosses, each cross indicating by its size the importance of what he had found. Thus, if he had little to report or if he had found little worthwhile, he sent a small cross, if he had found something of value he sent a large cross. At last he sent a very huge cross which aroused the curiosity of the friar who kept on going at a faster pace, but when he got close to the Seven Cities he learned that the Negro had been killed. Nevertheless, the friar went on until he got in view of the first of the Seven Cities, but fearing for his own life and more for the danger that had he been killed nobody would have known of his "fabulous" finding, he got as close as possible and what he saw was enough to satisfy him that the Seven Cities did exist. Back in Mexico City, his report aroused the curiosity, enthusiasm and greed of everybody, and an expedition was soon equipped to conquer those towns in the name of the King of Spain. We all know that after a march of some two thousand miles all the way to central Kansas, in a place called Quivira, now identified with the town of Lindsborg, some twenty miles south of Salina, Kansas, Coronado gave up and went back, defeated, to Mexico.

The importance of Coronado's and Niza's explorations cannot be overestimated, to judge by the numerous places named after the former, as far east as Philadelphia. ,I myself, stayed at the Hotel Coronado, a first class place, in St. Louis, Mo., for some months in 1929. But I know of only one place named after the friar, "Fray Marcos Mountain" in Arizona. Anyway, if Coronado had done nothing else than leave us the account of his exploration, especially of one of the towns in Cibola which one can still read with absorbing interest, just as I did recently, he deserves our gratitude. As Professor Bolton put it in his most scholarly and definitive history of the expedition, barring the discovery of unknown manuscripts, Coronado's description of Cibola is a "precious trophy . . . which will be prized through the ages."

As for Friar Marcos, even though his description was far from accurate, for which he was highly criticized by Coronado, and although Coronado was met with hostility at Cibola, as a whole the presence of the friar, who had been treated by the Indians "with the greatest care and tenderness" during his first expedition (Bolton), spared Coronado untold trouble. Actually, Fray Marcos was sent out on his first expedition after his bishop and the viceroy had asked the approval of none other than Emperor Charles V (only recently I saw again the statue of the emperor in Palermo, in Piazza Bologni, erected there 90 years after the Coronado expedition — in the same small square where the victims of the Inquisition were executed). In that report to the emperor, the friar was praised for his knowledge of cosmography (apparently exaggerated), his humility, his diplomacy and other qualities which were to endear him to the Indians. In a few words, Friar Marcos, regardless of his untrustworthy account, not through malice but because of human errors and other causes (I have not forgotten the mirages of which I was the victim when I rode along the alleged route of his expedition in 1950) the friar, I say, made Coronado's expedition much easier, aside from the fact that he had been there before and knew the way.

I must correct here some errors in my book, *Four Centuries* (1952), which was based on my 1934 book, as well as on Vol. II of my *Italian-American History* (1949), both of which were based on the sources then available. I mention this fact because some "experts" who have written about Niza and have copied what I published in my 1952 book, have repeated my errors without checking for additional material, such as for instance, *The Golden Conquistadores*, edited by Harry Rosen, Indianapolis, 1960, in which one will find the Instructions of the Viceroy to Fray Marcos, the report by Fray Marcos in 1539, the letter of the Viceroy to the Emperor, Coronado's report to Mendoza and Castaneda's account. There is another book, even more important, but I must refrain from divulging its title because of a litigation which has not yet been settled. It is in that book that I first learned that a photograph of the alleged inscription by Fray Marcos published on page 65 of my book, *Four Centuries of Italian-American History*, was a fraud.

As to the nationality of the friar, only a person not familiar with the history and geography of Italy would call him French, or a

Savoyard. To mention a few recent instances, in the 1972 coffee-table book published by the American Heritage Press, *The Discovery of North America*, we find that "Marcos de Niza had been born in France" (p. 10), which is ridiculous, because although Nice was ruled in the past by both France and Italy (actually the Republic of Genoa and the King of Sardinia at different times), it was not under French rule at the time the friar was born. Actually, Nice was ceded to France in 1859 by Victor Emmanuel II, King of Sardinia until 1861 and the first king of united Italy after 1861, in compensation for the assistance France gave Piedmont in its war against Austria in 1859.

What I find even more amazing is that an Italian-American professor who had served as United States consul at Genoa, Andrew Rolle, should repeat in his book, *The Immigrant Upraised* (p. 45), that the friar was "a colorful son of Savoy," just as we find in the *Catholic Encyclopedia* of 1967, a year before the publication of the Rolle book, except that in the *Catholic Encyclopedia* friar Marcos is called "a Savoyard." All of which is like saying that the Sicilians were also Savoyards because following the Treaty of Utrecht in 1713, Sicily was ceded to Vittorio Amedeo, Duke of Savoy, but only for seven years, as in 1720 Sicily was turned over to Austria, thus changing the Sicilians into Austrians by the same fiat, that is.

Aside from the fact that both the Spanish and French encyclopedias call Marcos de Niza "an Italian," and that Nice is east of the river Varo (mentioned by Dante, if I am not mistaken) which marks the boundary between France and Italy, or aside from the fact that Garibaldi also was born in Nice (by the same token he was not an Italian), and aside from many other factors which we need not go into here, there is the question of the language, for the people of Nice still speak Italian, as I noted with some fun years ago on a visit to its famous casino and had some pleasant verbal exchanges with some of the croupiers at that place. Incidentally, although the croupiers spoke in Italian to me, a better Italian than the salad spoken by Italian-Americans, they kept on warning me that they were not Italians, but Frenchmen. That, of course, is of no consequence.

One final thing, for the benefit of some misinformed or ignorant people, like the editors of the American Heritage Press who called the friar "Marcos de Nizza." "Marcos de," of course, is Spanish, whereas "Nizza" is Italian. To use the Spanish name, the correct form is "Marcos de Niza," but in Italian the correct way is "Marco da (small "d") Nizza," as one finds in the catalog of the Library of Congress. I suggest that form to the editors of the current *Catholic Encyclopedia* who, obviously, are not as well posted as our greatest library.

16

ENRICO TONTI

It has been said that La Salle would not be remembered today if Parkman had not written about him. I am not sure about that, but I am sure that, without minimizing in the least the achievements, the character, the integrity, the courage, and other superior qualities of La Salle, (he also had his share of faults), it can be positively stated that his lieutenant, Enrico Tonti, or Henri Tonty, as he signed his name, was not only his equal, but also achieved more because he continued La Salle's work for another seventeen years following the assassination of La Salle by his own men. Those seventeen years, furthermore, were not spent roaming around land that was already explored, although not minutely, but in consolidating the power of France in the entire Mississippi Valley. And that was not a small achievement, if we take into consideration the dissensions that existed among the French in North America and that La Salle's enemies were also Tonti's enemies, foremost among them Father Louis Hennepin, the great Jesuit priest and explorer.

The story of Tonti is told in many books, such as Parkman's *La Salle and the Discovery of the Great West,* but much more in detail in the fine monograph *Henry De Tonty—Fur Trader of the Mississippi* by Edmund R. Murphy, Baltimore, The Johns Hopkins Press, 1941, with a foreword by Professor Bolton, who concurred with the author about the neglect which Tonti had suffered at the hands of historians — "or perhaps injustice is a better word," as he put it.

As I may be charged with filiopietism (a word so dear to some presumptuous half-baked historians and sociologists or whatever) let me quote a few lines from the last two pages of Murphy's book.

After noting that Iberville, the co-founder, with Tonti, of New Orleans, was able to identify the Mississippi River by means of a letter which Tonti had written to La Salle fourteen years before, and how Tonti's *voyageurs* who reached the new settlement with a cargo of beaver pelts helped Iberville to cope with the problems connected with the new settlement, Professor Murphy concludes his fine study with the following words:

"By reason of Tonti's contributions, it may be said that he paved the way for the vanguard of Americans lured to the west by 'manifest destiny.' American advance into the Louisiana country was greatly facilitated by the economic development of that region under France, and in that development, Tonty had played a significant role. While Tonty's contributions are highly important, he has never been accorded the place, independent from that of La Salle, which he deserves. Yet, when the accomplishments of La Salle and Tonty are compared, it is Tonty who gains by the comparison. It is true that he seconded La Salle in all things, but while the latter conceived, Tonty achieved." Tonti's numerous achievements, including the signing of the *proces verbal* taking possession of Louisiana, follow. Then Prof. Murphy ends his study by asking, "How long is he destined to remain only the faithful lieutenant of La Salle, only the shadow of the explorer's greatness in the pages of history?"

The latest tribute to Enrico Tonti was given in 1953 by Marcel Giraud, the foremost historian of Louisiana, in his *History of French Louisiana*, translated by Joseph C. Lambert (an excellent translation, by the way) and published by the Louisiana State University at Baton Rouge in 1974. In one paragraph Giraud epitomizes Tonti's achievements, not only as La Salle's lieutenant, but as ruler of the Mississippi Valley during the 17 years following La Salle's murder. On page 6 of Vol. I of his work, he says: "Another example is Henry De Tonty, who sacrificed his security at Fort St. Louis in order to trade for pelts among the Illinois tribes. In the company of La Salle, and then in search of his ships and his unfortunate colony, he went through the Mississippi Valley and ascended the valley of the Red River, reaching the Cenis and Palasquessons, not far from the nearest Spanish missions. His years of observations of these lands and their peoples and his active participation in the campaigns against the Iroquois enabled him to maintain the prestige of France among the Indians without losing his profitable trade. He 'is the man who knows this country the best,' said the missionary Buisson de Saint-Cosme. 'He has been to the sea twice, he has been twice into the depth of the lands of the most faraway nations, he is everywhere feared and esteemed.'"

On the other hand, I must report that the fine article on Tonti in the 1940 *World Book Encyclopedia* (which I bought for my daughters) has been replaced by a worthless short item which is contrary to the evidence available in all recent works, including the facsimiles of documents in my *Four Centuries* which prove beyond the shadow of a doubt that Tonti was born in Italy, and not "probably in Paris," as stated by the Harvard contributor to that encyclopedia who, obviously, does not keep abreast of the literature in his fields of interest.

17

ALPHONSE TONTI
(Co-founder of Detroit)

Alphonse Tonti or Tonty, the younger brother of Enrico, was one of the two founders of the City of Detroit, and its governor for twelve years. Some writers conveniently forget the *indispensable* role played by him in the very beginning of the new settlement, for without him Cadillac would not have been able to remain in the new post, surrounded by enemy Indians and by disloyal Frenchmen ready to desert him or to turn any situation to their own account at the least possible opportunity.

Tonty has been pictured as dishonest and unfit to command a post, by some local historians who apparently are not aware of the fact that Detroit's early history cannot be studied without taking into due account the conditions that prevailed there, as throughout New France, in colonial days. Not only in New France, but in all colonial possessions, at all times and under all flags, not excluding Virginia under English governors. We need not mention India under the famous Clive. It is possible that Tonty plied the Indians with liquor, but how many American Indian agents did not? As for the charges advanced against him, one must remember that, with a few exceptions, all prominent men in New France were exposed to similar attacks at one time or another. La Salle was surrounded by enemies. Frontenac was recalled. Cadillac himself had plenty of trouble, not only with the civilians and soldiers at the fort, but especially with the Jesuits, against whom he advanced even more serious charges than he did against Tonty. Aside from that, none of the charges against Tonty was ever proved, as a careful study of the Cadillac Papers reveals. It is possible, on the other hand, that he had very influential friends at Montreal and in Paris who whitewashed them, but had they been very serious he would not have been reinstated and left in charge for a period of seventeen years. Tonty, moreover, was a foreigner (a Neapolitan, as Cadillac called him) and the easy target of other Frenchmen who wanted to replace him. Other Italians in other countries had to go through similar charges. Columbus, Vespucius, Sebastian Cabot, for instance. It is simply ridiculous to judge a man in the wilderness of 17th century America by the moral standards of our own days.

Timothy Severin, the brilliant 27-year-old English author of *Explorers of the Mississippi* (see notes to chapter on Enrico Tonti), has a very poor opinion of Alphonse Tonti, but it is quite possible that he has not seen all the documents available that I have examined. In any event, he modifies his opinion somewhat by adding that Tonti "redeemed his reputation by fighting gallantly against the Iroquois until he was reappointed to his old command at Detroit, where he remained for twelve years until he died in 1727. That explanation, to my mind, is rather simplistic and not satisfactory. Twelve years are quite a long time, indeed, and the fact that his financial affairs at Detroit were found to be in shambles after his death does not necessarily mean that he was responsible for them.

Alphonse Tonti was born in Paris in 1659 and came to America sometime before 1688. After serving in various capacities, including that of commandant at Mackinac, in 1700 he was chosen to accompany Cadillac as a captain, not as a lieutenant, as stated by some writers, to build a fort and start a new settlemen at Detroit. In 1704 he was put in charge of Fort Frontenac, but in 1717 he returned to Detroit, where he ruled as governor for eleven more years. His daughter, Theresa, was the first white child born in what is now the great city of Detroit. He certainly had more to do with the early consolidation and development of the rising village than Cadillac himself, if residence alone is considered. (See my book, *Italians in America Before the Civil War*, pp. 117-125.)

18

FATHER BRESSANI

Father Francesco Giuseppe Bressani was born in Rome on May 6, 1612, and died in Florence on September 9, 1672. The son of Pietro Bressani, a physician connected with the hospital of San Lorenzo, in the Eternal City, and of Cornelia De Rossi, he entered the novitiate of the Society of Jesus on August 15, 1626, completed his studies at Rome and Clermont, France, and for a while taught at Tivoli, Sezze, and Paris. In 1642 he was ministering to the French at Quebec, but during the following year he was already laboring among the Algonquin Indians at Three Rivers, in Canada. In 1644 he was transferred for missionary work among the Hurons and was on his way to take up his new duties, when he was captured by the ferocious Iroquois who inhabited the central and west parts of New York State and who subjected him to the tortures described by himself below. For two months Father Bressani bore all the torments with a fortitude becoming a true soldier of the Catholic Faith. Finally, when he seemed about to die, he was sold as a slave, for a few beads, to an old Indian who succeeded in selling him, soon after, for three hundred francs, to some Dutch sailors who happened to be at Fort Orange, on the site of which the present city of Albany is located. It was through the kindness and generosity of the Dutch that Father Bressani was sent to Governor Kieft at New Amsterdam (the present city of New York), who received him with utmost kindness and hospitality and gave him a letter of safe-conduct in which he wrote: "Christian charity requires that he be humanely treated by those into whose hands he may happen to fall. Wherefore we request all Governors, viceroys or their lieutenants and captains that they would afford him their favor in going and returning, promising to do the same on like occasion." Thus Father Bressani was able to return to France first and to Rome soon after.

One would imagine that the tortures he went through would have been sufficient to keep him away from the Indians, but Father Bressani was willing to suffer for his Faith, and a year after his return to Europe he was back at Three Rivers. There, at the confluence of the St. Maurice and the St. Lawrence, between Quebec and Montreal, he labored for four more years, until the mission was destroyed by the Iroquois.

According to Thwaites, "in the summer of 1648 he came down to Quebec with additional missionaries, returning to his field of labor with a reinforcement of five brethren. In the following year he went with the fugitive Hurons to St. Joseph (Christian) Island; but their situation was so perilous that Bressani was sent by his superiors to Quebec, to ask for succor,—a vain request, however, since the authorities there could spare none of the slender force of soldiers." The return to his mission, in the meanwhile, had become very difficult on account of the many dangers from the Iroquois, and he was compelled to remain at Quebec where he ministered for a while. In November, 1650, Father Bressani was called to Italy because of his failing health, and there he spent the last years of his life as a missionary and preacher.

Although Father Bressani labored chiefly in Canada, his name is connected with the early history of New York State. He was the first man to describe Niagara Falls, thirty years before Hennepin, and the second Catholic priest to visit the present site of the city of Albany, Jogues having been the first. Of the early Jesuits in New France he is certainly the most distinguished one, as mathematician, astronomer, geographer, and historian. He wrote *Breve Relatione d'alcune Missioni dei PP. della Compagnia di Gesù nella Nuova Francia, which was* published at Macerata in 1653, and which appears in English in Thwaites' Jesuit Relations, Vols. 38, 39, 40. He also wrote, in French, *Observations sur une Eclipse de Lune faites at Quebec le* 18 *Novembre* 1649, which was inserted in the proceedings of the French Academy of Sciences. On July 15, 1644, he sent to his superior in Rome an account of his tortures at the hands of the Indians, which follows, in part, as translated in the Jesuit Relations:

OUR VERY REVEREND FATHER IN CHRIST
PAX CHRISTI

I know not whether Your Paternity will recognize the letter of a poor cripple, who formerly, when in perfect health, was well known to you. The letter is badly written, and quite soiled, because, in addition to other inconveniences, he who writes it has only one whole finger on his right hand; and it is difficult to avoid staining the paper with the blood which flows from his wounds, not yet healed: he uses arquebus powder for ink and the earth for a table. He writes it from the country of the Hiroquois, where at present he happens to be a captive; and desires to give a brief report of that which the divine providence has at last ordained for him. I started from Three Rivers by order of the Superior, on the 27th of last April—in company with six Christian Barbarians, and a young Frenchman, with three canoes,—to go to the country of the Hurons. The first evening, the Huron who was guiding our canoe, wishing to shoot at an eagle, was the occasion of our wreck in the lake named for St. Peter; two Hurons, by swimming, dragged me to land, as I did not know how to swim, and a bad omen, and counseled to return, but I who suspected some superstition in this discourse, judged it best to proceed to another French fort, 30 miles farther, where I hoped that we might refresh ourselves. They obeyed me, and we started for that place on the following morning, quite early; but the snow and the bad weather prevented us from making much progress, there we spent the night, all drenched. The Hurons took the accident for and obliged us to end that day at noon. The third day, when not distant more than 22 or 24 miles from Three Rivers, and 7 or 8 from the fortress of Richelieu, we were taken captives by 27 Hiroquois, who, having killed one of our Barbarians, captured the others and me with them. We might have fled, or indeed, killed some Iroquois; but I, for my part, on seeing my companions taken, judged it better to remain with them,—accepting as a sign of the will of God the inclination and almost the resolution of those who conducted me, who chose rather to surrender than to escape by flight. Those who had captured us made horrible cries and after many thanks to the Sun for having in their hands, among the others, a "black robe,"—as thus they call the Jesuits—they changed our canoes. Then, having taken from us everything,—that is, provisions for all of ours who lived among the Hurons, who were in extreme necessity, as they had not been able for several years to obtain help from Europe,—they commanded us to sing. Meanwhile they led us to a neighboring river, where they divided the spoils, and tore away the scalp and hair, from the slaughtered Hurons, in order to carry it as in triumph, attached to a pole; they also cut off his feet and hands, along with the most fleshy parts of the body, to eat them, with the heart. Then they made us cross the lake, to spend the night in a place somewhat retired, but very damp,—in which we began to sleep, bound and in the open air, as during the remainder of the journey. On the following day we embarked on a river upon which we had hardly made a few miles when they commanded me to throw into the water my writings, which they had left with me till then,—as if these had been the cause, as they superstitiously believed, of the wreck of our canoe; and they were astounded that I showed some feeling on that score, not having shown any at the loss of everything else. We still voyaged two days against the current of the river, until we were constrained by the rapids to go ashore; and we traveled six days within woods. The second day,—which was a Friday, the sixth day of May,—we met other Hiroquois, who were going to war. They accompanied many threats with some blows which they gave us; and, having related to our party the death of one of theirs, killed by a Frenchman, the result was that my captors began to treat me more harshly than before.

When they seized us, they were dying with hunger; therefore in two or three days they consumed all our provisions, and for the remainder of the journey there was no food except from either hunting or fishing, or from some wild root if any were found. During the extreme hunger which we suffered, they found on the shore of the river a dead and putrid beaver, which at evening they gave to me, that I might wash it in the river, but, having thrown it away—persuading myself that this was their intention, so stinking it was—I paid for that with a severe penance. I will not write here what I suffered on that journey; enough to know that we marched, carrying burdens, in the woods, where there is no road at all, but only stones or young shoots, or ditches or water or snow, which was not yet everywhere melted. We traveled without shoes; fasting sometimes till three and four o'clock in the afternoon and often whole days; exposed to the rain, and soaked in the water of the torrents and rivers which we had to cross. At evening, my office was to gather the wood, carry the water, and do the cooking, when there was any; and if I came short in anything, or did not understand well, the blows were not lacking—and much less did these fail when we happened to meet people who were going either fishing or hunting; besides, I was hardly able to rest at night, for being bound to a tree and exposed to the severity of the air, which was still quite cold. We finally reached their lake on which—when they had made other canoes, at which it was necessary for me to assist them—we sailed five or six days, after which we landed and there we made three days' journey on foot. On the fourth day, which was the 15th of May,—about the 20th hour, being still fasting, we arrived at a river where about 400 Barbarians were assembled for fishing; being already apprised of our arrival, they then came to meet us.

At about two hundred paces from their cabins, they stripped me naked, and made me go first; on either side, the young men of the country stood in line, every one with his stick in his hand, but the first of them had, instead of the stick, a knife. Then, as I began to proceed this one suddenly stopped me; and, having taken my left hand, with the knife which he held, he made in it an incision between the little finger and the ring-finger, with so much force and violence that I believed he would split my whole hand and the others began to load blows as far as the stage prepared for our torment. Then they made me mount upon some great pieces of bark, about nine palms above the ground—in order that we might be seen and mocked by the people. I was now bruised all over, and covered with blood, which was flowing from all parts of my body—and exposed to a very cold wind, which made it suddenly congeal over the skin; but I greatly consoled myself to see that God granted me the favor of suffering in this world some little pain in place of that which I was under obligation, because of my sins, to pay in the other with torments incomparably greater. Meanwhile, the warriors arrived, and were magnificently received by the people of this village; and, when they were refreshed with the best that they had from their fishing, they commanded me to sing; it may be imagined how we could do so, fasting, weak from the journey, overwhelmed with blows and trembling with cold from head to foot. Some time after, a Huron slave brought us a dish of Indian corn; and a Captain, seeing me tremble with cold, at my urgency finally tossed me the half of an old summer garment all torn, which covered rather than warmed me. They made us sing until the warriors went away; and they left us in the hands of the young men of the place, who finally made us come down from that stage, where we had been about two hours,—in order to make us dance in their manner; and because I did not do so, or know how to, they beat me, pricked me, tore out my hair and beard, etc. They kept us in this place for five or six days for their pastime, exposed to the discretion or indiscretion of everybody. It was necessary to obey the very children and that in things little reasonable, and often contrary. "Get up and sing," said one. "Be quiet," said the other; and if I obeyed one, the other ill-used me. "Here, give thy hand, which I will burn for thee"; and the other burned me because I did not extend it to him.

They commanded me to take the fire in my fingers and put it into their pipes, and then they purposely made it fall four or five times in succession, in order to make me burn my hands by picking it up again from the ground. This was usually done at night. Toward evening, the Captains shouted through the cabins with frightful voices: "Up! assemble yourselves, O, young men, and come to caress our prisoners." At this invitation they arose and gathered themselves into some large cabin; and, lifting from my back that poor rag of clothing which they had returned to me, they left me naked. Then some pricked me with sharp sticks, others with firebrands; these burned me with red-hot stones, those with hot ashes and lighted coals. They made me walk around the fire, where they had fixed in the earth sharp sticks between the burning ashes; some tore out my hair, others my beard; and every night, after having made me sing, and tormented me as above, they would burn one of my nails or fingers for the space of eight or ten minutes; of ten that I had, I have now only one whole one left— and even from this one they had torn out the nail with their teeth. One evening, they burned one of my nails; on another, the first joint or section of a finger; on the next the second. In six times, they burned nearly six of my fingers, and more than 18 times they applied the fire and iron to my hands alone; and meanwhile it was necessary to sing. Thus they treated us till one or two hours after midnight and then they left me on the bare ground, usually tied to a spot, and exposed to the rain, without other bed or cover than a small skin, which covered not the half of my body,—even at times without anything, because they had already torn up that piece of garment; although, out of pity, they made of it for me enough to cover that which decency does not permit to be uncovered, even among themselves, but retained the rest.

I was treated in this way, and worse, for a whole month; but, at this first place, no longer than eight days. I would never have believed that a man could endure so hard a life . . . We started thence on the 26th of May; and, four days later we arrived at the first Village of this nation. On this journey,—made on foot, amid rains and other hardships,—my sufferings were greater than before. The barbarian who conducted me was more cruel than the first, and I was wounded, weak, ill fed, and half naked; more- over, I slept in the open air, bound to a stake or to a tree, trembling all night with cold and from the pain of these bonds. At difficult places in the road, I had need of some one to aid me because of my weakness, but all help was denied me; for this reason, I often fell, renewing my wounds; and to these they added new blows, in order to urge me to proceed,—thinking that I was feigning for the sake of staying behind, and then taking flight. On one occasion, among others, I fell into a river, and come near being drowned; however, I got out, I know not how; and all drenched with water, together with a quite heavy bundle on my shoulders, I was obliged to com- plete about six miles more marching until evening. They, meanwhile, jeered at me, and at my stupidity in having allowed myself to fall into the river; and they did not omit, at night, to burn off one of my nails.

We finally arrived at the first Village of this nation, where our entrance was similar to the former and still more cruel—because in addition to the blows with their fists,, and other blows which they gave me on the most sensitive parts of the body—they split for the second time my left hand between the middle finger and the forefinger; and I received beatings in so great number that they made me fall to the ground, half dead. I thought that I would lose my right eye, with my sight; and, although I did not rise from the ground, for I could not, they did not cease to beat me, chiefly on the breast and on the head. Indeed, without some other hindrance, they would have ended by killing me, had not a Captain caused me to be dragged —as it were, by force—upon a stage of bark, where they cut off the thumb of my left hand wounded the forefinger. Meanwhile a great rain came up, with thunder and lightning; and they went away leaving us there, naked in the water, until some one, taking pity on us, toward evening led us to the cabin. Here they tormented us with greater cruelty and impudence than ever, without a moment of rest: they forced me to eat filth; burned the rest of my nails and some fingers: wrung off my toes and bored one of them with a firebrand; and I know not what they did not do to me once, when I feigned to be in a swoon, in order to seem not to perceive something indecent that they were doing. Surfeited with tormenting us here, they sent us to another Village nine or ten miles distant, where, besides the other torments already mentioned, they suspended me by the feet,—sometimes with cords, again with chains, which they had taken from the Dutch; with these, at night, they left me bound—hands, feet and neck—to several stakes, or as usual upon the bare ground. Six or seven nights they tormented me in such fashion, and in such places, that I could not describe these things, nor could they be read, without blushing.

In this manner of living I had become so fetid and horrible that every one drove me away like a piece of carrion; and they approached me for no other purpose than to torment me. Scarcely did I find any one to feed me,—although I had not the use of my hands, which were abnormally swollen, and putrid; I was thus, of course, still further tormented by hunger, which led me to eat Indian corn raw—not without concern for my health,—and made me find a relish in chewing clay, although I could not easily swallow it. I was covered with loathsome vermin, and could neither get rid of them nor defend my self from them. In my wounds, worms were produced; out of one finger alone, more than four fell in one day. I had an abscess in the right thigh, caused by blows and frequent falls, which hindered me from all repose,—especially as I had only skin and bone, and the earth for bed. Several times the Barbarians, tried, but to no purpose, to open it, with sharp stones,—not without great pain to me. I was compelled to employ as surgeon the renegade Huron who had been taken with us. The latter—on the day which, as was believed, was the eve of my death —opened it for me with four knife-thrusts, and caused blood and matter to issue from it, in so great abundance and with such stench that all the Barbarians of the cabin were constrained to abandon it. I desired and was awaiting death, but without some horror of the fire; I was preparing for it, however, as best I could."

Father Bressani, however, was spared the supreme sacrifice and, as noted at the beginning, was sold to an Indian slave. A year later he was back in America.

19

THE INDOMITABLE FATHER CHINO

It is hard to write briefly about Father Chino and still do justice to his immense work. It is even hard to say whether he was greater as a farmer, as a statesman, as an explorer, as a chronicler or as a missionary. Of course, he was over and above everything else a Christian laborer, but since we in America — at least many Americans — love to measure everything in terms of dollars and cents, we shall start by attempting to estimate his work as a rancher.

It is not generally known that there were no domestic animals in the New World when the Spaniards first landed in Florida or in Mexico. They brought over horses, cattle, sheep, goats, and every other domestic animal which they considered necessary for the new American economy. As they advanced northward they took along with them or sent for the animals which were needed to start a new ranch, thus creating new nuclei from which the missions obtained the necessary food to carry on the work of God. The greatest of these missions was that of Dolores, in Pimeria, which Prof. Bolton calls "the Mother of Missions."

How many heads of cattle Father Chino furnished to the rising missions of Pimeria and of Lower California (Mexico) is not exactly known but may be guessed from the instances recorded by him in his *Favores Celestiales*, which Prof. Bolton has edited under the name of *Kino's Historical Memoir of Pimeria Alta*. It is certain that when the California missions were started, and the older missions came to their assistance, "Kino took the lead." What that meant we may guess from the fact that the district of Oposura gave one hundred head of cattle and a thousand head of sheep and goats. On another occasion, when he turned over the mission of Cocospora to another priest, he delivered to him some one thousand head of cattle, sheep and goats, and droves of horses, oxen, mares, etc. When he founded San Xavier del Bac mission he provided it with 1,400 head of cattle from the Dolores mission and in the same year he sent 700 more head of cattle to Father Salvaterra in California. As Prof. Bolton says, he was "easily the cattle king of his day and region." But he did more than that, for *out of the missions of Pimeria and California were born, in no small measure, the cattle industry of the Southwest of the future United States and the fine orchards of modern California.*

DOLORES MISSION

Dolores today exists no more; even the remaining wall which Prof. Bolton saw there in 1911 has disappeared. But in its days it set an example to the missions of California, both below and above the present border. It had a church, of course, gardens, orchards, ranches, farm buildings, but also workshops and homes for the help. Its description by Father Chino will help us to understand the structure of those missions. It has, said the great missionary, "its church adequately furnished with ornaments, chalices, cups of gold, bells and choir chapel; likewise a great many large and small cattle, oxen, fields, a garden with various kinds of garden crops, Castilian fruit trees, grapes, peaches, quinces, figs, pomegranates, pears and clingstones. It has a forge for blacksmiths, a carpenter shop, a pack train, water mill, many kinds of grain, provisions from rich and abundant harvests of wheat and maize, and other things, including horse and mule herds; all of which serve and are greatly needed both for domestic use as well as for expeditions, and for new conquests and conversions, and to purchase a few gifts and attractions, with which, together with the Word of God, it is customary to contrive to win the minds and the souls of the natives."

The community which in 1695, or eight years after its foundation, had more than ninety families had its own municipal government with its own "justices, captain, governor, alcaldes, fiscal mayor, alguacil, topil and other fiscals," and all the help needed, such as cowboys, muleteers, bakers, rope-makers, gardeners and painters. We should add that he also grew cotton, which later was woven into cloth.

THE EXPLORER

Father Chino's reputation as an explorer is based partly on his discovery (in a way it was a re-discovery) that California was a peninsula and not an island, as it was thought to be until then, and largely on his minute exploration and mapping of a good deal of Lower California and the whole of Pimeria, which, as we have seen, included the southern part of the State of Arizona.

From a special map prepared by Prof. Bolton we learn that Chino undertook thirty-six principal expeditions. On the average, during his twenty-four years of residence, he made some fifty trips, which ranged from 100 to 1,500 miles, as in 1695 when he travelled to Mexico city in fifty-three days. According to Clavigero, Chino, while a missionary, travelled more than 20,000 miles, always on horseback. Some of the trails opened by him had never been trodden by a white man before. He had a system, of course, both he and his men stopping for rest and long siestas, but even then his endurance was extraordinary if we bear in mind that he was close to sixty years of age when he took some of his longest journeys. One of them was over the famous Camino del Diablo from Sonoita to the Gila. "During the few years that this road was much travelled," we learn from a governmental report, "over 400 persons were said to have perished of thirst between Sonoita and Yuma, a record probably without a parallel in North America." Practically all those journeys, Prof. Bolton reminds us, were made without any military aid, and at times even without a single white man.

CHINO THE HISTORIAN

As a writer Father Chino was prolific, some of his writings having great historical value. They can be found listed in Prof. Bolton's *Rim of Christendom*.

THE MISSIONARY

Father Chino's greatest work, of course, was as a missionary. It is estimated that he built more than thirty churches or chapels and that he baptized more than 4,500 persons. He could have baptized more if he had been provided with the needed assistance.

Of the churches that he founded, that of San Xavier del Bac, nine miles south of Tucson, Arizona, is his monument. He built it in 1700 of stone and brick, with a mortar that has retained the consistency of cement. "Its inside dimensions are 105 feet by 70 in the transept and 27 in the nave. It has the form of the Latin cross. Directly in front of the church is an *atrium*, enclosed by a fence wall, where the Indians used to hold their meetings. The façade, profusely adorned with arabesques of varied colours and bearing the coat-of-arms of St. Francis, is flanked by two towers 80 feet high. From the top, made accessible by easy winding stairs cut in the thickness of the walls, a comprehensive view may be obtained over the verdant Santa Cruz valley, the distant city of Tucson and the circle of lofty pinnacled mountains." The church has been restored in recent years and is considered "the best example of the Spanish Renaissance mission style north of Mexico, and the best preserved of all the old mission churches in America." But, according to Prof. Bolton, both the Church of San Xavier del Bac and that of Humacacori, also north of the border in Arizona, as well as the other missions still standing in Pima Land "are in part or mainly Franciscan structures erected on foundations laid by the Padre on Horseback. They are monuments both to the Black Robes and to the Grey Robes who came after them."

Father Eusebio Chino (or Chini as the family name is spelled in Italy at present) was born in Segno in the Val Di Non, near Trent, on August 10, 1645, the son of Francesco and Margherita (Luchi) Chino. He was related to the Jesuit missionary Martino Martini, who won fame in China, where he taught the elements of Christianity and the natural sciences to the emperor and the members of his court. In 1665 he entered the Society of Jesus in Bavaria and for a while taught mathematics at Ingolstadt. He was even offered a professorship in that university, but his heart was set on missionary work and he refused. Yet he had to wait until 1678, when he was almost thirty-three years old, before he could get permission to go on missionary work. Even then there was an unexpected delay of more than two years before he and his companions could find accommodations on a ship sailing for Mexico. Finally he landed at Vera Cruz in May, 1681, reaching Mexico City about June 1. Almost three years had elapsed since he had left Genoa. But soon he was on his way, for in October he left Mexico City to join the expedition which Atondo was preparing for California. The expedition, which left the east coast of Mexico for the peninsula in January, 1683, met with failure, and Father Chino returned to Mexico City, but not for long. At the end of 1686 he started for his missionary work among the Indians of Pima Land, among whom he was to spend the rest of his life, or twenty-four years, as missionary, rancher and explorer. He died at Santa Magdalena on March 15, 1711.

What kind of man was Father Chino?

Father Velarde who was his companion for eight years says of him: "His conversation was of the mellifluous names of Jesus and Mary and of the heathen for whom he was ever offering prayers to God. When saying his breviary he always wept. He was edified by the lives of the saints, whose virtues he preached to us. When he publicly reprimanded a sinner he was choleric. After supper when he saw us already in bed he would enter the church and even though I sat up the whole night reading, I never heard him come out to get the sleep of which he was sparing. One night I casually saw some one whipping him mercilessly. He always took his food without salt, and with mixture of herbs which made it more distasteful. No one ever saw in him any vice whatsoever, for the discovery of lands and the conversions of souls had purified him. These then are the virtues of Father Chino: he prayed much, and was considered without vice. He neither smoked nor took snuff, nor wine, nor slept in a bed. He was so austere that he never took wine except to celebrate Mass, nor had any other bed than the sweat blankets of his horse for a mattress and two Indian blankets (for a cover). He never had more than two coarse shirts, because he gave everything as alms to the Indians. He was merciful to others, but cruel to himself. While violent fevers were lacerating his body, he tried no remedy for six days except to get up to celebrate Mass and to go to bed again. When he died he was almost seventy years old. [Actually he was sixty-six.] He died as he had lived, with extreme humility and poverty. In token of this, during his last illness he did not undress. His death bed, as his bed had always been, consisted of two calfskins for a mattress, two blankets such as the Indians use for covers and a pack-saddle for a pillow. Nor did the entreaties of Father Augustin move him to anything else. He died in the house of the Father where he had gone to dedicate a finely-made chapel in his pueblo of Santa Magdalena, consecrated to San Francisco Xavier. When he was singing the Mass of the dedication he felt indisposed, and it seems that the Holy Apostle, to whom he was ever devoted, was calling him, in order that, being buried in his chapel, he might accompany him, as we believe, in glory."

A statue of Father Chino (Eusebio Kino, S.J.) was unveiled in the U. S. Capitol on Feb. 14, 1965. It is in the Hall of Columns, House Wing.

See *Il Progresso*, New York daily, February 7, 14 and 15, 1965. The magazine *Arizona Highways*, of Phoenix, Arizona, devoted its March 1961 issue to Father Chino, with numerous illustrations by the Italian-American artist, Ted De Grazia, a native of the state.

For a bibliography on Chino see Schiavo, 1934, pp. 366-367; 1949, pp. 412-413; *Four Centuries*, 77-79 ill. The most recent account, with maps, a statue of "Kino" on horseback, and the discovery of his grave in 1966, see J. F. Bannon, *The Spanish Borderlands Frontier 1513-1821*, New York, 1970, pp. 65-70 and notes 25-29 on p. 244. See especially, Charles Polzer's A *Kino Guide, His Missions—His Monuments,* Tucson, Ariz., 1968.

20

WILLIAM PACA
Signer of the Declaration of Independence

In 1934, I wrote in my book, *The Italians In America Before The Civil War*, "Some Italians claim that William Paca, one of the signers of the Declaration of Independence, was of Italian descent, but no evidence has been produced yet on the subject with the exception of a statement by Paca, who, upon his return from a visit to Italy and England in 1760, wrote that he was in the land of his ancestors."

Since then nothing has been discovered to prove or disprove that Paca was of Italian origin or to prove that he was of English ancestry, regardless of the claims by some members of the Paca family, going back to the turn of the century, or by some students of the question, who advocate the English descent.

The only argument or evidence of those persons who believe that Robert Paca, the first member of the family to settle in Maryland, came from England and that his name was not Paca but Peaker rests exclusively on the will of one Robert Peaker made in 1681 in which he left his plantation to his son, Aquila Peaker, then under the age of eighteen. This bit of precious evidence, however, has more holes than an Italian *colapasta* (spaghetti colander).

To start with, the will that has reached us is not the original will with Peaker's or Paca's own signature. That document has been lost, or cannot be found. All we have is the fair copy by whoever recorded it in the will book, or register. Furthermore, to the best of my knowledge, we do not have the birth record of Peaker's or Paca's son, Aquila.

In the second place, we do not know when Aquila "Peaker" changed his name into Aquila Paca, but I doubt that there ever was any such change.

In the third place, I fail to understand why a proud Englishman in an English colony should have wanted to change a perfectly good English name into an Italian name.

In the fourth place, the only will by a person named Peaker in the eight volumes of wills edited by Jane Baldwin is that of 1681. I have scanned the names in every one of those wills which extend from 1635 to 1743, as well as hundreds if not thousands of names dealing

72

with residents of Maryland during the second half of the 17th century and later years and have found no Peaker, although there may have been one or two.

In the fifth place, in the July 1945 volume of the *Maryland Historical and Genealogical Bulletin*, vol. 16, page 52, I have found that one Mary Parker, daughter of William Parker, married "Robert Paca or Packer." That shows that the name was occasionally misspelled.

In the sixth place, according to Mrs. Hester Dorsey Richardson, noted genealogist and author of a column on genealogy in the Baltimore Sun, "in the early rent rolls, marriage records and elsewhere the name is spelled Paca." There is no reason to doubt Mrs. Richardson's word. Personally, in the same volume of the *Calendar of Wills*, edited by Jane Baldwin in which the "Peaker" will of 1681 is recorded (on page 99 of Vol. I), I have found (on page 39) that Robert Paca, not Peaker, was one of the witnesses to the will of William Eldridge of Ann Arundel County on March 11, 1665 and again on June 2, 1667.

If that were not enough, the Genealogical Society of England, headed by the Earl Mountbatten, Admiral of the Fleet, conducted extensive research on both Peaker and Paca at the request of Professor V. Belfiglio of Texas Woman's University at Denton, Texas, and reached the conclusion that no trace of any Paca could be found in England and that the name Peaker was very rare. (Letters by Mrs. C. M. Mackay, Secretary, dated August 28 and September 22, 1975.) Another leading genealogist, Robert W. Massey of Oxford, England, also conducted extensive research at the request of Prof. Belfiglio, but he, like Mrs. Mackey, was unable to discover any trace of any Paca or any Peaker in England. As Mrs. Mackay concluded in her letter of August 28, "The name Aquilla Paca is unquestionably Italian in origin and equally indubitably not English. The suggestion that Aquilla Paca was the son of Robert Peaker is on the face of it extremely absurd. If either the son or the father did change both the forename and surname to Italian names, there must have been some very unusual reason for doing so; but without evidence of any such reason, it is far more likely that there lies behind it a *slip of the pen* [italics added] or a misreading of documents, on some genealogist's or historian's part."

For good measure, there is the letter which William Paca wrote upon his return from Europe in which he said that he had been in the land of his origin. More than 30 years have elapsed since I last wrote that reference to Italy (a reference to England would have made no sense) but I can't find my original notes. Since, however, I first mentioned that letter (or letters) in my 1934 book, the reference must be in a printed book or article mentioned in my bibliography about Paca on page 371 of my Civil War book (from Hall to Andrews), which I cannot check now as they are not available to me in Dallas.

Besides what I have stated so far, there are other facts which support my conviction that William Paca was of Italian origin on his father's side, and they are: A) my interview with Paca's great-great-grandson in 1937; B) the fact that names often were spelled according to their sound; C) the fact that in Italy there has been for centuries a family named "Pacca"; D) the fact that Italians were specifically named in the Maryland Act of 1649 which allowed them to own land in the province. Finally, there is the coat of arms, which has nothing to do with Paca's origin.

A) In 1937, I wrote a letter to The New York Times in which I questioned an article which stated that all the signers of the Declaration of Independence were of Saxon-Celtic origin. "What about Paca," I wrote, "was he not of Italian origin?" (New York Times, July 11, 1937). Exactly a week later, on the 18th, The Times published a letter which said in part: "Giovanni Schiavo, whose letter you published, is correct in stating that my great-great-grandfather [he must have meant great-grandfather] William Paca, a signer of the Declaration of Independence was of Italian origin, or at least partially correct. The ancestors of William Paca were of Italian and English origin. The name is said to have been originally spelled Pacci. I am now 74 years old [the signer of the Declaration died 64 years before his birth] and can distinctly recall having seen some of the brass-bound chests that were used in importing silks, laces, and other finery for the ladies from English and Italian ports. Those chests were destroyed by fire in 1879 when the palatial residence of William Paca on Wye Island, was destroyed by fire . . ." (Signed) William S. Paca, Chestertown, Maryland.

Not long after the publication of that letter, I paid Mr. Paca a visit at his home in Chestertown. In those days the bridge that now connects Baltimore with the Eastern Shore had not been built and I had to go from Baltimore to Dover, Delaware, and then down to Chestertown. My interview added nothing of importance, except to confirm the family tradition about the Italian origin.

Of course, family traditions have little probative value. For instance, there was no name Pacci, but there was Pecci, which was obviously the name of Pope Leo XIII (1879-1903) whom Mr. Paca mentioned during our conversation. I think it was he who told me that it was Cardinal Gibbons of Baltimore to suggest the name Pecci, but it is also probable that Cardinal Gibbons may have had in mind Cardinal Pacca.

The trunks used to import finery from Italy have no special significance, as other Americans imported goods from Italy. On the other hand, is it not possible that William Paca visited Italy to meet some of his family's business connections in that country?

B) Foreign names were and still are spelled according to the way they sound to an English ear. Two cases in point are those of Taliaferro and Tasco. Taliaferro, originally Tagliaferro, is also spelled as Tailfer, Tolliver and in other ways. Tasco's name was spelled Tasker, as we learn from *The Travels of Andrew Burnaby* (1734?-1812). Burnaby spoke Italian, had been in Italy and could tell the difference. Incidentally, Tasco cultivated grapes and made fine wine in America before Mazzei. He had died by the time Burnaby drank his wine in 1759-60, but his book was printed in 1790, after he had served as chaplain at Leghorn, Italy. Hence his spelling of Tasker's name as Tasco, more likely Tasca. But there are numerous instances of changes in Italian names as I have shown in my book, *Four Centuries*, and in Chapter One of the present work. Of course, there is H. L. Mencken's *The American Language* (1937), Chapter VIII, and supplement.

C) The name Pacca can be found in any good Italian encyclopedia primarily because of Cardinal Pacca, already mentioned. The Pacca family, incidentally, was related to the Aquila family, although the name Aquila, as first name, is unknown in Italy, to the best of my knowledge (Aquilino is). As a first name, however, the name was used both in England and in the Colonies. There was, for instance, Sheriff Aquila Hall of Baltimore in 1763 and one Aquila Keen in 1732, and Abraham Aquila Johns in 1707. But there are other instances.

D) According to Mrs. Richardson's article in the Baltimore Sun of July 3, 1904, as well as other sources, "Robert Paca, the original settler in Maryland, came by way of England, but having made no effort to locate his residence there, it is sufficient to know that he was never naturalized in the province, but was as early as 1651 granted a tract of 490 acres in Anne Arundel County for transporting nine men into the Province, according to the conditions of plantations." The nine "men" were: John Hall, Samuel Fisher, John Chappell, Henry Wilson, Sarah Parke, Robert Parke, John Higgins, Abraham Watkins and Mary Wilkinson. (*Register of Maryland's Heraldic Families* by Alice N. Parran, Baltimore, Md., 1935, p. 285.) However, the Paca lineage in that book is not accurate. But that is not important. What is important is the statement that Robert Paca did not make any effort to locate in England — therefore he was not an Englishman. Coming from a very reliable archivist and genealogist, that is important. Since Mrs. Richardson could not have invented that fact or alleged fact, there must be a document somewhere in Maryland indicating it in black and white. Mrs. Richardson, as I have noted, said, for instance, that Paca — not Peaker — had acted as a witness to a will in 1665 and 1667, just as

I found out in the same volume which records the 1681 will of Robert "Peaker." If I were living in Maryland and could afford the time, I am very confident that I could confirm that what she said about the rent rolls and other documents is also accurate.

Even the transportation of the nine persons in order to obtain the land grant was not necessary because two years before the grant Maryland passed an act which allowed persons of "French, Dutch or Italian descent . . . [who] either are already planted or shall hereafter come and plant in our said province" to own land and enjoy the same rights and privileges of English colonists. Here one must remember that in those days there were quite a few Italians in England who held important positions, such as Julius Caesar (Cesare Adelmare, the son of a Venetian), who was chancellor of the exchequer and the Pallavicinos who were leading shareholders in the Virginia Company of London. (See my *Four Centuries*, pp. 95-98 for further details and facsimiles.) It follows, as it has always been customary with Italians whenever they travel abroad, that Paca may have contacted other prominent Italians in London, just as Mazzei did a century later.

E) The only argument that is valid, but only in part, is that William Paca, the signer of the Declaration, was Italian on his grandfather's side and English on his grandmother's, assuming that she was English on both sides of her family going several generations back. To go further is an exercise in confusion. Take the Taliaferro family. Many of the Taliaferro women married *into* families that were originally English or French or something else. The same thing may be said of the Danas or the Fondas or of Formicola (the Bankheads), and so on. By the same token, Winston Churchill was *not* an Englishman because his mother was American. The Roosevelts, whether Theodore or F.D.R., were not of Dutch or Jewish origin or whatever. The only standard one can go by is the ethnic origin of the first settler in America, for three or, at the very most, four generations. Even after that the ethnic or national origin of the first settler still remains the guiding index.

To put it another way, if the experts of the 1790 census figured that the vast majority of the white people in the thirteen colonies were of English descent, in accordance with their interpretation of the names, why not apply the same standard to Paca? Incidentally, I found no "Peaker" and no Paca in the names recorded for the 1790 census. Accordingly, we may throw in the ashcan all the arguments about the progenitors of Robert Paca as being of English origin — that is, until one can produce solid evidence to that effect. Such evidence does not exist today.

F) The theory or guess that the Paca family was an old English family, dating back possibly to the Saxons and the Normans, has no leg to stand on, assuming of course that the name had been Italianized in the 17th century or before. But why should an Englishman have wanted to Italianize his name?

COAT OF ARMS — I don't know what the argument regarding the Paca coat of arms is all about. As Mrs. Richardson explained it in her article, when the signer of the Declaration married Mary Chew, he was allowed to use the Chew coat of arms, as it was the custom.

To conclude:

1) There seems to be no doubt that the name "Peaker" was a slip of the pen, or an error in transcription.

2) Robert "Peaker's" original will, with the original signature, is lost. Therefore, an examination is out of the question.

3) The name Peaker is very rare, not only in England, but even in the United States. I have gone through many thousands of names and I have not come across any.

4) The name Robert Paca appears in various documents before 1681.

5) The birth certificate or record of Aquila Paca, or Aquila Peaker, the son of Robert, cannot be found. To the best of my knowledge, as of this writing, it, too, has been lost.

6) The name Paca is not English; far from it.

7) No Paca name can be found in England, after exhaustive research by reliable and authoritative English genealogists.

8) William Paca could have changed his name back to its original English spelling, if such had been the case.

9) The name Pacca, on the other hand, can be found in all good Italian encyclopedias.

10) Paca did not need to be naturalized because of the 1649 Act.

The Italians have contributed so much to America that they can do without William Paca. But why exclude him when other ethnic groups are trying to prove that they have deep roots in America by claiming every cat and dog that they can get hold of?

Until solid evidence is produced to dispute the points just mentioned, the fact remains that the name Paca was not and is not anything but Italian, unless one wants to include a Brazilian rodent, so called by an Indian tribe.

See also the Baltimore Sun for July 24, 1903, page 7, with a letter by a reader who said that Paca's name originally was Peaker, Mrs. Richardson's reply to her critic, and her column "Side-Lights" for that day. Also my *Italian-American History*, Vol. I, pp. 481-483 and bibl. p. 495.

21

PHILIP MAZZEI
and
THE DECLARATION OF INDEPENDENCE

In the spring and summer of 1825, an Italian nobleman, Count Carlo Vidua, visited the United States of America, well supplied with the necessary letters of introduction to the most prominent Americans of the day. Thus, he had dinner at the White House with President John Quincy Adams and later in Virginia with Jefferson and Madison. He did not write a book, but kept his father informed of what he saw or whom he met, leaving at his death numerous letters covering his voyages to various parts of the world. The letters, edited by the famous historian, Cesare Balbo, were published in Turin in 1835, in three volumes, but were never translated. Only recently, two Italian professors, Dr. Valeria Gennaro-Lerda of the University of Genoa, Italy, and Dr. Elizabeth Cimetti of West Virginia University, translated and published some of them in the *Virginia Magazine of History and Biography* (October, 1969, pp. 387-406), with excellent notes. The translation also seems to be excellent. (An article on Vidua by Joseph Rossi with some extracts from his *Lettere* had appeared in *Italica*, September, 1961, pp. 227-235.)

Count Vidua's observations are more than the superficial remarks of frivolous aristocrats. According to him, "Jefferson's intellect seemed to me the most brilliant, Madison's the most profound, Monroe's the least keen, and President Adams' the most cultivated."

What Count Vidua has to say about the Declaration of Independence should prove of some interest on the celebration of our Bicentennial, for, in my opinion, it is fundamentally correct. For instance, "In 1776, when England rejected the proposals of the Colonies and they made the momentous decision to separate from the mother country, Jefferson prepared a first draft of the Declaration of Independence. This document, which a severe critic would charge as being rhetorical and somewhat exaggerated in tone, is written with fire and elegance. Since the results exceeded the expectations, the document has become a national memorial which is publicly read each year. Its framed *facsimile* is found in almost every home and its author is regarded as the living *Patriarch* of the American Republic."

As I see it, Vidua said in a few words what historians and hack writers have not been able to say in a shelf of books about The Declaration, Thomas Jefferson, John Locke, John Adams, the Virginia Declaration of Rights and such matters, because the Declaration would have been forgotten if the Colonies had not won the war. Even now, aside from its literary and historical value, the Declaration is just a symbol, like a birth certificate, of a great event, and the Fourth of July is just a special birthday. Even if the Declaration had consisted of two lines, the Liberty Bell would have been rung as joyously as it did on that first Fourth, and the people would have celebrated it then and for the next 200 years, as it will be celebrated in all probability for years to come although, I am afraid, not as joyfully as when I was a boy. For that matter, we did not need a declaration or a majestic document for bedlam to break loose on the evening of November 11, 1918, when the announcement of the armistice came from France. I well remember that; I was in Washington on that evening, wearing the uniform of a doughboy.

A formal declaration of independence, nevertheless, was necessary, from both the political and moral point of view. In the first place, to make rebellion respectable, to justify that free men were entitled to separate themselves from a government to which they, as free men, owed no obligation. Politically, such a justification was imperative, so as not to alienate the governments of France and Spain which, notwithstanding their enmity towards Great Britain, still believed in the divine right of kings. They did so on moral grounds, in order to convince the American people that they, as free men born equal, had the right to rebel and separate. On this point, see the explanation by Carl Becker in his admirable, *The Declaration of Independence*, 1922, 1972 ed., pp. 6-9.

The Declaration was not the work of just one man, Jefferson, but of Congress, of a number of delegates who made so many changes that it could not be recognized from the so-called Rough Draft made by Jefferson. Aside from all that, the Declaration did not say anything that had not been said before, as claimed by Jefferson's enemies and friends alike, including John Adams. As James Madison put it, the purpose of the Declaration was to assert, not to discover truths (11*th Britannica* at Madison).

Jefferson himself recognized that there was nothing new in his Declaration. The Declaration had been criticized here and abroad from the first moment it was made public, but Jefferson was too busy or simply did not care. Two years before he died, however, he could not take it any longer, especially when his own friend, John Adams, joined the chorus of his adversaries, and shared the views of the supra-

Federalist, Timothy Pickering, who said in a Fourth of July address that the Declaration "contained no new ideas, that it is a commonplace compilation, its sentiments hackneyed in Congress two years before," which, wrote Jefferson in a letter to Madison, "may all be true. Of that I am not to be the judge. Richard H. Lee charged it as copied from Locke's treatise on government . . . I know only that I turned to neither book nor pamphlet while writing it. I did not consider it as any part of my charge to invent new ideas altogether and to offer no sentiment which had ever been expressed before."

More telling is his letter to Henry Lee dated May 8, 1825 (at about the same time he had Vidua to dinner and just about a year before his death on July 4, 1826—John Adams also died on the same day) in which he wrote:

"... when forced, therefore, to resort to arms for redress, an appeal to the government of the world was deemed proper for our justification. This was the object of the Declaration of Independence. Not to find out new principles, or new arguments, never before thought of, not merely to say things which had never been said before; but to place before mankind the common sense of the subject, in terms *so plain and firm* (italics added) as to command their assent, and to justify ourselves in the independent stand we were compelled to take. Neither aiming at originality of principle or sentiment, nor yet copied from any particular and previous writing, it was intended to be an expression of the American mind, and to give to that expression the proper tone and spirit called for that occasion. All its authority rests then on the harmonizing sentiments of the day, whether expressed in conversation, in letters, printed essays, or in the elementary books of public right as Aristotle, Cicero, Locke, Sidney, etc."

When all is said and done, Jefferson's glory and immortality rest on the first two paragraphs, the first at the very beginning, "When in the course of human events," which is as majestic as Aida's triumphal march, or as solemn as Lincoln's "Fourscore and seven years ago"; the second, "all men are created equal," a statement which a recent writer, R. B. Morris (*Seven Who Shaped Destiny*, New York, 1973, p. 145) called 'electrifying in its impact," is more than electrifying. I would say that it is like a clarion calling the people to the ramparts.

Of course, those words were nothing new. Recently, I was going through the *Virginia Gazette* for 1774-1775 and found numerous references to natural rights, the equality of men, and similar doctrines.

As a matter of fact, the doctrine of the equality of men goes all the way back to the Romans and possibly to the Greeks. The expression "all men are by nature equal" (*omnes homines natura aequales sunt*) goes back to the Roman jurist Ulpian in the *Justinian Digest* (6th century A. D.). It is, therefore, idle to say that Jefferson got the idea from Locke, anymore than it was for the late President, John F. Kennedy, to state that "the great doctrine 'All men are created equal' incorporated in the Declaration by Thomas Jefferson, was paraphrased from the writing of Philip Mazzei, an Italian-born patriot and pamphleteer who was a close friend of Jefferson." (John F. Kennedy, *A Nation of Immigrants*, Revised and enlarged edition, copyright 1964 by the Anti-Defamation League of B'nai B'rith, p. 16.)

According to some "authorities" on Jefferson and the Declaration, however, Jefferson got his idea about "all men are created equal" from the preamble to the Virginia Bill of Rights or Declaration of Rights which was drafted by George Mason. According to one writer, as a matter of fact, "the idea was Locke's but the felicitous expression was Mason's" (Robert Allen Rutland, *The Birth of the Bill of Rights*, Chapel Hill, 1955, p. 37). Others also trace the idea or phrase to Mason, and point out that a copy of the Virginia Bill of Rights had appeared in the Philadelphia *Evening Post* of June 6, 1776, as in *A Transaction of Free Men — The Birth and Course of the Declaration of Independence*, New York, 1964, by David Hawke, who was convinced that Jefferson had leaned on his friend, George Mason. According to Mr. Hawke, all the sentiments and most of the words of Mason's sentence came straight from John Locke's "Essay Concerning the End of Civil Government" concluding that "Though Jefferson knew Locke's work as well as his friend, he must have been *struck by Mason's succint summary of the natural rights philosophy* (p. 148, italics added). I should add here that the Virginia Bill of Rights appeared in another Philadelphia newspaper on June 12, 1776. Anyway, Hamilton Eckenrode also believed that the Virginia Bill of Rights "was drawn upon by Jefferson in the first part of the Declaration" (*The Revolution in Virginia*, New York, 1916). Professor Samuel Morison, on the other hand, is sure that "The principles and language of John Locke's *Second Treatise of Government* (1690) were so much a part of his [Jefferson's] mind that *unconsciously* (italics added) he thought and wrote like Locke" (*The Oxford History of the American People*, New York, 1965, p. 222 — but see also Prof. Morison's address "Prelude to Independence" in the October 1951 issue of the *William and Mary Quarterly*).

What we are prone to forget is that the Revolution did not fall like rain from the sky. Freedom was not only an abstract idea, but also a question of dollars and cents. That is, whether or not the British Government had the right to levy and collect taxes, while at the same time it had the obligation to defend the colonies, as it did against the French. Furthermore, the Revolution was actually a civil war, with hundreds of thousands of loyalists either openly or tacitly on the side of Britain. Some 50,000 loyalists found refuge in Canada alone. We are also likely to forget that the Declaration came three years after the Boston Tea Party, two years after the first Continental Congress, more than a year after the Boston Massacre, Patrick Henry's "Give me life or give me death," Lexington and Concord, Ticonderoga, Bunker Hill and the second Continental Congress, and almost a year to the day after Washington was chosen commander-in-chief of the Continental Army (July 3, 1775). Thomas Paine found the ground work already finished, for he put in a concise form what the people wanted to hear. But he did not prepare the ground. Actually, Mazzei had preached the same things Paine was clamoring about for more than one year, or probably two years, before Paine. But Paine hit pay dirt.

ENTER MAZZEI

Mazzei was a highly educated Italian who had spent 18 years in London before he was induced by Franklin and a Virginian business-man named Thomas Adams to try an agricultural experiment in Virginia. He came over in November, 1773, on a ship chartered by him, and preceded by such reports that he was welcomed to Virginia by its leading citizens, including George Washington, Thomas Jefferson, George Mason and anyone else who counted. Shortly after his arrival, however, he became so involved in America's struggle for freedom that he neglected his business and devoted all his time to explain to the Americans that they were ill-informed about Britain's alleged freedom. Jefferson was won to Mazzei's side (only so far as Mazzei's ideas agreed with his own) and it was decided that Mazzei would write a series of articles, based on his experience in London, where he had influential friends in the government and outside the government, as well as in other countries. Jefferson was to translate the articles into English, but after a while (after six or seven articles) he told Mazzei that his English was good enough (probably Jefferson got tired) and Mazzei was on his own. The articles were not printed in the local newspapers or as fliers or handbills, but in supplements that were inserted in the local *Virginia Gazette*. According to Camillo Branchi who saw some of them, they were signed "Furioso" and appeared in the supplements to *Pinkney's Virginia Gazette*. A search all over the country, however, has not produced a single copy, but I do not feel that the search, if continued, will be fruitless, especially if extended to Italy, Britain, France, and even Spain or the West Indies and Mexico.

In any event, while writing his memoirs (they were finished in 1813), Mazzei found one of the early articles, the first, and included it as an appendix to his recollections, which appeared as *Memorie*, in Lugano, Switzerland, in 1845-46 or almost thirty years after his death. It was while reading that book that I came across the article, and was struck by some words that reminded me of the preamble to the Declaration of Independence. I decided to translate it and published it in my book, *The Italians in America Before the Civil War*, in 1934. And that's how Mazzei's connection with the Declaration of Independence became known. In all fairness, however, Giovanni Mira, an Italian writer, had noted those very words, "Tutti gli uomini sono per natura egualmente liberi e indipendenti" 17 years before I did in *Nuova Antologia*, Rome, December 1, 1917, p. 228. I still have the tear sheets of that magazine article which I bought probably in January 1918, but I have my doubts as to whether it led me to the search for that article in Mazzei's *Memorie*. See notes.

In my opinion, Mazzei's article may have influenced Jefferson, as well as Mason, not only because of Mazzei's use of the words about the equality of men, but also because of the method followed by him in presenting his ideas. Whether or not such was the case, it is practically impossible to confirm, but the coincidence is certainly most remarkable. Aside from all that, if, according to Professor Morison and other writers, Jefferson had Locke in the back of his mind when he drafted the Declaration, is it not more likely that he may have had a better recollection of what he had translated a year or so before? What may be true of Jefferson may also be true of George Mason, as we shall presently see.

Be that as it may, here is what Mazzei wrote on pages 284-285 of Vol. II of his *Memorie*, as reproduced in facsimile in my study, *Mazzei*, New York, 1951, p. 146, and as translated by me on p. 147:

"In order to obtain our end it is necessary, my dear fellow citizens, to consider the natural rights of man as well as the basis of a free government. Such a discussion will show clearly that the British government has never been a free government at any time, and that ours was only a bad copy of the British, with so many other disadvantages that it was hardly above slavery.

"Then we shall examine how an impartial and lasting government can be established.

"The subject has been so amply treated by eminent writers that I desire only to deal with it in a popular and simple style; thus we can easily understand each other.

"Famous writers must forgive me; they do not need anybody to write for them. I write, instead, for those people of common sense who did not have the advantage of a higher education, and I wish to adapt my style to their capacity. I know very well that a sublime prose often appeals to men who unfortunately are willing to admire what they do not understand; but the time has finally come to change custom; our duty is to try to understand so that we can draw our own conclusions."

In other words, Mazzei wrote half a century before Jefferson, but not as concisely as Jefferson, that he was not saying anything new, but was trying to say it in a plain manner (Jefferson said, "in terms so plain and firm") what was in his mind so that everybody could understand him.

Mazzei then goes on:

"All men are by nature equally free and independent. Such equality is necessary in order to establish a free government. Each individual must be equal to another in natural law. Class distinction has always been, as it will always be, an effective obstacle, and the reason for it is very clear. When in a nation you have several classes of men each one must have its share in the government; otherwise one class would tyrannize over the others. But the parts cannot be perfectly equal; even if it were possible, human events show that they could not be kept in balance and no matter how little one exceeds the others, the whole must crumble.

That's why ancient republics did not last long. When thely were established the inhabitants were divided into [social] classes, always in conflict, each class striving to have a larger share than the others . . . I repeat it, a true Republian government cannot exist unless all men from the richest to the poorest are perfectly equal in their natural rights . . . The Government of England, from its earliest days to the death of Queen Elizabeth was either a despotic monarchy or an intolerable aristocracy or a mixture of both."

One will notice here that Mazzei did not say "all men are created equal" but "all men are by nature equally free and independent," just as one finds in the preamble to the Virginia Declaration of Rights, "That all men are created equally free & independent & have certain inherent natural Rights . . ." which is similar to the words used by Jefferson in his first Rough Draft. As noted by Julian Boyd in his book, *The Declaration of Independence. The Evolution of the Text*, Princeton, 1943, p. 15, "The first and other paragraphs of Mason's Declara-

84

tion of Rights have been quoted by respectable authorities as proof of Jefferson's dependence upon his fellow Virginian for that part of his declaration," but, still according to Boyd, "the similarity that exists is a similarity of ideas: Jefferson and Mason were both dealing with the concept of natural, inherent rights and on this subject both appealed, as all men of the day did, to Locke and other exponents of the idea of the social compact . . ." Jefferson, according to Boyd and other writers, must have read the Virginia Bill of Rights as published in the *Pennsylvania Evening Post* of June 6, 1776, as well as the *Pennsylvania Gazette* of June 12 as taken from Dixon and Hunter's *Virginia Gazette* of June 1.

All that is puzzling, because Jefferson had explained how he had sent to the Virginia Convention of 1776 a plan of his with a preamble similar to the preamble he later included in his Declaration. As reported by Kate Mason Rowland in her *Life and Writings of George Mason*, New York, 1892, Vol. I, pp. 252-253, quoting from *Jefferson's Works*, Vol VII, p. 405, Jefferson explained what had happened in a letter he sent to Judge Woodward a year before his own death. Briefly, Jefferson had sent his plan to the Convention which he could not attend as he was then in Philadelphia. Since the Convention had already approved a plan, and the committee of the whole could not be "induced to open the instrument again; but that, being pleased with the preamble of mine, they adopted it in the house, by way of amendment to the report of the committee; and thus my preamble became tacked on to the work of George Mason." Just in case someone might think that Jefferson's memory did not serve him right (he was 83 years old at that time), we have the confirmation of Mazzei who wrote on his *Recherches*, Paris, 1788, Vol. I, p. 163, that the preamble to the Virginia Bill of Rights "est d'ailleurs presque tout-à-fait le même dans la diction, puisque celui de nos concitoyens qui l'a rédigé, fut chargé de rediger aussi la declaration d'independance dans la quelle il y a quelque chose d'ajouté, à cause de quelques griefs qui n'étoient pas communs à toutes le colonies." Mazzei, according to Marraro's *Memoirs*, p. 221, says that the wording of the two declarations is almost the same, Jefferson being in charge of the preparation of the two documents, which, of course, is not true, but since I don't have the *Memorie* at hand, I don't know whether Marraro's translation is correct, that is, whether Mazzei was referring to the preambles, as it seems likely in his *Recherches*, and not to the Virginia Bill of Rights and the Declaration of Independence, as one might assume from Marraro's *Memoirs*.

In the same life of Mason, however, we are told that a year before, in June 1775, Colonel Mason had reminded the gentlemen of the Fairfax Company that, "We came equal into this world, and equal we shall go out of it. All men are by nature born equally free and independent." Does that mean that Mason had in mind Mazzei's article when he addressed the Fairfax Company in 1775? Who knows?

Mazzei and Mason certainly knew each other and had taken part in some of the round-table discussions that followed their "political" dinners. Mazzei admired Mason immensely, and was immediately impressed by him as soon as he met him. Here is what he wrote in his memoirs (Marraro's *Memoirs*, p. 205, for the easy checking by the reader): "The second day after my arrival in Virginia, Mr. [Thomas] Adams had introduced me to various worth-while (sic)) people, among them the afore-mentioned (sic) Mr. Mason. When we left his home, I said to Mr. Adams that such a man must surely be highly respected. 'But,' I added, 'I am of the opinion that he is not sufficiently well known. His is one of those strong, very rare intellects, which are created only by a special effort of nature, like that of a Dante, a Machiavelli, a Galileo, a Newton, a Franklin, a Turgot, an Helvetius, and so forth.'" Unfortunately, Mazzei's opinion of Mason was rather prophetic because Mason has been ignored by American historians who seem to be more concerned in how many times a day Jefferson went to the bathroom than in the role played by such men as Mason and Mazzei.

To better understand the relationship between Mason and Mazzei I must mention an account of one of those political dinners related by Mazzei in his *Memorie*. That particular dinner was attended by some 30 persons and must have taken place in 1774, because Mazzei says that the first issues of his second article had just been published and that the discussion was about the contents of that article of his in which he had shown "how fallacious are the bases of the alleged full public freedom in Britain." At this point, before going further, I should point out that the Marraro translation (*Memoirs*, p. 205, *Memorie*, p. 367) is not accurate. As a matter of fact it is misleading. Mazzei said, "supposta intiera libertà pubblica in Inghilterra," that is, "alleged full public freedom," whereas Marraro translated that passage only as "public liberty in England," omitting the words "full" and "alleged." And that makes a difference.

At any rate, during the discussion about Mazzei's article and his views on British freedom, "Mr. Carter Nickolas [Robert C. Nicholas], treasurer of the Colony, who was later confirmed in his office in the following administration (deservedly so, as nobody could be above him in integrity and accuracy), looking at me said: 'Mr. Mazzei, what I am afraid of is to loose (sic) the constitution.' And I, likewise looking back at him, replied: 'Mr. Treasurer, had I such constitution, I would think myself in consumption' [both question and reply in the original English]. All the guests appreciated my reply and laughed . . . Among the dinner guests was Mr. George Mason, a schoolmate and intimate friend of George Washington . . . Mr. Mason made several profound, appropriate and useful remarks, which the guests circulated throughout the country, for only two of them lived in the same county. In fact, everything that was said on the subject of liberty, which is one of the most interesting subjects to the human race, was quickly spread abroad" (Marraro translation, p. 205).

Later on, Mazzei tells how during the discussion about the abolition of slavery, which Jefferson and Blair wished that it take place without further delay, "Mr. George Mason and I were the only dissenters against the immediate abolition. I said that I wished ardently to see the plan put into execution as soon as possible, that is, as soon as circumstances permitted, but that, under the conditions then prevailing, such a step seemed too risky, since the number of colored people exceeded our own by two to one. Moreover, the benefit would seem even greater, in my opinion, if the slaves knew that their masters were inclined to bestow freedom on all those who deserved it; whereas by freeing them universally and unexpectedly, we might run the risk of their believing the act to be caused by fear, instilled by the circumstances. Mr. George Mason said much more . . . Everyone was convinced (and Jefferson first of all) by the reasons presented by Mr. Mason and myself. Wherefore it was agreed . . . The two laws were enacted as soon as they were proposed." (Marraro's translation, p. 222, as I don't have the Italian edition at hand, which should be consulted in case of differences.)

In conclusion, so far as the equality of man is concerned, there seems to be no doubt that the "felicitous" expression or phrase, "All men are created equal," no matter how modified or adapted, belongs to Mazzei and to no one else. I am not talking about the doctrine, but to the way it was enunciated in a few words by Mazzei at the very beginning of his article, following the introduction.

Yet that fact in itself is meaningless and Mazzei's "felicitous" phrase would have been completely forgotten if Jefferson had not inserted it in his Declaration, as my late friend, Vittorio Racca, correctly pointed out in his 1949 article in *Nuova Antologia*. Therefore, the credit should go to Jefferson and only to him.

On the other other hand, should not Mazzei also receive credit for having coined the phrase, having said in a few words what had not been done before him, and for putting those words at the very beginning of an article intended for popular consumption?

And that should put to rest all the speculations by unimaginative writers about Locke and similar nonsense. Furthermore, if Jefferson had Locke's ideas in the back of his mind, is it not more likely that, as I have already noted, Jefferson was more likely to have remembered the article he had translated two years before, a copy of which he may have kept around in his study? I am not going to waste any time on those who ascribe the phrase to Mason, as in the case of Robert Allen Rutland, who wrote in *The Birth of the Bill of Rights*, Chapel Hill, 1955, "The idea was Locke's but the felicitous expression was Mason's A comparison of the statement [in the Virginia Bill of Rights] with Jefferson's wording of the Declaration of Independence suggests that Mason exerted an influence upon the final phraseology of that statement" (p. 38).

At any rate, the few examples about Mazzei, Mason and the political diners I have quoted in the preceding pages should be enough to show that Professor Garlick was mistaken in assuming that Mazzei's influence was limited to what is now Albemarle county. Mazzei owned houses in Richmond, which is in Henrico county, and had financial interests in other places. Aside from all that, we must not forget that he had been in Virginia only eight months when he was elected a member of a committee of twelve to maintain order in the county and to correspond with the committee of the colony which corresponded with the other twelve colonies. As told by him, "In my county there were 1,200 voters, each of whom was eligible. The election took place 8 months after my arrival, during which I had spent more than half of the time out of the county. Nonetheless, only five candidates got more votes than I. Later I was elected a member of the committee of twelve overseers of the poor, and by my colleagues I was chosen one of the two administrators." The first office has special importance because of the contact with the other colonies, even though through the Virginia committee of correspondence. Strangely enough, Professor Garlick does not mention Mazzei's election to the committee which corresponded with the colonial committee. (Garlick, *Mazzei*, pp. 42-43, *Memorie*, pp. 359-360 and *Memoirs*, p. 198.)

Mazzei's influence or role in the Revolution was not limited, of course, to his talks and articles which affected audiences and readers, but extended to all the colonies through the Virginia gazettes and through the personal contacts, orally and by mail, of his Virginia friends, Thomas Jefferson, above all.

MAZZEI'S INFLUENCE ON JEFFERSON

Mazzei was close to 43 years of age when he came to Virginia in 1773. Jefferson was about 30. Mazzei was a much-traveled man, at home in London, where he had resided for 18 years, as well as in other European cities. Like all educated Italians, he was well-versed not only in literature, but also in politics and finance. He was the friend of ambassadors and politicians, to whose homes he was frequently invited. When he began to write his memoirs, for instance, he could recall how shortly after his arrival in London in 1756, during a "conversazione" at Dr. Sharp's house, the latter had reminded an arrogant young man that "we owe our Locke to their [the Italians] Marsilio Ficino. (*Memoirs*, p. 94.) His social position was such that when in Italy during a trip in 1765 he met the Grand Duke of Tuscany, who later became Emperor of the Holy Roman Empire (1790) and remained a friend of Mazzei until his death in 1792.

Jefferson, on the other hand, was well-read, with good sound training in the law, but was out of touch with the realities of life and especially with the devious ways of European politics, England's above all. So much so that when Mazzei pointed out to him the defects of the English form of government, Jefferson was amazed (*Memorie*, p. 366, *Memoirs*, p. 204). Mazzei's long residence in England, however, was at first a liability to him, because the people suspected that he would side with the British rather than with the Virginians. That suspicion was soon dispelled. Like the other fear that as an Italian he would try to introduce the "popery" among the colonists. Jefferson, of course, was largely responsible for the reassurance he gave the people as to Mazzei's love for freedom and dependability, vouching for his character and adding that his association with Mazzei had been useful to him. Whereupon Mazzei commented, brushing all modesty aside, "if he had said that I had been useful to him for all the information I had given him about England, he would not have been far from the truth" (*Memorie*, 385-386, *Memoirs*, p. 213). Of course, Jefferson had been more than useful to Mazzei especially regarding the state of mind of the people. One, however, has to read Mazzei's memoirs, preferably in the rambling Italian text, to get a glimpse of his many-sided activities.

The close relations between Jefferson and Mazzei continued with brief interruptions until Mazzei's death in 1813, as shown by the fact that Jefferson sent to Mazzei one of the five rough drafts of the Declaration (*The Papers of T. Jefferson*, edited by J. Boyd, Vol. I, p. 415) or by the famous letter from Jefferson to Mazzei in 1796, which Mazzei indiscreetly translated and had published in a Florentine paper, to Jefferson's discomfiture and his subsequent strained relations with George Washington.

As for the famous note that Jefferson wrote to Madison in which he feared that the return of Mazzei to Virginia in 1783 was going to cause him one of his frequent headaches, that was a mountain out of a molehill. What happened was simply that Mazzei desired to be named U. S. consul in some European city, but Jefferson's enemies who were then in power opposed it on the specious ground that those offices were to be filled by natives. I say specious because in 1794 an Italian, Filippo Filicchi, the friend of St. Ann Seton, was appointed U.S. consul at Leghorn, whereas Mazzei's application for a similar post was rejected even after Filicchi's appointment.

When all is said and done, Jefferson often asked Mazzei's opinion on subjects about which he had some doubt. One instance was the Virginia Convention of 1775, when Jefferson asked Mazzei's opinion on some particular questions (not on many matters, as translated by Marraro, *Memoirs*, p. 214). Mazzei wrote, "siccome io avevo fatto molte riflessioni su quel soggetto fin dalla prima gioventù e le avevo discusse in Inghilterra coi legali di prima classe, cominciando dal dottore Sharp, Jefferson mi mandava quelle sulle quali desiderava di conoscere la mia opinione, *Memorie*, Vol. I, p. 388 (since I had studied these questions from my earliest youth and had discussed them with first class jurists, starting with Dr. Sharp, Jefferson sent me those questions on which he wished to know my opinion). On Dr. Samuel Sharp (d. 1778), author of a book, *Letters from Italy*, see the *British Dictionary of National Biography*.

Needless to say, that was not the first, nor the last, time that Jefferson relied on his friend's opinion on current problems. Whether or not he accepted Mazzei's views is another story. Simply because we do not have any records (we must not forget that Jefferson and Mazzei were neighbors and met frequently socially and otherwise and that Mazzei's personal papers from 1773 to 1779 were destroyed while he was in Europe) does not mean that Mazzei exerted no influence on Jefferson's political thinking, as some myopic historians prefer to conclude.

In my study, *Mazzei*, as well as in my book, *The Italians in America Before the Civil War*, I have told how Mazzei was welcomed to Virginia by her leading citizens, including Washington, Jefferson, Madison, two future signers of the Declaration; how he went often to lunch with prominent Virginians, including Washington; how he was highly respected by John Adams, whom he met for the first time in Paris but who did not agree with him; how he advised Jefferson whom to see in Paris and how he introduced him to some of them (I published that long letter in facsimile in my *Mazzei*, before it appeared in *The Papers of Thomas Jefferson*, as I had to remind Prof. Dumas Malone in the *N. Y. Times Book Review*, Sept. 20, 1953); how he associated with the leaders of French society and government in Paris, from LaFayette to Vergennes, Condorcet and Lavoisier; how he was indefatigable in promoting and defending America's interests; how he was elected to public office in Virginia shortly after his arrival, getting more votes than local Americans; how in all probability he was influential in the rejection of Lord North's "conciliatory" proposal which he recognized as a trick, following two letters he received from London, one from Anthony Chamier, the top man in the London War Office, and another from the Minister of Saxony, von Bruhl, and so on and on. I also mentioned how probably the plan for bottling up Cornwallis's army at Yorktown may have been based on a plan which Mazzei thought out while a prisoner in New York City, and detailed in a report which the Count de Deuxponts brought over to Rochambeau, and Mazzei explained in a letter to Jefferson. As of this date, I am not in a position to express an opinion, one way or the other, as I am not a military man, but see the well-documented book, *Rochambeau* by Arnold Whitridge, New York, 1965, pp. 102, 137, 139-40 and 230. Also, Chastellux, *Travels in North America*, revised translation, Chapel Hill, N. C., 1963, Vol. I, p. 247, note 5. For the letter to Jefferson see my *Mazzei*, p. 152.

There is, however, a question which deserves serious consideration, as much as the similarity between the words "All men are by nature equal and independent," as in Mazzei's article and "All men are created equal" in the Declaration of Independence. That is, the similarity between Mazzei's advocacy of separation if the Colonies did not want to end into slavery and similar views found in the *Virginia Gazette* in 1774 and 1775.

We all know that notwithstanding the bloody clashes at Lexington and Bunker Hill, as already noted, the large majority of the colonists remained loyal to Britain and were simply defending their rights as loyal British subjects. Mazzei saw the danger of this attitude and warned his friends about it. Here is what he wrote in his *Memorie* (pp. 336-337, and p. 204 of Marraro's *Memoirs*):

"It was clearly seen by the policy of the Cabinet of St. James that in order to avoid becoming victims of the British Government the only solution was to prepare for an armed conflict. The inevitable result would have been, either full freedom, or the harshest slavery; that, once freedom was secured, a good government had to be organized; and that in order to do so, the prejudices of the people who believed that the British government was the model of perfection, had to be destroyed.

"Jefferson was surprised when I showed him the defects of the British government, and said that it had not crossed his mind. 'This is the only reason (I said) that has kept you from knowing them. You as a boy always heard that it was the best possible form of government; you must have read that an English writer showed that it was preferable to that of the Romans; you realized that such was the case when compared to other European governments; finally, not even dreaming of changing it, you saw no reason to look for flaws [Mazzei uses the Italian expression, *cercare il pel nell'uovo*]. But I, provoked by their insolent way of talking when referring to other nations *they are four hundred years backwards* [in English, in italics—Mazzei was referring to the way the English spoke about other countries] examined it carefully, and noted the essential defects I have shown you.' Then it was decided that I write another article so that the people would note them and understand them." (It is interesting in this instance to note that Marraro translates the words "foglio periodico" as "article," which is correct to my mind, and 'second volume of periodicals" in the preceding page 203, in which Mazzei says, "secondo foglio periodico).

What I find interesting, although it may have been mere coincidence, is the use of the words "either full freedom or the harshest slavery," for similar terms are to be found in several articles in the Virginia Gazette of those days. For instance, in *Rind's Virginia Gazette* for August 11, 1774, there is an article reading, "The times my dear countrymen, are critical, extremely critical, but we still have it in our power to counteract the machinations of our enemies . . . You now stand in a conspicuous point of view, and the event of this struggle will fasten around your necks the yoke of servitude, or forever secure your freedom and liberties. Can it, then, admit of any hesitation what alternative to chuse? . . . If you hesitate, you are ruined. The time admits of no hesitation." This article appeared a year and a half before Paine's *Common Sense* and eight months before Patrick Henry's famous battle cry but, the way I figure it, after the appearance of Mazzei's second article.

And again, in *Pinkney's Virginia Gazette* of February 9, 1775, more than a month before Patrick Henry's "Give me liberty or give me death," we read, "Men born and nurtured in the arms of freedom will, believe me, sooner lose their lives than to submit to a deprivation of their dearest rights and privileges. I would therefore expect that "free born Briton . . ." Here we see that the writer did not advocate separation except as a last resort and that, again, he was stressing British rights and privileges, but the consequence of the deprivation of those rights is clear. That is, harsh slavery.

Of course, I don't say that such articles were the result of Mazzei's preaching (he preached in churches, too, on political liberty) and of his articles, but who can say that such was not the case? Further investigation may clear up this and other points, especially if the other documents held in Italy are made public.

Mazzei was not always prophetic, as in the case of the French Revolution, although he may have been motivated by political and diplomatic reasons in writing that the people and the monarchy loved each other, but he certainly saw that the American storm was inevitable and so wrote to the Grand Duke of Tuscany long before 1776. In any event, he did his bit, with his voice and with his pen.

To conclude, let me quote two estimates of Mazzei, one by Camillo Branchi who saw and read some of the articles by Mazzei in *Pinkney's Virginia Gazette,* and the other by Baron Grimm. Branchi wrote or suggested in the introduction, preceding his first translation of Mazzei's memoirs in the *Columbian Monthly* for May, 1928:

"Yet Mazzei played his cards in a game that brought about the independence of the Colonies and the establishment of the Republic. A man of action as well as thought, he was among the pioneers of liberty who led in the revolt against the English and deserves to be remembered as one of the Fathers of our country . . . It will interest our readers to know that this great Patriot and friend of Thomas Jefferson helped to inspire the Declaration of Independence [this was written in 1928, but Garlick, Goggio, and Marraro ignore this very important point], an able diplomat in the service of the Virginian Government, and the author of the first history of the War of Independence."

Baron Friedrich Melchior Grimm (1723-1807) was a noted French-German critic, man of letters and diplomat, a man of the most brilliant literary society of the period, Baron of the empire (1787), minister of the Duke of Gotha at the French court and minister of Catherine II of Russia at Hamburg. Mazzei mentions him on more than one occasion in his memoirs. Here is what he wrote to the King of Poland on October 10, 1788, as quoted by Tognetti Burigana in her book, *Trasformismo Illuminato* (see Notes):

Le Toscan devenu citoyen de Virginie, doit déjà avoir donné à Votre Majesté des épreuves de sa pénétration et de la justice de son coup d'oeil. San être lié avec M. Mazzei je le connais depuis plusieurs années, et j'ai toujours fait un cas particulier de ses lumières, de sa tête et de son âme qui n'est pas froide."

Baron Grimm also defined Mazzei "a most sensible and expert judge, an uncommon diplomat" (Burigana, *op. cit.,* pp. 31 and footnote). Also according to Burigana, King Stanislaus II (Poniatowski) considered Mazzei who served him as his agent in France, a gift from heaven.

22

FRANCIS VIGO

Francis Vigo, a wealthy fur trader born in Piedmont, Italy, made possible the victory of George Rogers Clark at Vincennes and, as the result of that victory, the acquisition of the Old Northwest Territory which now comprises the states of Indiana, Ohio, Michigan, Illinois, Wisconsin and Minnesota. Had it not been for Vigo, Clark would not have dared to attack the British at Vincennes in the heart of winter when all odds were against him, and without Vincennes the Old Northwest Territory in all probability would be today a part of Canada. It is possible, of course, that later the United States might have conquered that Territory, or even purchased it, as in the case of the Louisiana Purchase, but that is pure speculation. On the other hand, all the Vigos in the world would not have won the Old Northwest had it not been for the audacity of Clark, one of the purest heroes in American history, regardless of his frailties and his drinking when he was abandoned by his own people and was forced to make mistakes common to all human beings. Furthermore, without the heroism of Clark's men, again regardless of all the rewards in land grants that they expected if victorious, there would have been no victory at Vincennes and no acquisition of the Old Northwest Territory. Everything else is fiction, or speculation.

Vigo, to start with, was not a Spanish merchant, or a native of Sardinia. Most certainly he was not a man who had acquired "a noteworthy reputation as an explorer because he helped to open the old Northwest to settlement," as stated by Prof. De Conde in that lopsided book of his, *Half-Bitter, Half-Sweet.* Nor was he "aide-de-camp" to George Rogers Clark, as stated by Prof. Andrew Rolle in two of his books, *The Immigrant Upraised* (1968, p. 49) and *The American Italians* (1972, p. 18) in which he copied Prof. Roselli's fantasies (in a hurry he cited Garlick as the author of the chapter, although Garlick was just the author of a chapter on Mazzei). Most certainly, Vigo was not an "Italian adventurer who, with George Rogers Clark, helped liberate the northwest regions during the American Revolution," as stated by Prof. S. J. La Gumina in a picture book for children, *An Album Of The Italian-American* (1927, p. 1). The irresponsibility of some Italian-American professors is simply unbounded! And Vigo was not the discoverer of the sources of the Mississippi, as stated by Giuseppe Prezzolini in *I Trapiantati*, p. 383.

Francesco Vigo was born in 1747 in Carrù, a "frazione" (hamlet) of the town of Mondovì, in the province of Cuneo, in Piedmont, a "regione" and not a province, of Italy, as some historians assume. Not even a county, but what we would call a state. Piedmont, at the time of Vigo's birth, and even after he died, was one of the "regioni" that made up the Kingdom of Sardinia, which included Piedmont, Liguria (the Genoa area with Nice), Savoy and the island of Sardinia proper.

In his youth Vigo enlisted in the Spanish Army and saw service first in Cuba (as a muleteer) and then in New Orleans. After his discharge from the Army he moved to Missouri where he soon became a prosperous fur trader and a partner of the Spanish Governor, De Leyba, but still a subject of Spain, later serving as a member of the Spanish militia, as a private, not as a colonel, a honorary title which he was given in later years. When George Rogers Clark got to Kaskaskia, in the Illinois Territory, Vigo came to his assistance, cashing his drafts, the last of them in order to purchase and equip a river boat which was to help in the attack against Vincennes. The boat, called *The Willing*, with six guns, however, proved of no value to Clark because it was detained along the way and arrived at Vincennes after Clark had captured it.

The invaluable assistance or service which Vigo rendered and which made the capture of Vincennes possible was of another nature. According to John Bakeless, the author of *Background To Glory — The Life of George Clark* (Philadelphia, 1957), the most scholarly book on Clark I have ever read (it is also beautifully written), Vigo was sent by Clark to bring some supplies to Captain Helm at Vincennes, without knowing that Helm had been made a prisoner by the British, commanded by Lieutenant Governor Henry Hamilton.

Before he got to Vincennes, however, Vigo was captured by a British scouting party or patrol and taken to Hamilton. Vigo had no trouble in convincing the British captain that he was a Spanish merchant, that is, a merchant in Spanish territory, and that he was on one of his regular business trips. Needless to say, the British took his horse, saddlebags, clothing and arms, worth about five hundred dollars (of those days). Before Hamilton let him go, however, he made Vigo promise that he would go straight to St. Louis, without stopping at Kaskaskia, where Clark was. Vigo kept his word, but once he reached St. Louis, he got back on his horse and quickly ran to Clark's headquarters. There he told Clark that Helm had been captured, that he (Vigo) had been allowed to wander around Vincennes, had noted the strength of the garrison, at first saying that Hamilton had about 800 men, but finally figuring that he had just about 30 regular soldiers (British), 50 French volunteers, and some 400 Indians. As figured by Bakeless, Hamilton had about 500 men, about 50 white men, the rest Indians, three field guns and two swivels. The British, in Vigo's opinion, did not anticipate an attack until the spring, so much so that Hamilton had postponed a campaign against Kaskaskia. As Clark wrote in a letter dated February 2, 1779, "In the high of our anxiety on the evening of the 29th of January 1779 Mr. Vague [Vigo] a Spanish Merch^t Arrived from St Vincents, and was there the time of its being taken, and gave me every Intelligence that I could wish to have."

Clark's account in his manuscript memoir is reprinted, in part, in *A History of Indiana*, by John B. Dillon, Indianapolis, 1859, in more formal language than in the original manuscript, "Memoirs of General Rogers Clark, composed by himself at the united desire of Presidents Jefferson and Madison." Dillon's book was reprinted in 1971 by the Arno Press, exactly as it was published in 1859. Here is what Clark wrote, with minor corrections in the spelling by Dillon, following his explanation of how Clark, after his own reduction of Vincennes before it was recaptured by the British, found himself in a perilous situation:

"I could see but little probability of keeping possession of the country, as my number of men was too small to stand a siege, and my situation too remote to call for assistance. I made all the preparation I possibly could for the attack, and was necessitated to set fire to some of the houses in town to clear them out of the way. But, on the 29th of January, 1779, in the height of the hurry, a Spanish merchant [Francis Vigo], who had been at Post Vincennes, arrived and gave the following intelligence: That Mr. Hamilton had weakened himself by sending his Indians against the frontiers, and to block up the Ohio; that he had not more than eighty men in garrison, three pieces of cannon, and some swivels mounted; that the hostile Indians were to meet at Post Vincennes in the spring, drive me out of the Illinois, and attack the Kentucky settlements, in a body, joined by their southern friends; that all the goods were taken from the merchants of Post Vincennes for the king's use; that the troops under Hamilton were repairing the fort, and expected a reinforcement from Detroit in the spring; that they appeared to have plenty of all kinds of stores; that they were strick in their discipline, but that he did not believe that they were under much apprehension of a visit; and believed that, if we could get there undiscovered, we might take the place. In short, we got every information from this gentleman that we could wish for, as he had had good opportunities and had taken great pains to inform himself with a design to give intelligence* [*Jefferson's correspondence, i, 451 — Clark's MS Memoir — at bottom of page as a footnote]. We now viewed ourselves in a very critical situation — in a manner cut off from any intercourse between ourselves and the United States. We knew that Governor Hamilton, in the spring, by a junction of his northern and southern Indians (which he had prepared for) would be at the head of such a force that nothing in this quarter could withstand his arms — that Kentucky must immediately fall; and well if the desolation would end there . . . We saw but one alternative, which was to attack the enemy in their quarters."

The rest is history. But see August Derleth's book, *Vincennes: Portal to the West*, 1968, pp. 57-70, for an excellent description of that epic march and victory.

No sensible person will thus dispute the fact that had it not been for Vigo's precise information (more or less), Clark would not have tried his desperate and heroic raid, for it was hardly more than that, with the exception of his gigantic bluff. But Vigo did more, as we can learn from various sources, including his memorial to Congress. Of course, such memorials are seldom taken at face value because the lawyer always tries to overstress the case, but the documentary evidence in the form of the drafts cashed by Vigo cannot be questioned. It is also true that Vigo was not the only person who helped Clark financially, but as I have shown in my 1934 book, *The Italians in America Before the Civil War* (p. 185), "the money advanced by Vigo alone represented almost one-fourth of the total amount received from about a score of individuals from the time of his arrival at Kaskaskia on July 4, 1778, to the time of his departure on February 5, 1779, or about one-half of the total amount cashed by Clark during the two months preceding his march on Vincennes. [That] should convince anyone that the example set by Vigo must have won over the population." Likewise, there is no doubt that the conquest of Vincennes dictated, in part, the Treaty of Paris in 1783.

Not everybody agrees, to this very day. Thus, Professor William E. Wilson says on pages 55-56 of his 1966 book, *Indiana, A History*, that "local pride" has led some historians to conclude that without Clark's victory at Vincennes the Hoosiers (people of Indiana) would be Canadians. "But the facts hardly support the contention, for the negotiators of the peace in Paris in 1782-83 *seem* (italics added) not to have taken Clark's exploits into consideration; at least there was no mention of them in any of their deliberations or journals or dispatches." But that's no argument. On the contrary, why should the Americans have said anything when they were in control, physical control, of the land?

"The fact remains," as John Bakeless succinctly puts it in his scholarly book (p. 340), "that the British were never able to resume possession. Had they been able to do so, it is as nearly certain as any "if" of history that the American boundary would today be the Ohio River. It was George Rogers Clark and the Illinois Regiment who destroyed the control without which Britain could not claim the country." And Vigo, of course.

Bakeless' conclusion is supported by recent research, as by Arnold Whitridge who shows in his fine biography, *Rochambeau* (New York, 1965, p. 230), that the British were anxious to conclude a treaty without delay. In other words, the British were as anxious to get out of that war as quickly as we were from Vietnam. Philip Mazzei had sensed that much a year before the Treaty of Paris was concluded. In a letter to the Grand Duke of Tuscany on April 18, 1782, he wrote that he firmly believed "that the desire for peace is general in England, and is shared by the King and his ministers, despite all apparent controversies on the subject and that some of the principal members of the cabinet have already agreed to recognize the independence of America, without which they know that peace cannot be secured." Actually, Mazzei had forecast the outcome of the war a year before, in 1781, in letter which in all probability he brought to the attention of Jefferson and probably Franklin. The letter, one of several is in Vol. II of Mazzei's *Memorie*, pp. 195-277. The translation by Howard R. Marraro was published in the *William and Mary Quarterly*, Vol. XXII, 1942, pp. 275-301, 361-380.

23

CARLO BELLINI

It is not generally known that the first chair of modern languages in an American institution of higher learning was established at the College of William and Mary in 1778 and that the first professor was Carlo Bellini, a native of Tuscany, who came over in 1774 to join his friend, Philip Mazzei. He taught for a quarter of a century, Italian, French, Spanish and German. This is the more interesting "when we learn that as late as 1814 George Ticknor could find in Cambridge, Mass., neither a good teacher of German, nor a dictionary, nor even a German book in the town or college. (Lyon G. Tyler in *William and Mary Quarterly*, Oct., 1905.)

No less interesting, Bellini "is perhaps the only man in history to have addressed the philosopher as 'My dearest Thomas'," outside, of course, of his immediate family. (D. Malone, *Jefferson the Virginian*, 1948.) However, the few letters from Jefferson to Bellini I have been able to read, begin with the formal "Dear Sir" or "Dear Mr." Also according to Prof. Malone, "Bellini's gratitude and affection for Jefferson were excessive." That is true, but Jefferson's affection for Bellini was not superficial, either. Personally, I have read few letters from one friend to another of the same sex couched in such affectionate and gentle terms as Jefferson's letter to Bellini of April 16, 1799, enough to reveal Jefferson's noble heart and loftiest sentiments. (*William and Mary Quarterly*, January, 1925, pp. 12-13.)

We do not know what Bellini did between 1774 and 1778, when he was appointed professor. Probably he took charge of Mazzei's affairs, as the latter was delving more and more into politics. One thing is certain: Bellini fell in love with America and her institutions, as shown in the letter he wrote to a friend in Italy in August, 1778. The letter begins with the words, "I am at last a free and independent man. As a consequence of liberty and independence in all these vast regions one finds not even a single being so stupid as to have the insolence to believe himself superior to another. The only superior is the law: the law is made by the whole people, so that the individual by obeying the law does nothing but obey himself. The lawmaker himself cannot disobey the law without becoming unhappy and ridiculous" and then about the war, "I can assure you that in every encounter we have won out over the enemy, who has waged war against horses, cows, chickens, corn, tobacco, houses, cities void of inhabitants, women, old men, children. When, however, he has to fight with soldiers in the open field, he has gotten rather the worst of it. In the course of this war, beginning at the battles of Lexington and Trenton we have taken from the enemy 18,940 men in dead, prisoners and deserters . . . We haven't lost even half as many people, which must not seem strange, because we have always struck on the run, rarely making a stand; and whenever it has come to making a stand, the enemy commanders with their whole army have thrown down their arms and surrendered unconditionally. If you don't believe me, ask the pompous English General Burgoyne what happened to him at Saratoga." How is that for a new American, just four years in the country?

In the same letter Bellini tells how in 1775 Mazzei, Bellini and a vigneron from Italy joined a company of soldiers, but the English withdrew and the company was disbanded. The story is told by Mazzei in his *Memorie*, but is repeated by Bellini in almost the same terms. According to him, Patrick Henry, who was the captain, told him, "You, Sir, render an important service to this state with your example, because barely arrived in this country, you voluntarily undertake to defend it as a soldier. You see what an effect your behavior produces on the minds of these citizens." Bellini may have exaggerated in saying that Henry addressed him, whereas he addressed the three Italians, as related by Mazzei, but the two versions agree as a whole. (Pace, A., "Another Letter to Carlo Bellini," *William and Mary Quarterly*, July, 1947, pp. 351-352.)

Later Bellini was named, as he put it, Secretary of this State of Virginia for foreign affairs, most likely a foreign correspondent, in the sense that he translated letters and other documents. However, according to Brant, *James Madison*, Vol. I, Bellini was actually Secretary of Foreign Affairs. The position, at any rate, was a responsible one. "From the accomplishments of Mr. Bellini," we read in a letter date May 13, 1778, from Patrick Henry, the Governor of Virginia, to Benjamin Harrison, Speaker of the House of Delegates, "there seems no doubt of his fitness to fill the office in which Secrecy, Fidelity and Knowledge were so essentially necessary." (*Official letters of the Governors of the State of Virginia*, ed. by H. R. McIlwaine, Vol. I, p. 272.)

Bellini spent the last years of his life as a poverty-stricken invalid. When his estate was liquidated in 1816, some 12 years after his death, the sum of $668.92 was sent over to his sisters in Italy. In 1924, a tablet in his honor, the gift of Prof. Luigi Carnevale of Chicago, was unveiled in the library of the College, where he taught for about 25 years.

24

RAZZOLINI, ARMOURER OF MARYLAND
(1732 - 1747)

Onorio Razzolini, a native of Asolo, a town north of Venice, was probably the first native of Italy to occupy an important post in one of the 13 Colonies. He died at Asolo in 1769 at the age of 70.

Razzolini came to America as tutor to Benedict Swingate, Lord Baltimore's illegitimate son, shortly before 1732, when he was naturalized a citizen of Maryland. Shortly after that, Charles II, Fifth Lord Baltimore, appointed him Armourer and Keeper of the Stores, a very important position, for he was practically in charge of the defense of the Colony. He seems to have been also a member of the Council and Keeper of the Council Chamber.

Razzolini married Elizabeth Fleury, a Catholic and the only daughter of a French officer who had served as President of the Parliament of Rouen, France, with whom he returned to Asolo in 1747, apparently after his wife's inheritance of considerable wealth which enabled him to build a fine villa which is still in existence. In 1761, after the death of his French wife, he married again and became the father of three daughters.

(See, Wallace, D., "Onorio Razzolini, Pioneer Italian," *Sons of Italy Magazine*, Boston, Nov.-Dec., 1942, Feb., 1943; *Maryland Archives*, Vols. 28, 37, 42; *Maryland Historical Magazine*, 1921, 1926, 1927; Bernardo, C., *Guida di Asolo*, Milan, 1949; C. P. Trieste de'Pellegrini, *Saggio di Memorie degli Uomini Illustri di Asolo*, Venice, 1780.)

25

SOME 18TH CENTURY ITALIANS WHO "MADE AMERICA"

In Italy, it used to be said of those immigrants who struck it rich in America that they "fecero l'America," literally, made America. Actually, the late Prof. Antonio Marinoni of the University of Arkansas wrote a book, *Come "ho fatto" l'America* (1932), but in a humorous sense because college professors don't get rich. With the usual exceptions. Please note that "ho fatto" is between quotation marks.

Hundreds of thousands of Italians, however, struck it rich in America, relatively speaking, that is, considering their economic status in Italy. Here I shall recall only half a dozen who achieved a degree of financial success during the last quarter of the 18th century: Formicola, Strobia, Giannini and Phinizy in the East, and Bouis, Berthold and Yost in St. Louis.

Serafino Formicola, a Neapolitan, is said to have come over with Governor Dunmore. Shortly after the hostilities he owned a hotel, the Charlton House, in Williamsburg, which is said to have been the fashionable meeting place of those days. (Hawthorne, H., *Williamsburg, Old and New.*) About 1780, when he was 37 years old, he moved to Richmond, where he owned the famous Eagle Tavern, on two different locations. It was patronized by Washington and other leaders. At that inn Aaron Burr was arraigned before Chief Justice Marshall in 1807. (*Diary of George Washington,* April 26, 1786; Dumbauld, E., *Thomas Jefferson, American Tourist,* 1946, 42-46.)

Formicola married one Matilda Newman in 1774. They had one daughter, Evelyn Formicola, who is said to have been one of the leading belles of Williamsburg. She married Stewart Bankhead, one of whose descendants is said to have been a leading motion picture actress. Evelyn's daughter, at any rate, married Col. Henry Garnett of Westmoreland in 1817 and her son, Thomas Bankhead, the grandson of the Italian immigrant, was killed at the Battle of Chancellorville. Be that as it may, Formicola became a man of consequence, just as the Marquis of Chastellux had foreseen when he stopped at his Richmond inn in 1781. In 1786 he subscribed the sum of $500 towards the erection of Quesnay's Academy of Science and Fine Arts. (Meagher, M., *History of Education in Richmond*, 1939, 22; Mordecai, S., *Richmond in By-Gone Days*, 1860, 206; Crozier's *Virginia County Records*, Vol. 9, 118; Little's *History of Richmond*, 73; *Virginia Magazine of History and Biography*, Vol. 10, 101, Vol. 27, 339, Vol. 30, 245; *William and Mary Quarterly*, II, 114; Series II, Vol. 9, 1929, p. 313; *Virginia Gazette* (Purdie), January 19, 1776; Chastellux, *Travels in North America*, 1828 ed., 276; *Virginia Independent Chronicle*, June 20, 1787; Schoepf, *Travels in the Confederation*, 1911, 64; Swem, *Virginia Historial Index*.

Giovanni Strobia seems to have been one of the gardeners who came with Mazzei in 1773. From a letter that Jefferson wrote to Bellini on April 26, 1799, we learn that he "has got rich as a grocer in Richmond . . . is in flourishing circumstances." His name appears frequently in the *Virginia Calendar of State Papers* (Vols. 4, 6, 8 and 9), between 1785 and 1802, when he resigned as a captain of the militia. He died in 1809. (*Richmond Enquirer*, March 17, 1809.) His son, John H. Strobia (1785-1856), married Ann Marie Lambert, the eldest daughter of Col. (later General) D. Lambert, mayor of Richmond. When he died he was buried with honors by the Richmond Light Infantry Blues of which he was active and later honorary member." He was one of the city's leading citizens (*Richmond Despatch*, Oct. 16, 1856) and is said to have been one of the patrons of local artists, including Robert M. Scully. (Dunlap, *Rise and Progress of the Arts*, III, 194.) Another of Giovanni's sons, Francis Strobia, was born in 1787 and died in 1815.

Jefferson, in his letter to Bellini mentioned above, tells also of Anthony Giannini, who "has raised a large family, married several of them, & after thriving for a while has become embarassed . . . Francis, his brother in law & Anthony Molina have done terribly well." Anthony Giannini in 1784 bought land on Buck Island Creek. "In 1792 he petitioned for liberty to build a mill on that stream. One of the same name, no doubt a son, became a Baptist minister in 1807." (Woods, E., *Albermarle County in Virginia*, 1901, 360.) Woods also mentions one Francis Modena, a carriage maker by trade, who died in 1826.

Antonio Sylvester Bilisoly (Bonisola, or Buonisola — literally translated, "good island") was born at Ajaccio, like Napoleon, in 1750, came to America with De Grasse in 1777 and served at Yorktown. After a brief residence in Haiti, where he married Adelaide Accinelli, the daughter of an exiled Acadian who owned a coffee and sugar plantation, he settled in Norfolk in 1799, later moving to Portsmouth, Va., where he died on October 6, 1845. His son, Joseph A., a native of Norfolk, was engaged in ship-building for about four years, but later became a merchant. Three of Joseph's sons became physicians. (*Eminent and Representative Men of Virginia and the District of Columbia*, 1893, 397-399.)

Ferdinand Phinizy (Finizzi), a native of Parma, Italy, also came with the French, with whom he served during the Revolution. After the war he settled in Georgia, where he became a prominent merchant. During the War with the Indians (1792-1794) he equipped a company of soldiers and received the rank of captain at first and major later. He died in 1818 at the age of 57, leaving an estate of $120,000 and five children (three sons and two daughters). Their descendants have been bankers, prominent lawyers, planters, publishers of newspapers, trustees of educational institutions, directors of railroad and insurance companies, and civic leaders. One of Ferdinand's sons, John Phinizy, graduated from the University of Georgia in 1811, served as mayor of Augusta, Ga., and was a prominent banker and merchant, as we have seen in a preceding chapter. (See also F. P. Calhoun, *The Phinizy Family in America*.)

Antoine Vincent Bouis was born in Genova, Italy, in 1752 and emigrated to New Orleans in 1780, but did not stay long and moved to St. Louis, where in 1782 he married Madaline Robert of Garandolet. Their children married into families which were prominent in Creole society. Their son, Pascal, graduated from the U.S. Military Academy in 1806 and died in a duel in 1812. A great-great-grandson of the Genoese immigrant became Secretary of State of Missouri and a newspaper editor. His name was Alexander Leseur.

Bartholomew Berthold was born in Trento, which until 1918 was a part of Austria, in 1780. He was an officer in the Italian Army at the Battle of Marengo, where he was wounded and taken prisoner by the French. In 1798 he came to America by way of England, lived in Baltimore for a few years and in 1809 moved to St. Louis. He married into the family of one of the founders of St. Louis. He soon became a prominent fur trader, as owner or co-owner of the American Fur Company, one of the largest in the country. His daughter married William L. Ewing and was the mother of a mayor of St. Louis.

Emilian Yosti was born at Novara, in Piedmont. He was one of the prominent persons in the early annals of St. Louis. He was a member of the first grand jury summond in 1804. He was a land speculator, and ran also a lime kiln and stone quarry in 1799. At his tavern, a meeting was held in 1808 for the formation of a volunteer company. He died at his house, on the SW corner of Main and Locusts Streets in 1818 at the age of 78. His widow died in 1824 at the age of 55.

One must bear in mind, however, that the name Yost, Yohst, Yoest, Youst appears in the 1790 census as one of those with more than 100 heads of family with such or similar name. It seems likely, therefore, that Yost's name may have followed the spelling of the older Yost.

26

THE FILICCHI BROTHERS AND
ST. ELIZABETH ANN SETON

The canonization of St. Elizabeth Ann Seton on September 14, 1975, makes timely the story of two Italians, Antonio and Filippo Filicchi, whose financial assistance, friendship and, above all, exemplary Christian life were responsible in the conversion of Mrs. Seton to the Roman Catholic faith.

Antonio and Filippo Filicchi were the sons of a patrician of Gubbio, in the province of Perugia. Filippo had travelled in the United States in the years 1785-1788 and was a sponsor at one of the earliest baptisms in the Church of St. Peter on Barclay Street in New York City, that of Philip Ghiradini, the son of Vincent Ghiradini and Elizabeth Kearny, who was born on October 10, 1787. Filippo married an American woman, a Miss Cowper, "and was so thoroughly acquainted with American conditions that he was appointed consul-general of the United States at Leghorn in 1794, serving until 1798. He died on August 22, 1816. Antonio died thirty years later on February 3, 1846.

There is not one of the several biographies of St. Anne Seton that does not stress the generosity and the noble hearts of the two Filicchi brothers. Wealthy business associates of Mrs. Seton's husband, they took care of her and her children after the death of Mr. Seton in Italy, with a munificence that seems almost unbelievable, at least to us moderns. "In addition to the orders left with you on my departure from America," wrote Antonio Filicchi to John Murray and Sons, his New York agents, in 1806, "you are requested to furnish Mrs. Seton with whatever further sum she might at any time call for, to support herself and family." Mrs. Seton, however, does not seem to have made use of that privilege.

Later on, in 1808, when she needed some money for her institution, Mrs. Seton proposed to Antonio Filicchi that he buy in his name the property she needed, so that he could always retain control over it. He replied that he could not think of it and asked her to draw $1,000 on his New York bankers, "charging the same to the account in the world to come of my brother Filippo and of your brother Antonio. If something more should be wanted, you are commanded to quote it to me plainly and positively." After all, he added, Mrs. Seton's prayers had bettered their financial position "here below," so much that they could easily afford it. He repeated the same refrain two years later when Mrs. Seton took $1,000 in gold from an Italian priest who was going back to Italy, Father Zocchi, and asked Antonio Filicchi to pay the same amount in gold to him. The financial assistance never stopped, until it was no longer needed.

Much more important than the financial assistance was the example which the two brothers set for her Protestant friend while she was their guest in Leghorn after her husband's death. "The name of this noblehearted Italian," wrote Mother Seton's biographer, Madame de Barberey, "can never be forgotten by those who venerate the name of Seton, for where Seton lives, Filicchi cannot die." "O Filicchi," Saint Ann Seton was wont to say, "may you shine as the stars in glory."

Both brothers, we may add, maintained close relations with the American prelates of their days, especially with Bishop Carroll, as well as with John Adams, Madison, Jefferson, and Washington, who appointed Filippo Filicchi American Consul General at Leghorn.

There are quite a few books on Saint Ann Seton. One of the best, with a generous account of the friendship between Mrs. Seton and the Filicchi families, is *Mrs. Seton — Foundress of the American Sisters of Charity*, foreword by Francis Cardinal Spellman, Preface by Amleto Cardinal Cicognani, New York, 1962, ill., including 3 photographs of the Filicchis. But see also, Annabelle M. Melville, *John Carroll of Baltimore, Founder of the American Catholic Hierarchy*, 338 pages, New York, 1955.

27

CERACCHI

Giuseppe Ceracchi was "unquestionably an artist of the first class," as Thomas Jefferson informed the Commissioners of Washington in a letter dated April 9, 1792. He was born in Rome, not Corsica, as stated in some dictionaries, in 1751, but by 1775 he was in London, where he was commissioned to execute several statues for the old Somerset House and several busts, including those of Lord Shelbourne, Admiral Keppel, Sir Joshua Reynolds, now in the Royal Academy, and one of Mrs. Damer which now stands in the vestibule of the British Museum. (Whitley, W. T., *Artists and Their Friends in England*, 1928, I, 317.) From London he then went to Holland and later to Vienna, where he received a few orders from Maria Theresa and Emperor Joseph II. Back in Rome in 1785, he made the busts of Pope Pius VI, Cardinal Albani, Metastasio and Winckelman. In 1790 he was back in Amsterdam, where he obtained a letter of introduction to Thomas Jefferson from the banking house of N. and J. Van Staphorst. Since that letter was dated October 11, 1790, it would seem that Ceracchi came to America towards the end of that year, or early in 1791, when he was in Philadelphia. On January 20, 1792, he was elected a member of the American Philosophical Society. Two months later he went to New York with two letters of introduction to Chancellor Livingston, one from Jefferson (March 6, 1792) and the other from his fellow-countryman, Count Andreani. On March 25 of the same year Jefferson gave Ceracchi another letter of introduction, this time to John Hancock.

Four months later he was back in Holland, as we learn from two letters he wrote to George and Martha Washington from Amsterdam on July 6, 1792. In 1793 he wrote to Jefferson from Munich offering him the bust he had made of him. A year later he was once more in the United States, for in March, 1794 ,he asked Jefferson for more letters of introduction. As his plans did not materialize, in March, 1795, he returned to Europe. There he took part in the French revolutionary movement siding with Napoleon at first, but plotting against him as soon as he became convinced that the great Corsican was not interested in the independence of Italy. Because of that plot he lost his head on the guillotine on January 30, 1802.

Ceracchi's American activities deserve a special monograph, for there is plenty of material about him in American archives, especially in the Washington and Jefferson papers in the manuscript division of the Library of Congress. He had come to America primarily to erect a national monument in honor of George Washington and the other leaders in the Revolution. The monument was to be one hundred feet high, with a goddess of Liberty, as Ceracchi stated in his announcement, "represented descending in a car drawn by four horses, darting through a volume of clouds which conceals the summit of a rainbow.

The main figure, of course, was to be that of George Washington, surrounded by the men who took part in the War of Independence. To that end, Ceracchi asked a number of men to sit for him, and actually made 37 models of the great men of America. Washington sat for him early in 1792, and so did Jefferson, Madison, Hamilton, John Paul Jones, John Jay, George Clinton, David Rittenhouse, and others Later, when the plan did not materialize, Ceracchi asked the men who had posed for him, whether they wanted to purchase the busts he had made of them. Jefferson and a few others accepted the offer and paid the sculptor. Washington, however, refused to accept his bust as a gift and offered to pay for it, but Ceracchi resented the tone of Washington's reply (in Washington's own handwriting, but signed and sent in the name of his secretary, Bartholomew Dandridge) and took the bust back.

It is said that the bust was then sold to the Spanish minister in Philadelphia, Jaudenes, who sent it to Spain, as a present to Godoy, the Spanish prime minister. At any rate, it is now in the Metropolitan Museum of Art of New York. In the Gibbes Art Gallery of the Carolina Art Association of Charleston, however, there is another bust of Washington which is said to be also by Ceracchi, apparently the bust mentioned by Appleton in his letter to Jefferson from Leghorn, dated April 15, 1816. In connection with that bust, it is interesting to recall a letter dated March 1, 1793, from Amsterdam, Holland, quoted in the *New York Magazine, or Literary Repository* for May, 1793, pp. 317-318. According to it "The celebrated sculptor, Mr. Ceracchi, who returned from America last summer, arrived at Rome, and soon after he arrived commenced the sculpture of the bust of the President of the United States. The populace being informed thereof surrounded his house and threatened him with destruction. He providentially made his escape and has since arrived safely at Munich." Why the Rome populace should have tried to harm him is not clear.

It has been said also that Ceracchi in order to meet his debts had given his creditors notes for the busts "for which he had already been paid" (*William and Mary Quarterly,* January 1945, pp. 73-74). Such an impression is not well founded. Even a cursory reading of the correspondence about Ceracchi in the Jefferson and Washington papers in the Library of Congress should be sufficient to show that nobody paid the sculptor a penny and that although he made those busts as his own request, so that they could be used in the monument he was planning (Ceracchi to Clinton, Vienna, August 25, 1792, *Emmett Collection,* New York Public Library) nobody was under any obligation to pay for them. Later, when Ceracchi's dream was shattered, he asked the various men whose busts he had made whether they wanted to keep them and pay for them, as already pointed out. (See the letters by Ceracchi's vidow in the Library of Congress, Dec. 31, 1802, March 10, 1805, uly 5, 1805; also Appleton to Jefferson, July 5, 1805, and April 15, 1816.)

The monument, at any rate, was never erected because, as the sculptor stated in a letter to Washington dated March 28, 1795, "malicious ignorance has attacked my project" and "I am the innocent victim of intrigue" (Ceracchi to Dandridge, April 28, 1795, and to Jefferson, March 11, 1795, MS. *Library of Congress.*) His plan, however, had met with the approval of several men, including George Washington himself who had taken four shares, for the sum of $120.00. Jefferson was in favor of it. "I have seen the model of the monument in honor of the Revolution," wrote John Jay to Egbert Benson, the first president of the New York Historical Society, on March 31, 1792. "The design appears to me to be a noble one, worthy of the attention of the United States, and honorable to the taste and talents of the artist. I think the expense proper . . . I confess to you that the effort which the measure would noturally have on the President's feelings is with me an additional inducement. It is only while he lives that we can have the satisfaction of offering fruits of gratitude and affection to his enjoyment; prosperity can have only the expensive pleasure of strewing flowers on his grave." (Johnston, H. P., *The Correspondence and Public Papers of John Jay,* Vol. III, pp. 417-418.)

Dejected and disgusted, after wasting a considerable amount of money and labor, in May, 1795, Ceracchi sailed for France, where seven years later he was to be executed on a public square with Arona, Le Brun and other plotters.

Ceracchi's busts, however, remain among the finest works of arts ever modelled in America. Of his bust of Hamilton, for instance, it has been said that "It has been Hamilton's good fortune that his lineaments have gone down ennobled by the genius of Ceracchi and that solemn and majestic face, which would have not been particularly striking under any ordinary hand, is literally part of his fame. (Elson, H. W., *History of the United States of America,* N. Y. 1905, Vol. II, p. XI.) Engravings of Ceracchi's bust of Hamilton were made by Lency in

1815 and Durand in 1897. General Trumbull made a painting of Hamilton, but he did not succeed and he copied Ceracchi's bust. Trumbull, however, made a fine miniature portrait of Ceracchi, which is now in the Yale Collection of Art.

Even if we did not have the Hamilton busts (there are at least four of them, one in the New York Public Library, one in the Federal Museum at Wall and Nassau Streets in New York, one in the New York Historical Society, and one the property of the Hon. Andrew . Sordoni of Wilkes-Barre, Secretary of Commerce of Pennsylvania), those of Madison, Clinton, Jay and Washington should be sufficient to show that Ceracchi was an eminent sculptor. Some art connoisseurs even prefer him to Houdon.

Yet there is something else which should endear Ceracchi to Americans. While in Philadelphia in 1791 and 1792, Ceracchi, William Rush, and Charles Willson Peale tried "to form a collection of paintings and sculptures and to found a school of art." From this school, established by Peale, descended the "Columbianum" which in 1805 gave way to The Pennsylvania Academy of the Fine Arts. (Henderson, H. W., *The Pennsylvania Academy of the Fine Arts*, Boston, 1891, pp. 1-2.)

28

JAMES PHILIP PUGLIA
(Political Pamphleteer)

With the possible exception of descendants of colonial Italian immigrants, there have been only two Italian-born political pamphleteers in America before 1800. The first was Philip Mazzei, the second James Puglia, one of the most active writers the Federalists had on their side. He wrote numerous articles, several pamphlets, three plays based on current political events, and at least two books.

We do not know exactly where Puglia was born, but he seems to have been a native of Italy, although his family had emigrated to Italian Switzerland some two hundred years before his birth. His father, John Dominick, was born at Blenio, in the Canton Ticino. From 1775 to 1782 young Puglia studied at Savona, a city near Genoa, after which, apparently, he travelled, as his father wished him to do, until he reached America. At any rate, he was here as early as 1792, for we find him listed as "Spanish interpreter" in Hardie's *Philadelphia Directory and Register* for 1793. In 1794 he was a private in the local militia. (*Pennsylvania Archives*, Series 6, Vol. 5, 509.)

It was in that year, 1794, that Puglia's first book printed in the United States, *El Desengaño del Hombre*, in Spanish, appeared in Philadelphia. A year later he published a *Federal Politician*, a book of 284 pages, and *The Blue Shop, or Impartial Humorous Observations on the Life and Adventures of Peter Porcupine*. Porcupine was the pseudonym of William Cobbett, as students of that period know, Puglia often attacked him under the name of Quick Silver.

We need not dwell here on all that Puglia wrote during the next quarter of a century, or until his last book known to us, *El Derecho del Hombre*, a translation of Paine's *Rights of Man*, appeared in Philadelphia in 1822. It is in that book, a copy of which I consulted at the Huntington Library in San Marino, Cal., that one will find a list of Puglia's published and manuscript writings and a reference to his Italian nationality.

Puglia is said to have served as health officer for the city of Philadelphia and to have lived for a number of years in Harrisburg, where he was "worshipful Master" of Perseverance Lodge No. 21 of the Masons, (*Notes and Queries*, Harrisburg, 1894, Series I, Vol. I, 51.) From a letter he wrote to Jefferson, to whom he dedicated his comedy, *The Embargo*, we learn that William Warren, the manager of the Chestnut Street Theater, refused to produce it because he was opposed to Puglia's political ideas. (Puglia to Jefferson, June 21, 1808, and Jefferson to Puglia, June 24, 1808, *MS Library of Congress.*) That he never became a rich man we learn from his *Short Extract* (also in the Huntington Library), or summary of his *Desengaño del Hombre,* which he wished to publish in an English translation, provided he could get enough subscriptions. "The low circumstances of De Puglia ((who must get his living like the birds of the forest) are great impediments to his sparing time for study." Whether Puglia's *Embargo* was ever produced on the stage we do not know. (See Hornblow's *History of the Theatre in America*, 1919, I, 212, and Quinn's *History of the American Drama*, 2nd ed., 1943, 136.)

The New York Public Library has a copy of *Federal Politician,* Philadelphia, 1795, by James PH. Puglia, Teacher of Spanish and Italian Languages. For a list of other works by, or attributed to, Puglia, under the pseudonym of Quicksilver, see Gaines, Pierce Welch *Political Works of Concealed Authorship*, Third Edition, Revised and Enlarged, Hamden, 1972, p. 212.

29

GIOVANNI BATTISTA SARTORI

Giovanni Battista Sartori, a business man of Rome, Italy, founded the first Catholic church in New Jersey.

Sartori was born in Rome in 1765, came to America in 1793, married a Miss Musgrave, and returned to Italy in 1794. In 1797 he was in Rome, from where on March 14 he sent a letter to Robert Morris in which he applied for the position of consul in Italy. Three months later he received his appointment, a position which he retained for a long time, although he returned to America in 1800. During his absence from Italy his brother was the acting consul and, later, consul until March 3, 1823, when he was succeeded by Felix Cicognani.

Sartori returned to America after the death in 1800 of his first wife. On March 8, 1804, he married at Lamberton, N. J., the former Mary M. Henrietta L'Official de Woofouin, a natie of Hispaniola. They became the parents of fourteen children, eleven of whom, six sons and five daughters, reached maturity. One of the sons, Louis Sartori, became a commodore in the United States Navy. His daughter Eugenia married Peter A. Hargous, one of the incorporators of St. John's College (Fordham) in 1846. One of his grandsons, Monsignor Luigi Sartori, the son of Edmund Sartori, worked for twenty-five years in the diocese of Baltimore, notably at Upper Halls, Md., where he built and was pastor of the Church of St. Stephen. Later he settled at Grigno, in the Trentino, Italy, where he died in 1924. Giovanni Battista's last surviving grandchild, Frank A. Sartori, died in Philadelphia in October, 1934.

Giovanni Sartori erected the first calico factory in Trenton (1877) and a macaroni factory. In 1832 he returned to Italy and settled at Leghorn, where he died in 1853.

(For additional data see my *Italian-American Mistory,"* Vol. II, pp. 101-103, 416.)

30

PAOLO BUSTI
(Founder of Buffalo, N. Y)

Paolo Busti, a native of Milan, Italy, came to America from Amsterdam about 1798, as the general agent of the Holland Land Company, which at that time owned some 3,000,000 acres of land in the northern part of New York State and Pennsylvania. Why he should be considered the rightful founder of Buffalo has already been told in my book, *The Italians in America Before the Civil War* ,pp. 215-220, and need not be repeated here. Here I shall add only a brief passage from a biographical sketch of Busti which I found in manuscript form in the archives of the Historical Society of Pennsylvania. It was written in 1886 by one Loren Blodget, who learned many of the facts about Busti from a relative who was a neighbor of Busti and knew him personally. It reads:

"The first General Agent of the purchasers of land made by citizens of Amsterdam, Holland, in Western New York and Western Pennsylvania was Theophilus Cazenove, who acted as such from 1793 to 1798; but he did little toward the settlement of the lands, and he was succeeded in 1799 by Paul Busti, who established his general office in Philadelphia beginning at once an active system of survey and settlement of all these lands. He directed all the work of Joseph Ellicott, the chief surveyor who had gone to Canandaigua, New York, in 1798, and who subsequently laid out in proper form, all the lands of the Holland Land Company's purchase in New York State. Agent Busti also had the direction of the survey and settlement of the purchases in Western Pennsylvania made by the same Amsterdam merchants, and sent H. J. Heinekoper as the first resident agent to Cassewago, now Meadville, in 1804. From this time forward, and during the entire period of the settlemnt of the seven or eight large counties occupied by the Holland Land Company as proprietors, the firm and enlightened policy of Agent Busti is to be credited with all the important results. These liberal acts of management and settlement of the millions of acres embraced in these purchases, and forming now the richest portions of Western New York and Western or Northwestern Pennsylvania, constitute the enduring memorial of Paul Busti, who, during all this period was a resident and prominent citizen of Philadelphia."

Busti, wrote the *American Daily Advertiser* of Philadelphia on August 17, 1824, at the time of his death, "possessed a refinement of manners — a comprehensive knowledge of things, and in intelligent spirit, which contributed to the delight of the learned and the pleasure of social intercourse. He spoke several of the European languages well, which enabled him to maintain a correspondence with foreigners of the first distinction . . . In the infancy of these settlements he extended every patronage and encouragement to promote their success. To his judicious management, prudence and circumspection, and to the liberal policy, uniformly enforced, are these regions, so lately a wilderness, mainly indebted for their rapid progress in population and improvement — rapid, perhaps, beyond a parallel and now assuming the first rank in physical strength and respectability."

Busti, one might add, was also one of the first prominent real estate operators in the Philadelphia area.

NOTES

CHAPTER 7 — A FLORIDA TRAGEDY

Stephen Vincent Benet, a descendant of one of the Minorcan settlers, wrote a novel about the ordeal of his ancestors, *Spanish Bayonet*.

Professor Bruno Roselli wrote a small pamphlet on Italian families in Florida before 1821, but I can't recall anything about it, except that it was a pamphlet. According to Prof. De Conde, it is unreliable but I would not take his word for it, as it would take much time to check the facts in Roselli's pamphlet before expressing an opinion about it, which De Conde did not have, to judge by his hasty statements.

Other descendants of the Italian settlers are mentioned in A. J. Hanna's *Flight Into Oblivion* (1938, reprinted in 1959), pp. 188-200-205, 222 and 273). The book, which is well-known, deals with the flight of the former members of the Confederate Cabinet to Florida and Cuba and England. One of them, General Breckinridge, finally made it to Cuba, where he and his 5 companions were given a dinner by another refugee, a descendant of one of the New Smyrna Italian settlers, Gumersindo Antonio Pacetti, a former mayor of St. Augustine, Fla. Another Italian, either Adolphus Pacetti or Ramon Canova (a strictly Italian name) was the captain of a boat in which the former attorney general of the Confederacy, George Davis, tried to escape to Cuba, but could not make it and was arrested by the Federals. Since he had no money and he did not reveal his identity, the captain put him to work to pay his passage, doing menial chores, but one can imagine his surprise when he learned the identity of his passenger. Still another Italian mentioned in the Hanna book, one Captain Frederick Tresca, a "native of France" (!) (the Italians sided with the Union during that conflict, thus one can imagine how it was possible for Tresca to say that he was born in France, although that's possible, but the family was strictly Italian). Captain Tresca arranged for the flight to the Bahamas of former Secretary of State Benjamin, who finally made it to England. His son, Rev. W. B. Tresca, is also mentioned in a reference to a book published in 1933 by Lillie B. McDuffee, who apparently had interviewed him. But one has only to go to St. Augustine to see how Italian names are present everywhere. I have read in a recent Federal Works Project book that there still is in that town a Minorcan Quarter or barrio.

In any event, I would recommend those early settlers to N.B.C.'s know-it-all David Brinkley, according to whom the inhabitants of the United States in 1790 were only Wasps (obviously there must have been some Anglo-Savons who were not white!), and then Irish, German, Spanish and one per cent Swedes. Nobody else, you can believe Mr. Brinkley as to that.

CHAPTER 10 — FIGHTERS FOR AMERICAN INDEPENDENCE

For an excellent description of the Battle of Yorktown which lends support to the Mazzei plan, alleged or otherwise, see Charles Botta's *History of the War of Independence*, translated from the Italian. I have the

116

seventh edition which was published in New Haven in 1837, but the work first appeared in Italy in 1809. It contains a map showing the position of the Gatinais regiment at Yorktown and an excellent account of the encounter between De Grasse and Rodney, with a mention of the ship Pluton on which the *Royal Italien* regiment was embarked.

The back of the *Haym Salomon-Financial Hero* commemorative stamp reads: Financial Hero — at top. Then, below, "Businessman and broker Haym Salomon was responsible for/ raising most of the money/ needed to finance the American/ Revolution and later to save/ the nation from collapse." That's a stinking lie, as I have shown in this chapter. One more example of the shameless pushiness of some brazen people and of the stupid servility and cowardice of some politicians and bureaucrats who are willing to falsify American history.

I am especially incensed at the stupidity and ignorance of some (fortunately not all) Italian-American jellyfish who are afraid to lift a finger and assert the contribution of their people to American civilization, not at the usual banquets they give to themselves or to promote some two-bit politicians — at a cost of millions of dollars a year — but in a tangible and all-American visibility. I am afraid it will take another 100 years before the Italians get their toes on the American scene. *VERGOGNA!*

CHAPTER 11 — COLUMBUS

Every year, almost invariably, a few days before Columbus Day a new book or two tries to put Columbus down. Usually such books get a little publicity for a day or so and then they fall into the obscurity which inevitably will follow. Occasionally, however, one of those books lasts a little longer, especially when it is backed by a highly reputable institution, as in the case of the Vinlad Map published by the Yale University Press in 1965. As stated in the coffee-table book, *The Discovery of North America* by W. P. Cumming, R. A. Skelton and D. B. Quinn, American Heritage Press, First American Edition, 1972, p. 32, "its publication caused a great stir, since it was regarded as casting doubts on the priority of the dicovery of America by Columbus, with which, however, it was not concerned." That's preposterous, because a glance at the map will show the alleged existence of Vinland, leading to the conclusion that if the map was genuine, Columbus and others might have known about Vinland before Columbus started on his voyage of discovery. Here it should be stated that one of the three authors of the *The Discovery of North America*, R. A. Skelton, was one of the three authors or editors of the Yale University book, *The Vinland Map and the Tartar Relation.*

A number of Italians, both in Italy and in the United States, attacked the map as false, particularly the late Justice Michael A. Musmanno, who went to Yale, examined the map, became convinced that it was a fraud and wrote a book about it (*Columbus Was First*, New York, 1966). Musmanno, in turn, was criticized by some professors, including Samuel Morison, who brushed his book aside as emotional, or something of that kind, and by Professor A. De Conde, who called it passionate (what's wrong with that?) in his book, *Half-Bitter, Half-Sweet* (p. 353) and one of those things which "made Italian-Americans look foolish." And that, to my mind, is poppycock because a fraud is a fraud, and should be exposed as a fraud, as the Vinland map eventually proved to be (The New York

117

Times, January 26, 1974) even though one of the perennial defenders of the Viking discovery of America, O. G. Landwerk, continued to insist that the map was genuine in his book, *Runic Records of the Norsemen in America*, N. Y. 1974. The editor of *Heritage* magazine, Oliver Jensen, likewise tried to defend the Vinland map, on the ground that although the copy published by Yale is false, it still is a copy of the now lost original map (*Heritage*, June 1974, p. 2). Mr. Jensen, however, does not say how he happened to know that there was such a map.

Incidentally, a book by the previous author, Landsverk, in collaboration with another expert, was ridiculed by Professor Morison in his own book, *European Discovery*. As for Prof. De Conde's opinion of Judge Musmanno's book, *The Story of the Italians in America*, see Appendix A in this volume.

While I am at it, I do agree with Prof. De Conde that the picketing of the FBI headquarters in New York by Joe Colombo and his League made the Italians look foolish, I would say stupid, but the FBI did not think that the picketing was funny, to say the least. Colombo was shot down by a Negro who in turn was killed by "unknown" assassins at a huge rally of the League at Columbus Circle in New York in 1971, surrounded by people who must have seen who shot him (think of it, that is not "omertà"), but nobody has even been indicted for the murder of the Negro, nor has a motive been found for his shooting. Not as of this writing, almost five years later. But what has Prof. De Conde done to counteract in a dignified and scholarly way the smearing of his people? He, too, is an Italian-American.

The latest assault on Columbus has been promised for the near future (as of this writing) by an assistant professor of African studies at Rutgers University who is planning to publish sometime in 1976 a book, *They Came Before Columbus*, in which he promises to show that Africans discovered America long, long, before Columbus. He gave a small indication of what his book is going to be in an article, "Bad News for Columbus, Perhaps," which appeared on the Op-Ed page of the New York Times on December 4, 1975. The principal proof seems to be the finding of two Negro skeletons in a grave in the United States Virgin Islands which had been used and abandoned long before 1492, as shown by a test of the soil. Which is like finding Roman coins in a North Dakota grave in order to prove that the Romans had been in America 1,500 years before Columbus. The book, I am positive from my knowledge of ancient geography, will be brushed aside like those about the Irish in America, also before Columbus, or the Phoenicians, or similar tall tales. What I find regrettable is the irresponsibility of the Op-Ed page editor of the Times who fails to ask the opinion of responsible authorities on any subject before giving it wide publicity.

CHAPTER 12 — AMERICO VESPUCCI

For a brief summary and illustrations see my books, *The Italians in America Before The Civil War* and *Four Centuries*. To the bibliography one may add Germàn Arciniegas, *Amerigo and the New World*, New York, 1944. Professor Samuel Morison's references to Professor Pohl's writings about the Vikings in America are not flattering (Morison, *The European Discovery of America—The Northern Voyages*, New York, 1971, pp. 75, 78, 89), but Pohl's errors or alleged errors about the Vikings should not detract from his work on Vespucci, even if Arceniegas disagrees with him. See also in Morison, p. 324, how Vespucci's conclusions about the New World did not differ sensibly from those of Columbus. Also pages 243-244. For the last word on Vespucci, however, see G. Caraci, *Questioni e polemiche vespucciane*, Parts I and II, Rome, 1955-56.

In 1970, a New York rare book dealer, Hans P. Kraus, donated to the Library of Congress a contemporary copy of Vespucci's letter to Soderini in 1504 (The New York Times, January 10, 1970).

The author of the Italian verse was Monsignor, Chev. Francesco Sciocchetti (pseudonym Fides), *Scherzi in Rima*, San Francisco, Cal. n.d. but c. 1936.

For whatever it may be worth, in a brief contribution to John A. Garraty's book, *Unforgettable Americans*, Great Neck, N. Y., 1960, Professor Irving A. Leonard expresses the belief that Amerigo Vespucci was entitled to have the new world named after him rather than after Columbus, because he was convinced that it had nothing to do with Asia, which is not what Professor Morison believes, and rightly so, in my opinion. Of course, Professor Leonard is justified in his confidence in Vespucci as a scholar, a first class navigator, and a man of integrity.

On the other hand, according to Alistaire Cooke's *America*, New York, 1973, p. 25, Vespucci was a "businessman and promoter who promoted himself so well that he got his name . . ." etc., etc. That's an asinine statement for imbecilic readers. Mr. Cooke is so careless that he even calls Verrazzano a Genoese like Columbus (p. 47). Anyway, his book is not even a panorama of American history, but only his personal view of a few aspects of American life, according to his whims, or more correctly, his fantasy.

Mr. Cooke's book has been praised by the usual book reviewers (you scratch my back, I scratch yours), and his television programs on which the book is based were attacked by some Italians because when referring to representatives of some ethnic groups he pulled out some famous name out of a drawer, but in the case of the Italians he pulled out only Capone's name. That's malice or stupidity. Anyway, his own paper, *The London Times Literary Supplement* after saying on November 30, 1973, that his book is "grandiose in extent but deficient in substance" concluded that "an admitted absence of formal scholarly credentials is too often confirmed by error and lack of precision." His interpretation of such events as the Revolution or the Civil War, for instance, is just garbage, like his opinions of Vespucci and John Cabot.

CHAPTER 13 — JOHN CABOT

The most authoritative article on John Cabot to this day is Alberto Magnaghi's article in the Italian encyclopedia (Treccani), 1930. The best account in English is in Samuel Morison's *The European Discovery of America*, New York, 1971, even though it does not add anything of any importance to what is said by Magnaghi in Italian, except for some speculations regarding navigation and other geographical questions. The bibliography is up to date, including the author's comment on the alleged discovery of America by Bristol men before 1497 (p. 208). If the Bristol sailors had discovered America, argues Professor Morison, why "would that prudent Prince, Henry VII, have granted a new *isle* in 1497?"

As for the pension which was paid until 1499, it seems that it was probably paid to Cabot's widow; therefore, the argument on page 53 of my book, *Four Centuries*, is not valid.

Professor Morison's passage from the translation of the 1496 letter-patent is from the new version (1962) of Williamson's *The Voyages of Cabot*, while mine ((that is, the translation in my *Four Centuries*) is from the 1929 edition.

As for the year John Cabot went to Bristol, according to Magnaghi he may have gone there as early as 1491, although he began to plan a voyage to the New World after he learned about the discovery by Columbus.

It is beyond the province of this study to comment on Professor Morison's unjustified attack on Sebastian Cabot, in complete disregard of the solid arguments by such outstanding authorities as Alberto Magnaghi and Roberto Almagià, even though he cites the works in defense of Cabot by the latter. But then, for Almagià, according to Prof. Morison, "an Italian-born discoverer could do no wrong."

According to foreign correspondent Alistaire Cooke, *America*, 1973, p. 31, Queen Isabella decided to back Columbus, first because the war against the Moors had ended, but also because she was reminded that John Cabot had convinced Henry VII that the "Spice Islands could be reached by sea." If such was the case (I had never heard that story), why did Henry VII wait until 1496 to give Cabot and his sons permission to fit out an expedition at their expense, which took place a year later? It is strange, indeed, why Mr. Cooke does not say that England's right to North America was based on Cabot's voyage and how Sebastian Cabot's position as head of the Company Adventurers of England from 1553 to the time of his death in 1557 led to the colonization of North America. Of course, he could find room for Capone and Torrio, but not five picas for such men as Chino or Tonti. Even Marcos de Niza was just a Franciscan friar. That's American history, as some New Yorker would put it? See also chapter 12, Vespucci notes.

CHAPTER 14 — VERRAZZANO

The six-inch headline in my 1952 book, *Four Centuries*, was used to spearhead the campaign for naming the new bridge over the New York Bay "Verrazano-Narrows Bridge (with one "z") in 1964. For the description of the unveiling of the monument to Verrazzano at Battery Park in 1909 see my 1952 book, pp. 60-61, together with a photograph of the statue, and my 1934 book for a brief account of the various attempts to discredit Verrazzano. The Battery Park monument was removed in 1940 for the construction of the Battery-Brooklyn tunnel, but was re-dedicated in 1952 on the original spot with a new pedestal and legends in both Italian and English, whereas it was only in Italian on the old pedestal. For a full story of the movement sponsored by Il Progresso, New York daily (the money was subscribed by New York Italians) see A. Bosi, *Cinquant'anni di vita italiana in America*, New York, 1921, pp. 390-397.

The attempts to belittle Verrazzano have continued to this very day, as in the case of a "commentator" on the staff of the Detroit News, to which the Italian consul in Detroit, Eric Da Rin, took exception with the following letter which was printed by The News on April 23, 1959. Consul da Rin, unfortunately, has been one of the very few Italian officials in the

United States who have defended the name of his compatriots in this country. Here is what he said in part, as reprinted by the Italian weekly, La Tribuna of Detroit, Vincent Giuliano publisher and editor, on April 24, 1959:

"On your issue of Tuesday, April 21, I read the Commentator's column, 'Why Not Captain Kidd?' concerning Giovanni Da Verrazzano. It appears that, for once, his well stocked reference library failed to provide him with more accurate information needed to support his objection to a well-deserved recognition of New York Harbour's discoverer.

"Whether Verrazzano was able or not to spell his own name, seems rather irrelevant in the history of great discoveries, where what really counted was the ability of reading the still mysterious language of the stars and unknown seas. Verrazzano's own report to King Francis I of France (whose original manuscript can be seen at the Morgan Library in New York City), leaves, however, no doubt as to his proficiency not only in the problems of navigation but also in those of orthography. Far more important is the fact that in this same document he accurately described New York Harbour in the following words (a passage from Verrazzano's report follows).

The consul's letter ends by recalling that Verrazzano died at the hands of cannibals in the Gulf of Darien (Panama) when "Hardly bothered by the correct spelling of his name, his cannibal captors devoured him and other six companions, while his brother Girolamo was helplessly watching from the deck of the ship. As for Enrico Tonti [he meant Alfonso], I heartly applaud the Commentator's suggestion for a public tribute to Cadillac's gallant companion. And there will certainly be streets and bridges left to be named after Captain Kidd, whose biography at least does not require accuracy of more extensive research."

I would recommend this letter and the article by the Detroit News "Commentator" to the reflection of those Italian-American historians, like Professor Vecoli of Minnesota, who charge with filiopietism and paranoia those writers who resent the distortions of irresponsible people who smear or belittle any Italian who may come within reach of their venomous arrows.

The attempt to belittle Verrazzano's achievement continued even after the Legislature of the State of New York in March, 1960, approved unanimously (58 senators and 151 assemblymen) a resolution in favor of giving the name of Verrazzano to the new bridge which was to connect Brooklyn with Staten Island. Following the assassination of President John F. Kennedy some individuals proposed naming the bridge after him, but they did not get very far, largely because the arguments against Verrazzano were based on ignorance and prejudice. In this connection, I may be allowed to mention a long letter of mine, "Expert Answers Salmon's Attack on Italian Explorer" in the *Brooklyn Spectator* of March 13, 1964. Mr. Salmon, a Brooklyn businessman, to the best of my knowledge, had fought the naming of the bridge after Verrazzano on worthless grounds and on evidence that had been found worthless, such as the Buckingham Smith pamphlet of 1864 and the Henry C. Murphy pamphlet a few years later, so that I had to remind him of Socrates's warning to his shoemaker to mind his last.

Since then the story has been told in two authoritative books, first in 1949 by Jacques Habert, *When New York Was Called Angouleme,* a biography, and in 1970 by Lawrence C. Wroth, *The Voyage of Giovanni Da Verrazzano,* 1524-1528, Yale University Press, for the Pierpont Morgan Library. To them one must add the scholarly booklet, *Giovanni Da Verrazzano, The Discoverer of New York Bay* by Lino S. Lipinsky, with numerous drawings and other illustrations, together with bibliography, New York, 1958. Mr. Lipinsky also wrote an article, in Italian, in Il Progresso Italo-Americano of November 28, 1964. Also on the same page, which was entirely devoted to Verrazzano, one will find two additional articles on the navigator as well as the bridge. See also Mr. Lipinsky's letter to *The Sons of Italy Times,* a Philadelphia weekly, on May 25, 1964. The last word on Verrazzano was said in 1971 by Professor Samuel Morison, the eminent historian, in his book, *The European Discovery of America,* pp. 277-325, with beautiful illustrations, maps and other drawings. The translation of the Verrazzano report, reprinted from the original translation in 1910 will be found in the Lipinsky booklet.

As for the spelling of the name, it is true that there are various documents which show the spelling with one "z," but those errors are common in old manuscripts, because of the carelessness and other errors on the part of the copyists. The fact is, however, that the Verrazzano family goes back to the 13th century. There is even a Verrazzano castle which belonged to Verrazzano's family, and possibly to himself, in Greve di Chianti. We can afford, therefore, to disregard two letters by an Italian-American orchestra manager in two New York periodicals and similar "proofs."

In Italian, the best source is Alberto Magnaghi's article (with bibliography) in the *Enciclopedia Italiana Treccani* at Verrazzano, in which he questions the death of the navigator at the hands of the cannibals, but on this point there is no doubt as to how Verrazzano died. The most recent article in Italian is Roberto Almagia's *L'importanza geografica delle navigazioni di Giovanni da Verrazzano,* Florence, 1962. Almagià died a few years ago.

CHAPTER 15 — MARIO DA NIZZA

The article on Marco da Nizza in the *Dictionary of American Biography* says "Nice in the Duchy of Savoy" which is technically correct, but would be more so if "then in" were added. Nice, of course, was in the Duchy of Savoy, but so was also Piedmont. By the same token, Nice later was in the Kingdom of Sardinia.

Professor Bolton says that Fra Marco lived in Nizza, which is also correct, but see my *Italian-American History,* Vol. II, pp. 44-48, 409-410, as well as my *Four Centuries,* pp. 65-66, for illustrations.

John Bartlet Brebner says that Marcos was "French by nation," which is nonsense, because politically Marcos was a Savoyard, not French. (*The Explorers of North America,* 1492-96, 1933, reprinted in 1955 by The World Publishing Company, Meridian Press, p. 69.)

The account in *The Eyes of Discovery* by John Bakeless (New York, 1950, reprinted 1961) is too journalistic and far below the excellence of the scholarly *Background To Glory* by the same author. See Chapter 21 in the present volume.

There is nothing new in *The Seven Cities of Cibola* by Stephen Chissold, London, 1961, Chapter Seven, "Friar Marcos Views the Promised Land," which is based largely on Winship's *The Coronado Expedition*, Washington, 1896. Chissold also calls the friar a Savoyard by origin, p. 77.

CHAPTER 16 — HENRY TONTY

The finest account of Enrico Tonti's life and achievements I have read was written in 1966 by a 26-year-old Englishman, Timothy Severin. It is beautifully written, concise, accurate, and to the point. As I have stated in this chapter, and as I noted in my Civil War book in 1934, Tonti was a most remarkable man and would have figured more prominently in the exploration and consolidation of French power in the Midwest, as well as the real explorer of the Mississippi, had he been the commandant and not a lieutenant. As Mr. Severin puts it in his book, *Explorers of the Mississippi*, New York, 1967, pp. 162-184, all the adjectives used in praising Tonti are "accurate and well-deserved, but the historians and commentators usually miss the essence of Tonti's personality; he remains a half-figure, the second-string player on a team whose captain steals the glory and captures everyone's attention" (p. 166). Of course, Severin does not tell anything about Tonti that was not known, but it is the way he tells it, and his grasp of all the events, great and small, that give us an excellent view of Tonti's personality, of his achievements, of the difficulties he had to overcome, and at the same time of the intrigues, plots and lies which surrounded him. Not for nothing, his following chapter about Father Hennepin is entitled "The Mendacious Friar," the only man, as I have said, who did not speak well of Tonti.

John Upton Terrell says in his book, *La Salle — The Life and Times of an Explorer*, New York, 1968, that Tonti's father, Lorenzo, and his fellow-countryman, Mazarin, "an expert in obtaining money, ostensibly for the church, by extortion and blackmail" invented a way of making money which they kept in their own pockets, through a system of insurance which was called Tontine royal. In fact, according to Mr. Terrell, that was a big swindle and Tonti spent eight years in the Bastille. The cardinal went scot-free because of his red hat (p. 101). Mr. Tirrell's ignorance of French history in general and of the Tontine insurance in particular is so obvious that I need not bother to confute him, as the facts can be easily ascertained. See, for instance, the article under "Tontine" in the 11th edition of the *Encyclopaedia Britannica*, Vol. 27, p. 12, but also Vol. 14, p. 672b. Tonti went to jail, as explained by Prof. Murphy, because he incurred the displeasure of the King.

In recent years some historians have reappraised or reevaluated La Salle's work, but whether rightly or wrongly their conclusions are subject to serious examination. W. J. Eccles, for example, says in his book, *France in America*, N. Y., 1972, that Parkman's *The Discovery of the Great West* remains a literary epic but has little merit as history, and cites W. R. Taylor's article in the *William and Mary Magazine* (1962), pp. 202-37. E. B. Oster is even more critical in his book, *La Salle*, Toronto, 1967, and quotes Jean De Langlez (1938), who is said to have destroyed Parkman's "great man," but fails to mention that De Langlez was a Jesuit whose Order opposed La Salle at every step.

When all is said and done, regardless of Tonti's undying loyalty, his opinion that La Salle was one of the greatest men is worth more than the opinions of some debunkers, for Tonti spent years by La Salle and had ample opportunity to detect his faults, if they really were so notorious. Leave that to a Neapolitan.

What I find even more inexplicable and stranger is the fact that Professor De Conde (see Appendix A) who cites Severin's book in connection with Beltrami, to whom he (De Conde) devotes about half a page (p. 12 and not page 16 as in his Index) has nothing to say about Tonti, except that he was an explorer and the first Italian to set foot in Arkansas, and that in connection with the naming of Tontitown. Personally, I fail to see how in a history supposedly about the Italians in America, a man like Beltrami should rate higher than Tonti. For Tonti helped to open up the Midwest to civilization, whereas Beltrami's exploration of the Mississippi (his discovery of its sources is still in doubt) was of little consequence, geographically or otherwise. Severin, on the other hand, may have been a little severe about Beltrami, whom he ridicules, but whether he is entirely wrong deserves an investigation that I cannot afford at this time. My opinion that De Conde's book is lopsided, however, remains.

See also *Wilderness Manhunt — The Spanish Search for La Salle*, by Robert S. Weddle, University of Texas Press, 1973.

CHAPTER 20 — MAZZEI

All false modesty aside, the only scholarly work on Mazzei as of this date (February, 1976) is my own study, *Mazzei — One of America's Founding Fathers* (1951), with 3 photographs, 40 facsimiles and 244 notes. This study must not be confused with the chapter on Mazzei in my book, *Four Centuries of Italian-American History*, of which it was intended to be a chapter, but as the book turned out to be much larger than I had anticipated, I was forced to cut down the chapter from 54 pages to 7 as noted elsewhere.

Next to my work, I would list Professor Richard C. Garlick's *Philip Mazzei, Friend of Jefferson — His Life and Letters*, Baltimore, 1933, 179 pages, a scholarly job, even if I can't agree with some of the author's conclusions. Professor Garlick also wrote the biographical sketch of Mazzei in the *Dictionary of American Biography* and a chapter in the book, *Italy and the Italians in Washington's Time* (1933). Before Prof. Garlick, the only article in English I know of was Helen Zimmern's, "The Story of Mazzei" in the *New England Magazine*, October, -1902, pp. 198-221. Then came Prof. Emilio Goggio's article "Italy and the American War of Independence" in *The Romanic Review* for January-March, 1929, pp. 25-34 and a brief reference to Mazzei in his 17-page pamphlet, *Italians in American History*, 1930.

Helen Zimmern (apparently an Englishwoman) wrote many articles on Italy and the Italians, including a book, *Italy of the Italians*, 1906, 6th revised edition, 1920 (which I have had since 1930). Goggio's article (five pages) is based on Mazzei's *Memorie*, which led him to the conclusion that "his contribution was a valuable one, and worthy of much greater consideration than it has generally received." And, again, "the fact remains, however, that as a zealous republican, as a lover of freedom, and an enemy of intolerance, Mazzei made a very important contribution to American democracy."

Goggio also quotes the letter written by John Adams about Mazzei's "attachment and zeal for the American honour and interest, which would have become any native of our country" and Jefferson's eulogy of Mazzei on his death, and how "his early and zealous cooperation in the establishment of our independence (having) acquired for him here a great degree of favor." In his pamphlet (15 pages, with less than two small pages about Mazzei), Goggio does not add anything to what he had already said in his article, repeating that "Mazzei made a most precious and last contribution to American democracy," thereby revealing a remarkable perception of Mazzei's role in the Revolution, before the Garlick book and the publication of the documents by Marraro in later years. Needless to say, Goggio said more in a few lines than all the nincompoops who have been babbling about Mazzei in recent years.

In Italian, the only account of any importance still is G. Mira's article noted in this chapter. Alessandro D'Ancona's *Scipione Piattoli e la Polonia*, Florence, 1915, is uninformed, so far as Mazzei's activities in America are concerned, but well-taken regarding his literary style. Mira's article, on the other hand, is the only discerning article on Mazzei I have read in Italian regarding Mazzei's contribution in the Revolution. Enough to say that he places Mazzei "among the founders of the great Republic, whom their offspring worship as the Founding Fathers." To the best of my knowledge, Mira is the only writer who noted Mazzei's connection, directly or indirectly, with the Declaration of Independence. As he puts it, he, Mazzei, "knew how to shape into lucid and polished language the ideas which were the essence of the American people's doctrine and faith. 'All men are by nature equally free and independent. This equality is necessary in order to establish a free government.'" I don't know who Mira was and whether he was familiar with the background of the Declaration of Independence, but his reference to Mazzei's wording of the ideas about the equality of men is certainly striking, when compared to what Jefferson's admirers have called and do call "felicitous expression" or "succint summary."

Since Mira, there have been three books and one article before 1940: Mazzei's letters to the Polish Court, *Lettere di Filippo Mazzei alla Corte di Polonia*, edited by R. Ciampini, Bologna, 1937, of special value because of Mazzei's letter to the King of Poland, dated October 13, 1788 (pp. 31-39) in which he recalls his activities in Virginia and how he had predicted to the Grand Duke of Tuscany that Europe would soon be stunned by a revolution in America, and other matters pertaining to the American Colonies; two books, one by Angelo Flavio Guidi, *Relazioni culturali fra Italia e Stati Uniti*, Padua, 1940, and one by D. Visconti, *Le origini degli Stati Uniti d'America e l'Italia*, Rome, 1940, with nothing new about Mazzei's American activities; a brief reference by Benedetto Croce in his magazine, *La Critica*, 1927, pp. 329-335, in which he calls Mazzei dependable and trustworthy, as he concluded from some episodes with which he was personally acquainted. And that's about all, with the exception of the book, *La Cultura americana e l'Italia*, Turin, 1938 (not listed in Marraro's bibliography), by Angelina La Piana, a professor of Italian at Wellesley and the sister of George La Piana, professor of church history at Harvard for many years. More than a decade later, as noted in this chapter, the article in *Nuova Antologi* in 1949 by Vittorio Racca of Yale University.

Dr. La Piana has some intelligent and discerning remarks about Mazzei in her book, even though she finds his two thick volumes, *Memorie*, verbose, boring and hard to read (she was a professor of languages, not a historian). However, she recognizes that "even if he[Mazzei] exaggerates a little, it cannot be denied that Mazzei rendered important services to the American revolution." She says, quoting my mention in my Civil War book of the hypothesis about Mazzei's possible role in the plan to bottle up the British at Yorktown, that Mazzei would have mentioned it had he had anything to do with it. However, she failed to note that I credit Prof. Garlick for the hypothesis. Anyway, Mazzei wrote about it to Jefferson on May 20, 1780. Her opinion of Mazzei "a 'figura simpatica' [likeable fellow] among so many unscrupulous Italian adventurers . . . his is the only Italian name that deserves to be mentioned in the annals of the American Revolution, side by side with those of his great friends who later filled the greatest office in the land, Jefferson, Madison and Monroe" [she forgot Vigo]. The famous letter that Jefferson wrote to Mazzei on April 24, 1796, is a glaring proof, according to her, that Jefferson and Mazzei "shared the same ideas on the fundamental principles of Jeffersonian democracy which have remained the keystone of the American political system." But, she adds, "did Mazzei exert any influence, somehow, in arousing or intensifying Jefferson's passion for egalitarian democracy? It is very probable; in any event, it is interesting to note that in his 1796 letter Jefferson refers to England and the English government system almost with the same contempt and hatred that Mazzei had used twenty years before. However, if Jefferson received from his contacts with Mazzei a stimulus toward more radical democratic concepts and less favorable feelings toward British traditions beyond those he had before he met Mazzei, it is also true that Jefferson, once he became convinced that the democratic idea was the just one, went far beyond Mazzei's concepts, as in his views regarding the abolition of slavery" (pp. 60-62).

Among the recent books and articles published in Italy, I would single out a small volume by Sara Tognetti Burigana (the name is entered as Burigana in the New York Public Library catalog card, although it would seem that Burigana may have been her second surname, the first being Tognetti, but on the frontispiece of the book the name is without the dash, as in Tognetti-Burigana). The little volume, only 127 pages, *Trasformismo illuminato e dispotismo napoleonico*, does not say anything new about Mazzei's activities in America, but is especially valuable for Baron Grimm's estimate of Mazzei, as noted at the end of the present chapter. An object of curiosity is a letter by one F. M. Gianni to "Pippo l'Ortolano (Philip the [vegetable] gardener), Mazzei's nickname by some of his friends.

Other recent books about Mazzei in the New York Public Library: Wandruska, Adam, *Leopold II*, 2 vols., Vienna-Munich, in German — nothing of any importance or new about Mazzei's American activities, as already noted in his *Memorie;* Carlo Francovich, "La rivoluzione americana ed il progetto di costituzione del granduca Pietro Leopoldo" in *Rassegna Storica del Risorgimento*, 1954, pp. 371-377, reviewed by G. Berti in *Rivista Storica Italiana*, Vol. LXXVI, pp. 823-829. Carlo Francovich, *Albori socialisti del Risorgimento*, Florence, 1960, a history of Italian political secret societies, as possibly influenced by Mazzei as a freemason; G. Berti, *Russia e stati italiani nel Risorgimento*, Turin, 1957 ("Mazzei, the only Italian signer of the Declaration of Independence," p. 231); A. Gerbi, *La disputa sul nuovo mondo — storia di una polemica*, Milano, 1955 (idle talk about America's savages, animals, and such things); Carlo Bernari, "Filippo Mazzei, un toscano fra due rivoluzioni" *Letteratura*, Roma, July-October, 1965, pp. 3-15 ("if Mazzei was not remarkable for his literary style, he was nevertheless a keen writer, always well-documented," p. 4); Giovannetti, A., *L'America degli italiani*, Modena, 1975, nothing new, even if the author is kind enough to praise my *Italian-American History*.

The chief source, besides the letters to, from, and about Mazzei noted below, are his memoirs, or *Memorie della vita e delle peregrinazioni del fiorentino Filippo Mazzei*, 2 volumes, over 900 pages, published in Lugano, Switzerland, 1845-1846, some thirty years after his death, reprinted in Milan in 1970, 571 pages. The memoirs were translated in part by Prof. Howard R. Marraro and published as *Memoirs of the Life and Peregrinations of the Florentine Philip Mazzei* by Columbia University Press in 1942, 447 pages, including bibliography and index. Professor Marraro, obviously, reprinted only those parts which he considered important or useful, so much so that he omitted Mazzei's valuable reports to the Grand Duke of Tuscany, which he translated later (*William and Mary Quarterly*, July and October, 1942, pp. 275-301 and 361-380). He omitted much more, including the article with the phrase "All men are by nature equal," parts of which he translated and published on the first page of the *Memoirs*, preceding the Foreword, but eight years after I had noted that article, translated it and published it in my book, *The Italians in America Before the Civil War* in 1934. Because Mazzei's recollections jump from one thing to another, without any chronological order, Marraro tried to place the events as they took place, from one year to the next, with the result, for instance, that he jumps from page 375 to page 383 and back to 376 (p. 208) or from page 396 to page 407 and back to page 396 (pp. 220-221).

Marraro's translation, furthermore, is not always dependable. In one place, for instance, he translates "governo libero" as "liberal government," whereas it is obvious that Mazzei meant "free government.' In another place, he refers to Robert C. Nicholas, the treasurer of Virginia, as Nicholas Carter, even though Mazzei, more or less correctly, said Carter Nickolas (page 367 of *Memorie* and p. 205 of *Memoirs*). He fails to identify important persons, such as Anthony Chamier, top man in the British war office, who informed Mazzei about Lord North's so-called conciliatory proposals. He does not identify Count von Bruhl, who also was important, and when he does in his translation in the *William and Mary Quarterly* he lists a man who had been dead a number of years at the time Mazzei heard from von Bruhl. He spelled the name of Lavoisier, the celebrated father of chemistry, without identifying him, as Lavoisier on page 293 and Lavoisière on page 346, as if they had been two different persons. He translates Abbè, as abbot, and so on (for other errors see the notes in my *Mazzei*). I don't mention those errors in order to criticize (I have made and will continue to make mistakes) but in order to help the student of Mazzei.

Professor Marraro translated numerous documents and letters, some of which were published in the *Bulletin of the New York Public Library* in 1934 (later in book form in 1935); others in the *William and Mary Quarterly* in 1942, 1943 and 1944, in the *Virginia Magazine of History* in 1943 and 1955, in the *Mississippi Valley Historical Review* (now *Journal of American History*) in 1943, and in the *Bulletin of the Polish Institute* in 1944.

A few extracts from Mazzei's memoirs were first translated into English by Camillo Branchi when he was teaching at the College of William and Mary in Williamsburg. At first, his translation appeared in the *Columbian Monthly*, a publication of The League for American Citizenship of New York, in May and July 1928 and later, more at length and in a revised form, in the *William and Mary Quarterly* for 1929 and 1930. The latter translation, however, does not have some of the notes in the *Columbia Monthly*, such as note 2 in the July 1928 issue in which he says that "Mezzei's supplements were published in *Mr. Pinkney's "Virginia Gazette"* (1774-1775) below the pseudonym of "Furioso." That's where I first learned about "Furioso" and *Pinkney's Gazette*, as I first pointed out in my Civil War book in 1934. After me, everybody else began to prattle about "Furioso" and *Pinkney's Virginia Gazette*, including Professor Marraro at the beginning of his *Memoirs*, already noted. Actually, Professor Garlick also mentioned that fact or alleged fact in his chapter on Mazzei on page 24, note 17, but omitted it in his book. A passage from a long letter which he sent me from the University of Virginia on January 20, 1934, may prove on this point of some interest to the reader:

"Your criticism, I think, is justified, certainly from your point of view. I believe that Mazzei did help to mould a public opinion against England; but I believe his influence was small and entirely local, probably confined to what is now Albermarle County. Mr. E. C. Branchi, formerly professor at the College of William and Mary, translated a portion of Mazzei's memoirs (see *William and Mary Quarerly* . . .)." In connection with this, Prof. Garlick refers to Mazzei's articles in the *Virginia Gazette*. "Elsewhere," he goes on, "I cannot put my hand on the reference, Mr. Branchi refers to Mazzei's articles in 'Mr. Pinkney's Virginia Gazette' and says that his nom-de-plume was 'Furioso.' In my short article on Philip Mazzei which appeared in *Italy and the Italians in Washington's Time*, I referred to these articles by Branchi. I have since tried to check up on Mr. Branchi's reference, but like you, can find no such articles. I have searched thoroughly at the Virginia State Library, at William and Mary and in the Congressional Library. I tried to get in touch with Mr. Branchi, but he had moved to Chile, of all places, and apparently there was no way of reaching him. Mr. Branchi is considered a reputable scholar. He did not make up 'Furioso' or 'Mr. Pinkney's Virginia Gazette.' I believe that those articles exist, and that he has seen them. I hope your search for them will be more fruitful than mine has been. As a result of my not being able to find the articles, I left out (or thought I did) all mention of them in my *Philip Mazzei*, and also in my article on him in the *Dictionary of American Biography* . . . I am enclosing herewith a picture which I took of "Colle" just before it was pulled down. To the left of the picture, where the fir-tree intrudes into the ground there had been added an enormous wing to the house, which obviously was not in the original plan . . . I have found out that the School of Architecture here made a measured drawing of "Colle" and have made a colored rendering of it as it probably looked in its prime . . . By the way, you need not return this wretched photograph, since I have another copy."

Dr. Camillo Branchi (1883-1962), the author of many books in Italian,

Spanish and English, was a good friend of mine. I still have a snapshot I took of him and some friends of ours in Dallas, of all places, where I now live, way back in 1924. I saw him in San Francisco in 1936, where he was secretary of the local Italian Chamber of Commerce, but I don't recall whether I asked him about Mazzei. In 1950, however, as I was working on my study on Mazzei, I wrote him about it and he replied on October 14, 1950, from Santiago, Chile, that he was unable to tell me anything. Then he added that he expected to be in New York at the end of the year and then we would talk about it. When he came to New York two or three months later we spent a couple of days together, as he was going to Italy with his wife, but then he was unable to tell me where he had seen the Mazzei articles. I really do not know what happened. Incidentally, Mazzei's supplements must not be confused with the broadsides, such as those in *Southern Broadsides Before 1877* by R. O. Hummel, Jr., 1971, which are handbills, with notices of funerals, articles for sale, petitions and similar announcements. On Branchi see, *Italian-American Whos Who*, 1944, under California, as well as in other editions.

To get the facts about the *Pinkney Gazette* articles straight, Mazzei wrote: "Si convenne di pubblicare per mezzo delle gazzette un foglio periodico tendente a dimostrare al popolo il vero stato delle cose e la necessità di prepararci per non essere colti all'improvviso in caso di attacco (e conoscendo io le vedute del Gabinetto di S. Iacopo e particolarmente gli attori)) ch'io lo scrivessi nella mia lingua, ed egli lo traducesse in inglese." In English, as translated by me, "it was agreed to publish through the gazettes [newspapers] a periodical sheet [supplement] which would show the people the real state of things, and the urgency to prepare ourselves so as not to be surprised in case of attack (and since I knew the views of the Cabinet of St. James and especially its members) that I write it in my language and [Jefferson] translate it into English." Marraro, instead, translated that passage as, "We agreed to announce through the newspapers the publication of a periodical, by which we aimed to show the people the true state of affairs and the necessity of preparing ourselves so as not to be caught unawares in case of attack. As I knew the views of the cabinet of the Court of St. James and particularly of the persons involved, I would write . . ." (p. 198). Here, obviously, Mazzei and Jefferson did not intend to announce through the newspapers the publication of a periodical, but to publish a periodical sheet or supplement to be inserted in the local newspaper. I have read many of those supplements in the rare book room of the New York Public Library and in the Library of Congress way back in the 1930's, at the Newberry Library in Chicago in photostatic copies, and elsewhere in microfilm and, as I have just noted, they were not broadsides or handbills. As for the views of the cabinet and of persons involved, Mazzei said, "the views of the cabinet and the (not *of* the) persons involved.' After all, Mazzei had left London just about a year before and he knew good many English people, in the government and out.

So much for the truth about the origin of the pseudonym of "Furioso," and the name of the newspaper in which articles allegedly appeared, which so many self-styled "experts" and "scholars" toss around, from right to left and from left to right, like coconuts, as if they had known all about it.

Getting back to Mazzei's American experts, what I find really aggravating is the gall of so many presumptuous ignoramuses who steal with complete effrontery, passing off as the sweat of their brow, without citing their source, what has cost me and others many years of research and thousands upon thousands of dollars. I have especially in mind the reference to Mazzei's article with the words "all men are born equal" which I first found, translated and printed in my Civil War book in 1934, as already noted. Since I came out with it, even the late President John F. Kennedy got into the act, as inaccurately as the rest. And that goes also for the publishers of his book, A Nation of Immigrants, the Anti-Defamation League of B'nai B'rith, the paladins of he 20th century.

Personally, I have an idea as to who or where President Kennedy got his information about Mazzei, (like the presumed Italian origin of the Fitzgeralds, also mentioned by me when he was in high school). Way back in 1939, Louis Adamic, a fine writer of Yugoslav birth and the radical protegé of Mrs. Eleanor Roosevelt, so far as I know, wrote me a letter (which I still have) inquiring about my books, especially the Civil War book in which I told about Mazzei and his possible connection with the Declaration of Independence.

Since quite a few of Adamic's articles appeared in periodicals which are not listed in Reader's Guide, I can't tell when Adamic began to write about Mazzei. For the record, after the publication of my book in July, 1934, The New York Times published (Dec. 2, 1934) a very long letter of mine about Mazzei (20 inches), with a double-column heading, "MAZZEI'S ROLE CITED IN OUR CONSTITUTION — with a three-line subhead also on two columns — "Italian Is Held to Have Preceded Paine In Urging Complete independence from Great Britain." The title, of course, is wrong because I was referring to Mazzei's activities during the Revolution, or before 1789, actually between 1774 and 1779, but the headline writer mistook my reference to the British constitution for the American constitution, as I have noted in the present chapter in connection with Carter Nicholas. A month later, an article of mine appeared in the January 1935 issue of Atlantica and since in both places I referred to my chapter on Mazzei in my Civil War book, that may explain why Adamic wanted to get that book for further details.

In any event, the first book in which Adamic wrote about Mazzei that I know of, was Two-Way Passage, New York, 1941, in a chapter entitled "The Plight of an 'Italian' Boy," pp. 149-155, in which he tells how an Italian boy tried to commit suicide because Mussolini's troops were losing battles and other boys were teasing him and he felt miserable. Whereupon, Adamic assured the boy that the Italians fought well when they were fighting for a good cause, and . . . In America, too, the Italians did well, Adamic told the boy. Mazzei, for instance. "In 1774 he wrote some essays in the Italian language on liberty and democracy. Jefferson translated them, and the phrase about all of us being 'created equal' seems to have been originally Mazzei's — it came from the essays and found its way into the Declaration of Independence" (p. 153). Here, I must assert once more that no one, but no one, had referred to such a phrase as used by Mazzei and that it was only in my book that it was to be found (on page 165). Adamic's book appeared in 1941, one year before Marraro's translation of Mazzei's memoirs and eight years after my own book.

In 1944, Adamic began to write a series of articles for Woman's Day—

the A & P Magazine, one of them on the Italians, in which he dealt at length with Mazzei. His account is rather accurate, as it is based largely on my book, as are other facts mentioned by him, like the founding of the U.S. Marine Band, on page 25, which is incorrect, although taken from my book, as incorrect as his tale about Haym Salomon which responsible Jews have denied (see, for instance, the *Encyclopaedia Judaica,* 1971, Vol. 14, p. 695). Adamic was no scholar and made no claim to scholarship. He was an excellent popularizer who picked his facts here and there without checking their accuracy, so long as they made good copy, and without crediting his source. So much so that when he copied my translation of Mazzei's article, without even mentioning my name, and I threatened to sue him and the magazine, *Women's Day* immediately published a correction and apologized (November, 1944 issue).

Regardless of Adamic's petty omissions of my work (he listed my book in his bibliography), the fact remains that it was Adamic and no one else (including myself) who put Mazzei on the map.. Through me, of course, as in the case of my translation of Mazzei''s article. Later, he used the Marraro's translation (1942), notwithstanding the fact that Marraro had limited Mazzei's influence in the American Revolution to his work as agent of Virginia in Europe. And that's how, in all probability, President Kennedy got to know about Mazzei. I may add that for a time I thought that the President may have learned about Mazzei from his assistant, Prof. Arthur Schlesinger, Jr., to whom I sent a copy of my study on Mazzei, which he acknowledged with a note of thanks from Harvard on March 2, 1951 ("most interesting and handsome"). Frankly, I don't think so, and I have not bothered to ask Prof. Schlesinger, as the similarity between the titles of the Kennedy and Adamic books leads me to a different conclusion.

Since Adamic's story of Mazzei in his book, *A Nation of Nations,* which in my opinion he would not have written, had it not been for the similarity between Mazzei's article and the preamble to the Declaration of Independence — which I and no one else made public in 1934 — everybody and his or her uncle has been babbling, as I have said, about Mazzei, but no one has published or written anything in English worth mentioning. Usually, rehash or trash, as I shall presently show.

The only exceptions have been Marraro's translations of documents and notes (still holding to his thesis that Mazzei's role was just that of Virginia's agent in Europe), a scholarly article by Antonio Pace in the *Proceedings of the American Philosophical Society* in 1946 (it seems that the article was enlarged and published as a book, but I have not had the opportunity to check) and Sister Margherita Marchione's translation of the first volume of Mazzei's four-volume *Recherches, Philip Mazzei: Jefferson's "Zealous Whig,"* American Institute of Italian Studies, New York, 1975, 350 pages, 120 illustrations and facsimiles, including the portraits of Lafayette, William Paca, Poniatowski (the King of Poland), John Adams, Patrick Henry, George Washington, and other noted Americans. Some of the facsimiles were not published before. Most of them I did in 1951.

I have already said what there is to be said about Mazzei's *Recherches* in my 1951 study, *Mazzei,* pp. 161-165, and I need not go into further details. Mazzei's book was a complete flop in America (see Garlick's *Mazzei,* p. 163 and *interim*) yet it remains as the first history of the American

Revolution ever written. To Americans it is of little value, although historians may find here and there some nuggets which may confirm or deny some doubtful points in American history, as in the case of the preambles to the Virginia Bill of Rights and to the Declaration of Independence. Of course, one may find other references of value to researchers, but that requires a close study. Certainly, the translation can do no harm and as such it should be welcomed.

Be that as it may, Dr. Marchione's translation seems to be excellent, from what I have been able to gather by checking a couple of items and from other comparisons. Her bibliography about Mazzei is the most complete as of this date, although she missed a few worthwhile works. On the other hand, I fail to see why she included the books by such writers as Rolle, Pisani (not Pisano), Lo Gatto and similar compilers, who are no authorities on Mazzei, by any stretch of the imagination. That, however, is not a sin. What I fail to understand is why titles of Polish books in an English bibliography are followed by an Italian translation. On the other hand, I find her acknowledgment of indebtness to her three chief sources commendable, although in a footnote on page 32.

Some of the claims advanced by some Mazzei "experts" in support of Mazzei's title to immortality, or at least recognition, are bound to belittle his historical importance. For instance, one young lady (I suppose she is young) wrote in a 1967 book that "Jefferson gave an American immortality to Philip Mazzei when he sharpened his Italian friend's phrase 'All men are by nature free and independent' into five words that shaped the attitude of the emerging nation and ring down loud and clear through the ages, 'All men are created equal,'" (p. 44).

I need not bother with Mr. Lagumina's *An Album of the Italian-American,* (according to him Mazzei was a political philosopher), since his book is for children who are used to fairy tales. Or with professors De Conde and Rolle and other colleagues of theirs, as I do refer to them elsewhere in the present volume.

Be that as it may, some kind of prize for the most mephitic piece of garbage about Mazzei (as well as other Italian pioneers) should go to one Doctor Robert C. La Briola who has copied and copied from my books, directly or indirectly, but whether or not he distorted his "facts" deliberately in order to avoid the charge of plagiarism, or through his obvious sloppiness, I am unable to say. But let me quote some of his asininities about Mazzei, as printed in a Denver, Colorado, weekly on January 31, 1976.

Mazzei, so Dr. La Briola tells his readers, was the most prominent of many intellectuals and revolutionaries who left Italy hurriedly for America because of political oppression in Italy, "he brought a large number of his followers, artisans, musicians and farmers to assist him in his projects . . . But the American Revolution came into the scene and Mazzei turned his undivided attention to the 'Cause.' Most of his followers immediately enlisted in the Continental Army. Jefferson and Washington refused to allow Mazzei to enlist — they had other plans for the Italian revolutionary! Mazzei having been elected to the Virginia county committee carried on correspondence with the other 12 colonies" [that would have been a really important contribution, if we had any proof of such correspondence] and similar "fesserie" as an Italian would say. Other Italians would use a vulgar but picturesque term and say "coglionerie."

I am omitting the rest of his asininities in the same and in the previous issues.

American historians of non-Italian extraction have generally either ignored completely or minimized Mazzei's role in the Revolution, usually overstressing Jefferson's letter to Mazzei, without realizing that Mazzei must have exerted some influence on Jefferson if he had chosen him to let off steam. That was seventeen years after Mazzei had left America (he returned for a short while) and the problem that bothered Jefferson was such that he could confide it only to a man who had shared his struggle for independence and for a truly democratic government. American historians, I regret to say, are not usually famous for their insights, or for what Baron Grimm called Mazzei's *coup d'oeil*, or good judgement at a glance.

Aside from that, I fail to understand why American historians ignore Mazzei and extol men like Kosciusko or Pulaski or De Kalb who did no more than Cosimo Medici (see Chapter 10) and other American officers. (Von Steuben is something else.) I have especially in mind such eminent historians as Samuel Morison, Dumas Malone, Julian Boyd, I. Brant, Carl Becker, Edward Dumbauld and their peers. I would not give two cents for a presumptuous and arrogant biographer of Jefferson at the University of Virginia, notwithstanding his thick but pedestrian tome. And, while I am at it, that goes also for Vigo. Most certainly, ignoring men like Mazzei and Vigo, two stars in the American Revolution firmament, does not add to the reputation and good name of American historians.

The few non-Italians who mention Mazzei usually refer to him as a viniculturist, as in the case of a book, *Thomas Jefferson, A Biography In His Own Words* by the editors of Newsweek Books, in which we find a photograph of Mazzei over a caption reading, "A Florentine who had settled near Monticello in 1773 and cultivated vineyards." Such is the cultural profundity of some of America's self-styled purveyors of culture to the American people! Another author, one Phillip Russel, says that Mazzei was a wine grower, and nothing else, in his book, *Jefferson, Champion of the Free Mind*, New York, 1956. Fawn M. Brodie devotes countless pages to Jefferson's sexual prowess in her *Thomas Jefferson — An Intimate Look*, New York, 1974, but recalls only a few petty incidents regarding Mazzei and ignores his influence on Jefferson. To her, Mazzei was only a Florentine grape-grower and friend of princes, who introduced Jefferson to Lavoisier and Condorcet. No one else.

Nathan Schachner's *Thomas Jefferson* is rather an exception, even though the author does not look deeply into the Mazzei phenomenon, for it was a phenomenon, everything considered. In his three-volume biography of Jefferson (1070 pages) he notes "the advent of one Philip Mazzei whose career was intimately connected with Jefferson" and then adds that Mazzei was forced to quit Italy, which is nonsense, as Mazzei returned to Italy time and again. He is more accurate when he says that "Mazzei was a true European liberal, his head filled with the gospel of the Enlightenment and the more radical teachings of the philosophes," just as one finds in the recent books by Italian writers (Burigana, Francovich, Bernari, mentioned by me in the preceding pages). That is a pleasant surprise in an American book. Then he adds, "He [Mazzei] threw himself heart and soul into the turbulent career of his adopted country.

133

He was to influence Jefferson considerably though the reverse influence was more profound." I agree. Bravo! That's a break. Moreover, authors like Schachner restore one's faith in American scholarship and revive one's hope that sooner or later America will do justice to her long-forgotten patriot.　　　　＊　　＊　　＊

A few references on some points I have dealt with in the text:

On the criticism of the Declaration by contemporaries, the best book is still M. C. Tyler's, *The Literary History of the American Revolution*, 2 vols., 1897, reprinted in 1957, chapter XXIII, pp. 494-521.

On Mason, the Virginia Bill of Rights and the preamble of both the Bill of Rights and the Declaration, I. Brant's *James Madison*, Indianapolis, 1941, Vol. I, pp. 190 and 240, seems to be the only book which recognizes that the preamble in both was by Jefferson. I am not sure whether I understand correctly what Dumas Malone means in his book, *Jefferson, the Virginian*, Boston, 1948, when he says that Jefferson could have drawn on George Mason for his own statement.

Mason's most recent and staunchest supporter, R. Carter Pittman,, exaggerates a little when he refers to Mason as "the forgotten architect of our liberty." He says that in his review of John C. Cooper's *Sources of Our Liberty*, New York, 1959, in the *Virginia Magazine of History* for 1960. I am a great admirer of Mason, one of our really eminent men, but he was not the only architect of our liberty, as others, including Mazzei, did their bit.

I have mentioned David Hawke's "succint summary of the natural rights philosophy" in the text, but here I may mention also that Jefferson, according to him, may have been influenced by Cesare Beccaria when he drafted the Virginia Constitution. I am inclined to agree, but largely through Mazzei who read Beccaria's celebrated little book, *Dei Delitti e delle Pene* (on Crimes and Punishments) in London as soon as it came out in 1764. (*Memoirs*, p. 81.) It is true that the English translation of Beccaria's work appeared in 1768, five years before Mazzei came to America, but that does not preclude the possibility that Mazzei and Jefferson may have discussed the problem. On Beccaria see my chapter, "Cesare Beccaria and the Reform of Criminal Jurisprudence in America" in my 1934 book, *The Italians in America Before the Civil War*.

According to Robert D. Meads, *Patrick Henry, Practical Revolutionary*, (1969), "That George Mason wrote the first fourteen of the sixteen articles [of the Bill of Rights] is virtually unquestioned." Of course, that's far from unquestioned. On the contrary, the question of the preamble was settled by Jefferson himself, as noted in the present chapter.

Few writers mention that Jefferson sent Mazzei the first or one of the five rough drafts of the Declaration. Cornell Lengyel, for instance, mentions Lee, Wythe and Patrick Henry in his book, *Four Days in July*, 1958, p. 77, but so far as Mazzei was concerned, he did not exist. But see *The Papers of Thomas Jefferson*, ed. by J. Boyd, Vol. I, p. 159. As noted by Claude Bowers, *The Young Jefferson*, N. Y., 1945, Mazzei gave his copy to the Countess de Tessé, Lafayette's cousin and the wife of the famous marshal.

And that should give some historians food for thought, for two reasons:

First, because of the obvious close relationship between Jefferson and

Mazzei, and especially Jefferson's respect and high regard for Mazzei's opinion, even if none was asked.

Second, because of Mazzei's powerful connections in Parisian social, political and economic circles, just as he had in London and in Italy) because, even today, only men of the highest level are admitted to the highest circles. That, incidentally, also explains why Mazzei was chosen to represent the King of Poland in Paris.

A recent book, *The King's Chevalier: A Biography of Lewis Littlepage*, by Curtis Carroll Davis, Bobbs-Merrill Co., Indianapolis, Ind., 442 pages, 1971, based on unpublished material in the Polish archives, adds more light on Mazzei's work in the service of the King of Poland. Littlepage, a soldier of fortune who also served the same king, and Mazzei had a poor opinion of each other, for reasons which become apparent. The book is rather sympathetic toward Mazzei.

CHAPTER 21 — VIGO

Back in 1927, my friend, Vincent Ferrara, who was then and until his death a few years ago national treasurer of the Italo-American National Union, asked me if I would join a small group of national officers who were going to East Chicago, Indiana, to install the officers of a new lodge of the Union. I accepted gladly and went along. During the ceremony, the president, who was then Judge Barasa, made a speech in which he said to the new members and their families, "Do you know that an Italian gave 50,000 dollars to the State of Indiana?" or something like that. On the way back to Chicago I asked Judge Barasa who that man was, but he had absolutely no information about him or the occasion. At that time, however, I was working on my book, *The Italians in Chicago*, which appeared a year later and, curious as I have always been about such things, I began to look into the matter. Time was short, I had much work to do, and could not do much, as my book was to be turned in, as it was turned in, in April (it was published in July, 1928). Nevertheless, in February I was able to do a little research and finally came out with the name of Francis Vigo, who until then was usually known as a "Spanish" merchant, and, at best, as a Sardinian. To this very day, some people call Vigo a Sardinian, as in the 1952 book, *George Rogers Clark*, by Walter Havighurst, because of their ignorance of the fact that "Sardinian" in the past meant both native of the island of Sardinia and a citizen of the kingdom of Sardinia (incidentally, Prof. Oscar Handlin also called some Genoese immigrants as Sardinians in a book of his). At any rate, the results of my preliminary and hasty research appeared for the first time in a work dealing with Italian pioneers in America, in my book, *The Italians in Chicago* (1928). Only about half a page, mostly taken from Vol. IV of the *Encyclopedia of the History of St. Louis*, 1899.

In May of the same year, as I related in a long article in the weekly newspaper, The Italian News of Boston, for April 1, 1930, my friend Ferrara was going to Indianapolis and I asked him to get in touch with the Italian consular agent in that city, Dr. Lapenta, who, however, did not suspect that Vigo was an Italian. Another year went by, and nobody had done anything about Vigo until, while working on my next book, *The Italians in Missouri*, I took a trip to Vincennes, Indiana, to get more data, if possible. It was on that occasion that I called on the president of the

University of Vincennes (a junior college founded in 1801) who showed me a large portrait of Vigo hanging from a wall. Then and there I decided to have a photograph of that portrait, which until then had not been made, although I had seen a similar portrait in a book. In any event, the president and I carried the portrait to a photographer and had six or eight photographs made. They cost $8.00, which the Italian consulate general paid for, to my regret because it was on account of those photographs that Professor Roselli got into the picture through the consul general, Dr. Castruccio. The first time that portrait appeared in a magazine, to the best of my knowledge, was in *Atlantica* (March, 1930) as a frontispiece, in connection with an article of mine about Vigo, the first in an Italian-American publication. From then on I continued my search, from Terre Haute to Jefferson City, Missouri, all the way to the Library of Congress, with a long account and an extensive bibliography in my book, *The Italians in Missouri,* which was published in September, 1929.

Before the publication of my book, however, I had sufficient material on hand and had written an article which I offered to *Current History,* but it was turned down. Then I gave that material to my late friend, Edward Corsi, who acknowledged it in a letter dated April 27, 1929. Actually, he wrote an article based on my material which appeared in the New York Italian language daily, Il Progresso, shortly after. I should add that on May 22, 1929, I called on Professor J. A. Jameson, the editor of the Clark Papers at Northwestern University, who read my manuscript and encouraged me to go on. Which I did getting, on the way, a serious nervous breakdown when, after I had finished my book on Missouri, I went to Detroit to study the Vigo manuscripts in the Askin Papers in the Burton Historical Collection at the Detroit Public Library. My interest in Vigo continued unabated, following up my March, 1930, article in *Atlantica* with another in the September issue of the same magazine, with a lengthy bibliography. The first article was summarized in the New York Times, on September 14, 1930, Section VIII, page 12. A letter of mine to the New York Times appeared on August 16, 1931, further exploring the subject. Professor Roselli followed my trail with an article of his in the magazine *Gerarchia* of Rome, Italy, October, 1929, more than a year after the publication of my Chicago book and some months after the publication of the Corsi article which, as I have said, was based exclusively on the material which I had offered to *Current History.* I should add that shortly before President Roosevelt dedicated the national memorial to Clark at Vincennes, I wrote him a letter, together with a memorandum about Vigo, which was acknowledged on May 26, 1936, by his assistant secretary, M. H. McIntire. A year before, however, President Roosevelt had written me a personal letter about Catalano, an Italian who helped America during the Tripoli war and whom I discovered.

As for Professor Roselli's claim that he preceded me, notwithstanding my book on Chicago which appeared before he had written one line about Vigo or had even suspected that Vigo existed, and later in my Missouri book, the following facts speak for themselves:

On March 7, 1930, *The Italian News,* a Boston weekly newspaper, published an article on Vigo based on my March, 1930, article in *Atlantica,* without mentioning the source. That article elicited an immediate protest by Prof. Roselli who, incidentally, was not a journalist who visited New

York in the 1920's, as imagined by Prof. Rolle in his book, *The Immigrant Upraised*, 1968, pp. 83 and 122, and in his later book, *The American Italians*, 1973, p. 7. Prof. Roselli was a distinguished educator, the head of the Italian department at Vassar for many years, and a good orator with a full command of both English and Italian. I first saw him in 1917 when, wearing the uniform of an Italian officer, he lectured on Italy's war effort at Baltimore City College which I was then attending. So much for the infinite knowledge of Italian-American experts on the Italians in America.

In his protest, Professor Roselli first admonished the editor of the Italian News in a friendly way, claiming that his story had been plagiarized, with the result that the News published an article on March 21, 1930, with a front page headline reading, "Prof. Roselli Charges His Story Plagiarized." Of course, as soon as I learned about Roselli's claim I hastened to send the *Italian News* my own account of what had really happened, whereupon the editor asked Professor Roselli for his comment. Here let me quote the introduction to my letter, as it appeared in the *Italian News* on the front page on April 4, 1930, with a prominent headline reading NEW YORK WRITER CLAIMS / HE, NOT PROF. ROSELLI / IS AUTHOR OF VIGO STORY: "Mr. Schiavo's letter was preceded by one from Mr. Lamonica of 'Atlantica,' a New York monthly publication, in which he took us to task for crediting Prof. Roselli instead of Mr. Schiavo as the real author of the Vigo article. We thereupon communicated with Prof. Roselli, informed him of the situation and requested a reply. That was nearly two weeks ago. As yet we have not heard from the professor . . . To repeat, the Vigo article was one of the most interesting and most important that ever appeared in these columns. Prof. Roselli had us believe that he originated it, but now, owing to his reticence and the proofs before us, we pass the laurels to Mr. Schiavo." My letter, full of details, took up almost four columns.

In his book on Vigo (see below), Prof. Roselli claims that he began to write and lecture about Vigo in 1927 (p. 3), but the professor's memory did not serve him right, to be charitable about it, because in his own "Rassegna Cronologica" which he sent to my good friend, Vincent Giuliano, who published it in his own weekly newspaper, *La Tribuna Italiana D'America* (Detroit) on July 3, 1936, he begins his chronology with "1929 — Prima monografia su Vigo — *Un Italiano Donatore di Regni All'America*, di Bruno Roselli, Tipografia del Popolo D'Italia. That, incidentally, was not a monograph but a seven page article with hardly any more information than I had in my 1928 book. The article had originally appeared in the Fascist magazine, *Gerarchia* of Rome, Italy, for October, 1929, or a month after I had gone to press with my book, *The Italians in Missouri*, and several months after I had gone to Indianapolis, where I had the assistance of Miss Dorothy Riker, of the Indiana Historical Bureau, and of Mr. Coleman, who became secretary of the Rogers Clark Memorial at Vincennes authorized by President Coolidge in 1927, as stated on page 34 of my book on Missouri.

After that, Professor Roselli wrote a "biography," *Vigo: A Forgotten Builder of the American Republic*, Boston, 1933, 280 pages — more fiction than hard facts. He himself explained that much on page 35, in which he wrote "the gap will have to be filled by using logic in lieu of direct evidence." Of course, Professor Roselli taught languages.

137

As for other writings on Vigo, I might mention a full page advertisement in *Life* for October 14, 1940, by the John Hancock Insurance Co., and a drawing by Frederick Polley in the Indianapolis Star of November 10, 1929, showing Vigo's tombstone and grave. I should add that the Indianapolis Italian consul and his Italians did nothing except trying to get some publicity for themselves, whereas a non-Italian, Mr. Frank Culbertson, purchased with his own money Vigo's Old Farm House and donated it to the Rogers Clark Memorial Commission. I, myself, tried to raise some money for the purchase of some 2,000 letters by, to, or about Vigo, then available (they may still be), but no Italian would advance a red cent.

The New York Times for Sunday, January 21, 1973, had a long article on Clark, with a large photograph of Vigo's statue, by Raymond and Marion Carmel, entitled "The Old Frontier Often Seems Near / On the Banks of the Wabash, Far Away." Mr. Carmel, we are told, is an amateur historian, his wife is a reporter. That's why one may overlook their reference to Vigo as "an Italian from Sardinia," while appreciating their sympathetic story about Vigo. One thing I failed to notice which is brought to the attention of the reader by the two authors is a small pile of empty bags on which Vigo rests his right arm, that is, on the monument. Those bags, according to some people, are supposed to be "a stack of empty money bags." How true, indeed, and how symbolic of Vigo's generosity to his adopted country! As good Hoosiers, they do not fail to recall that "Clark's capture of Vincennes guaranteed that the western American border after the Revolutionary War, would be the Mississippi instead of the Allegheny Mountains," which is absolutely true.

As a whole, however, both Clark and Vigo are ignored in most American history books, as by Professor Samuel Morison in his *Oxford History of the American People* (1965) in which he calls Clark's heroic expedition "a patriotic version of Governor Dunmore's War," but, basically, a land grab. Professor Wilson, on the other hand, feels that all the sweat and blood before and after Vincennes were for the fur trade, which in part was also true, although it is hard to see why the fur trade would have been more profitable to the traders under American rule than under French or Spanish, or English rule. Vigo acquired his wealth before Clark's arrival. After that, he lost everything and died in poverty.

What is not generally known is the fact that Clark's expedition to the Illinois Territory had the secret support of both Patrick Henry, who was then Governor of Virginia, and of Thomas Jefferson, both of whom were already dreaming of America's expansion westward. Professor Morison himself admits that as the result of Clark's victory at Vincennes, "Thus Virginia implemented her old charter claims to the whole Northwest" (op. cit., American Library edition, Vol. I, p. 364), but isn't that the same thing that has been said and is being said by those persons who maintain that it was because of Clark's victory that the Old Northwest became a part of the United States rather than of Canada?

Appendix A
A BIBLIOGRAPHICAL ESSAY

During the last few years, in small part because of the approaching Bicentennial, there has been a kind of stampede to publish a book, or at least an article, on the Italians in America. Unfortunately, there has not been one single writer, to this very day, who seems to be aware of the magnitude of the task, with the result that all that has been published so far, with the exception of a few articles or translations, is based on material in the English language which has been rehashed time and again. In other words, no original research to amount to anything, so that when one has read one book, one has read them all. With the usual exceptions of insignificant details.

Years ago, to be exact after my Mafia book in 1962, I decided to write a history of Italian immigration, but the more I delved into it, the more I realized that the problem was too vast, notwithstanding my long experience and study as shown by my books, and that a history could not be written without a study of literally hundreds of articles and books in the Italian language, most of which could be found only in Italy.

Of course, there were many articles and books in the English language dealing with the Italians in America, but with a few exceptions, such as the articles by Gino Speranza and by the Rev. Mangano, they are nothing more than observations of friends or detractors of the immigrant. What is needed is the story of the immigrants as seen also by Italian observers familiar with the history of Italy, its geography, its customs and traditions, and, above all, with the mental habits of the immigrants. As, for instance, such books and articles as those by Amy Bernardy, Adolfo Rossi, and, over and above everybody else, of Amerigo Ruggiero, whose book, *Italiani in America*, is very rarely listed in one of the many pretentious bibliographies by Italian-Americans. Not to mention the indispensable consular reports from 1863 to 1928 (they are no longer published, as imagined by Professor Iorizzo) and the book by Mayor des Planches.

Even that, however, is not enough, for no student of the Italians in America can afford to ignore the Italian-language press which is still well represented in American libraries, as well as in Italy, as in the *Eco d'Italia* (1850 to the 1890's), *La Follia* (still being published), *Il Carroccio, Atlantica, La Parola del Popolo, Il Grido della Stirpe* (fascist weekly), *Giovinezza* (later *Impero*), *Controcorrente* (anarchic), not to mention the many weeklies, such as *La Gazzetta del*

Massachusetts, La Tribuna Transatlantica of Chicago (utilized to a small extent by two students), *La Tribuna* of Detroit (still going). Of course, there are the daily newspapers, in New York, Boston, Cleveland, Chicago and, above all, San Francisco, which tell the real story of the Italians in the United States. Since those publications have been searched only in very rare instances (I have read practically every issue of *L'Eco d'Italia* up to the 1880's), the writers of books and articles on the Italians in America which have appeared during the last few years have simply repeated the same stories, the same fallacies, the same fables, the same clichés written before them, with a very, very, rare original thought or observation.

Take, for instance, the question of fascist activities in America. I lived through that period. I knew everybody who was anybody, on both sides of the fence, directly or indirectly, and I do know what really happened, at first hand. (Incidentally, I wrote the first article on fascism for any encyclopedia I can think of, for the *Americana, Annual* 1922, which appeared about four months after Mussolini's rise to power. My article was signed.) That's why I must brush aside as unilateral the accounts by such experts as De Conde and Nelli who have ignored the fascist publications as well as the anti-fascist periodicals, with rare instances.

To give an instance of Professor De Conde's alleged familiarity with fascist activities in the United States, according to him (*Half Bitter-Half Sweet*, 1971) it was Count Di Revel, a friend of mine from way back, who disbanded the Fascist League, whereas it was Ambassador De Martino. As the ambassador told me in Washington, "La Lega Fascista l'ho sfasciata io" (I, and nobody else, broke up the Fascist League). I remember the words well, because of his use of "sfasciare" as compared to "fascio." Italian-American professors are afraid, so it seems, to use fascist sources. And that is not history.

Be that as it may, some knowledge of the language and a glance at a work is not sufficient, for one must read a book or article carefully, so as to do justice to the author. For instance, Professor De Conde cites the translation of Count Vidua's letters to his father by Elizabeth Cometti and Valeria Gennaro-Lerda in *The Virginia Magazine of History and Biography* (October, 1969 — the translation seems to be first-class and so are the footnotes) but notes only Vidua's unfavorable references to some aspects of American life. He fails to note, however, the count's discerning remarks about the Declaration of Independence and his opinion of Jefferson, Madison, and John Quincy Adams who invited him to dinner (at the White House by Adams). Besides, Vidua did not simply meet them, as stated by De Conde, but on this point see Chapter 21 in this volume.

To give another instance of inadequate bibliographical reference, according to Prof. De Conde (*op. cit.* p. 409), "Amy A. Bernardy wrote two books describing the torment, as well as some of the satisfactions, of Italian immigrant life, which criticizes American life in general [she also admires America]. See *America Vissuta*, 1911, and *America Randagia*, 1913." Bernardy wrote more than two books besides some very important articles which I have either in the original form or in photoduplication. *America Randagia* does deal with the Italians in America, but *America Vissuta* devotes only 24 pages out of 501 to Italian immigrants. I obtained a copy only a few months ago, as of this writing, in July, 1975, in a second-hand bookstore in an alley off Piazza De Ferrari in Genova. The first book, in any event, should be listed under "Italian travelers in America" and not under books on Italian immigrant life.

To mention another instance, also from De Conde's book, page 410, according to the California professor, Howerth's article "Are the Italians a Dangerous Class?" (*Charities*, 1894) was one of those articles which defended the Italians and refuted their criminal activities. Howerth did defend the Italians, but his article has nothing to do with crime (as I myself was inclined to believe when working on my book on the Mafia — whereupon I read it carefully), except for a few lines, as it deals mainly with Italian life in Chicago, that is, living conditions, etc. To give one more instance, on page 419 Professor De Conde says that Branchi's *Il primoto* (sic) discusses anti-Italian bigotry and, accordingly, he lists it under books dealing with immigration restriction. Branchi gave me a copy of his booklet in the 1920's, but Marcantonio borrowed it from me, together with my precious little volume on Spinola, then he had a heart attack on a New York street, and I never got my books back. Therefore, I can't check to what extent Branchi referred to anti-Italian bigotry, a subject that is ever-present in any Italian book on Italian immigrants in America. My recollection, however, is that the booklet dealt with Italian achievements in the world and to a very small extent in America (nothing that was not generally known in the latter case). Therefore, the listing under restriction is misleading, except for the brief reference. At this point I should add that the listings under Branchi, C. (690) and Branchi, E. (1051) in Cordasco's bibliography, refer to the same author, Camillo Branchi, sometimes also known as Eugenio Camillo, as correctly listed in Velikonja's bibliography. As for Branchi's subtitle, "Breviario degli Italiani in America," the word "breviario" in Italian means both "breviary" and "Guide" or "outline." In other words, Branchi's book has nothing to do with religion, except for the mention of some Italian missionaries.

Let me mention another example from De Conde's book. I prefer to single out that book, first because it has been overpraised by some people who are not familiar with the history of Italian immigration, and, secondly, because the professor is too cocksure of himself, struts while sitting down (as someone said of the late Thomas E. Dewey), pontificates, ladles out opinions right and left by just looking at some title or leafing through a book or article. After all, if he or his assistants had to read every article or book listed in his impressive bibliography, it would have taken them a lifetime. But when a man does not have the time to do a job, he should limit his research to just one particular field, or section of a field (see the outline at the end of this essay), as I have done with my forthcoming *History of the Mafia*.

Be that as it may, on page 402 De Conde says that Moreno's pamphlet, "History of a Great Wrong," 1905, is "a pamphlet attack on the *padrone* traffic in children." I read that pamphlet in the Boston Public Library some years ago and I still remember that on the same day I was telling my late friend, Giacomo Grillo, about it. Recently I tried to get a photostatic copy of that pamphlet but the librarian wrote me that it could not be found. Anyway, that little book is not just an attack on the *padrone* traffic in children, which had disappeared following the legislation enacted twenty years before the publication of the pamphlet, as it is an attack against the Italian minister in Washington, Baron Fava, "A Hebrew like his wife" (used by Moreno in a derogatory sense), who had sued Moreno for libel and had him sentenced to three months in jail. Hence Moreno's defense of himself and his claim that it was he who had first attacked the traffic in children, which is not true because, to the best of my recollection, it was Secchi de Casali, the editor and publisher of the weekly newspaper, *Eco d'Italia*. It would seem, however, that Moreno may have been justified in claiming that it was the who first used the term *padrone* which later was applied to labor agents. It is only because of this claim, as well as for Moreno's history of the exploitation of children in the 1860's and 1870's, that the pamphlet is of interest.

I could mention numerous cases of similar nature, that is, that a title is often misleading and in some cases absolutely meaningless, not only in De Conde's book, but also in other books, such as Andrew Rolle's *The American Italians*, 1972, which confirm the assumption that the author, or whoever compiled the bibliography, did not read the book or took a good look at the contents, if he or she ever saw it at all. Far more deplorable is the fact that often the author, or his assistant, does not check elementary facts. For instance, according to Professor De Conde (p. 388), I am "an immigrant journalist from Sicily," which is simply laughable and irresponsible, because I came to America in January 1916 at the age of 17, and I began as a cub reporter with the

Baltimore Evening Sun in the summer of 1918. Then I was allowed to join the Army, as a volunteer, et cetera, et cetera. The professor could have checked those facts without any trouble in one of the 21 volumes of my own *Italian-American Who's Who* and in other biographical dictionaries. Or in the case of Adolfo Rossi (p. 84) who, according to De Conde, was "an immigrant journalist [who] tried to find a job on an Italian newspaper . . . in the middle eighties" — a proof that the professor did not bother to read Rossi's book, one of the fundamental books for the study of Italian immigration in the United States. The fact is, as told by Rossi himself, that he had been a postal clerk before he came to America in 1879 at the age of 20. As for his journalistic career, he had had a story published in a magazine, but knew nothing about journalism. Then Carlo Barsotti founded *Il Progresso* (New York Italian daily, still being published as of this writing) but there were no Italians who knew anything about making an Italian newspaper, with the exception of Secchi De Casali and possibly some amateurs and Rossi was called to do his best by reprinting some stale articles from old Italian newspapers which had been collected — four pages in all, of which two of advertisements. Rossi was with *Il Progresso* from December 1880 to July 1881, when he left for Colorado with a crew of laborers. He returned to Italy in 1884, or *before* the middle 1880's.

Far more reckless are some of the hasty opinions of the California professor or of his assistant researchers. According to him, or them (p. 391), my study on Mazzei (1951) was or is "the reprint of a chapter from a larger work." That is not correct. When I published my study I had planned to include it in my *Four Centuries,* but when I got to it, the book turned out to be larger than I had anticipated and I was compelled to cut down my chapter on Mazzei from 54 pages to just seven. It is true that my 1951 study said that it was "a chapter from *Four Centuries,*" but only a hasty and superficial "researcher" could have missed the difference.

On pages 388-389, De Conde lists five volumes of mine, I am not interested in his opinions because it is obvious that he just glanced at my books, if he did happen to see them at all (on this point, see the opinions of leading authorities, in Appendix C of the present volume). For instance, he lists my two volumes of *Italian-American History* and my volume on the *Italians in Chicago* under general works, and that's misleading, for the first volume of *Italian-American History* deals with musicians and the second with missionaries and other priests. The Chicago book should have been listed under local works. He forgot, most likely he had never heard of , my book on *The Italians in Missouri.* His bibliography on the Italians in Music is simply ridiculous. Only a short history of opera (1965), a history of the Metropolitan (1969), a book on opera in Chicago (1966) and Dorothy Caruso's book about her celebrated husband. Even a high school girl could have done better (again, see Appendix C). As for the Italian missionaries, they are nonchalantly dismissed with just a few lines (p. 16) and with only two books and three articles in the bibliography, compared to 405 pages of text, 36 pages of notes and 22 pages of bibliography in my *Italian-American History*, Vol. II.

Let us examine now another type of bibliography compiled in the summer of 1975 by a young Italian-American, Professor Luciano Iorizzo, for the Balch Institute of Philadelphia.

I would have ignored Prof. Iorizzo's bibliography as it is of little account, were it not for the fact that the Balch Institute, a highly reputable organization, is distributing it, together with bibliographies for other ethnic groups, to high schools and colleges.

The Iorizzo-Balch bibliography, however, is not the only bibliography compiled by Professor Iorizzo, for one will find a much longer one (83 books and 105 magazine articles) at the end of a volume *The Italian-Americans* he wrote in 1971 together with Professor Salvatore Mondello. Obviously, the task was too big for only one of them. As for the Balch bibliography, I have seen two, both published in the Philadelphia *Sons of Italy Times* on August 18 and September 22, 1975. We may dismiss, however, the first one, only 12 titles, all of which but one are included in the latest list.

A glance at the Iorizzo-Mondello bibliography, which is necessary to get an idea of the familiarity of the two authors with the subject, reveals at once to the experienced eye that they have very much to learn about Italian history, geography, customs, traditions and, above all, the Italian language.

For instance, at the very beginning of their bibliography, on page 53, the entry "Bacci, Massimo Livi, *L'Emigrazione* is wrong, for in Italy whenever there are two surnames, with or without an hyphen, the first surname is the family name and the second surname is the name of the mother. Thus, in this case, the surname is Livi, the name of the mother is Bacci and the first name (or Christian name if the Livis were not Jewish) is Massimo. The same thing may be said of "De Calboli, R. Paolucci," in which case the correct name is Paolucci and not Calboli. By the same token, Denis Mack Smith's surname is Mack and not Smith (p. 256).

To mention another instance of Prof. Iorizzo's lack of familiarity with things Italian, he says in his bibliography for the Balch Institute that the reports of the *Bollettino Dell'Emigrazione* (according to him they are still being published whereas they stopped in 1928, as I have already noted) were written by "consular agents." That's amazing, for a professor of history should know a few things about diplomacy and international law. In any event, a consular agent is not a career man, but a local man, usually a professional or business man (often a grocer) who represents the vice-consul, or the consul general, in a small town. That does not mean that the reports of a consular agent could not be at times even better than those of a consul,for the consular agent knows exactly what is going on. I remember for instance the excellent reports by the consular agents at Scranton (my late good friend Tiscar), Albany, Buffalo, St. Paul, Minnesota and other communities. Should one quibble about the term agent, one will find the definition of "consular agent" in *Webster's Third New International*.

Another glance at the Iorizzo-Mondello bibliography reveals two books by Brenna (the second is only a revised and updated edition of the first) and five books in the Italian language which are not as important as others which are omitted, with the single exception of the Ruggiero book.

The list of the writings in the English language includes a few good books, but many which are even more important are not included. For instance, it is ridiculous to include a book, *The Godfather*, plus an article, by Mario Puzo who is an unqualified and patent jackass, so far as anything about Italy and the Italians is concerned (he himself admitted to a *New York Times* reporter that had he known anything about the Mafia he would not have been able to write his novel).

What I find absolutely out of proportion is the inclusion of two books about La Guardia (not the most significant ones at that, because *The Making of an Insurgent* by the Little Flower and Cuneo's fine sketch of his former boss tell more than a dozen books put together. I knew La Guardia for many years and I have a few letters from him). And why two books about Marcantonio and not a single book about some of the more prominent governors and mayors or judges of Italian descent? I do realize that all those books do not belong in a short bibliography, but neither do the La Guardia and Marcantonio books, even if they are mentioned in the text. They even refer to obscure authors without indicating who they are or were, as in the case of one Thomas (p. 252, note 17).

To go one step further, the two authors include several recent books on art in America, which can be found without any difficulty in any small library, but not one single book on music, especially opera, although they include my Volume I of *Italian-American History*, but without indicating that it deals with Italian music and musicians. Probably, they expected the Holy Ghost to tell their readers all about it. Iorizzo refers to two books of mine in the Balch bibliography, but he must have been in a great rush, for he got the facts mixed up.

According to him, my book on the musicians is my *Italians in America Before The Civil War*, whereas that book has only one brief chapter about musicians.

Furthermore, I fail to see why an author who includes Brace (again, he has the facts mixed up, just as Foerster did) does not include the two rather famous books by Jacob Riis, or Ernst's book, for that matter. And what has Gramsci got to do with Italian emigration or immigration? Why not include also Karl Marx or Turati or Malatesta or Borghi? He includes Nitti's book on emigration, but omits his more important *Nord e Sud* and *La Ricchezza d'Italia*. Why include a book about Frank Sinatra and nothing at all about Valentino or Caruso or Adelina Patti? And why not list my *Four Centuries* which is the most important work on the Italians in the United States ever written, whether some envious upstarts like it or not? As I think I have said before, writing about the Italians in America without a reference to my *Four Centuries* is like writing about the Catholic Church without mentioning the Pope. Again, if that is immodest of me, so be it.

As for his criticism of my books, which he calls filio-pietistic (the usual garbage by upstarts in search of fame who cannot pinpoint a charge), I fail to see why he should have found it necessary to cite some of them 15 times in his book, including the bibliography, on pages 224, 225, 226, 227 and 255.

Of course, it is very easy to criticize — "dees is a free condry," as Italian immigrants used to say, and so it is. So, what would I have done if the Balch Institute had asked me to compile a bibliography on the Italian-Americans?

In the first place, I would have told the Balch people that a division into secondary, undergraduate and graduate is out of the question, so far as the Italians are concerned, because the few books that are available could be divided into two groups: one for specialists, and the other for the average reader. The specialists need only an extensive bibliography like that compiled by Cordasco, or the works listed in such books as Foerster's *The Italian Emigration of Our Times*, or Grazia Dorè's *La Democrazia italiana e l'emigrazione in America* (1964) which is included in Cordasco's compilation, or the more succinct and therefore more valuable bibliography in his *Studies in Italian American Social History*, 1975, pp. 234-251 or the bibliographies in my works.

For the average reader, I would have included just about a dozen books or so, at the most, with my *Four Centuries* heading the list, so far as the pioneers are concerned. Then I would have included a book or two on backgrounds, like *South Italian Folkways* by Phyllis H. Williams (it must be handled with great care, because the reader may be inclined to believe that local customs are all alike throughout southern Italy, whereas such is not the case), Silone's *Bread and Wine*, Levi's *Christ Stopped at Eboli*, Francesco Perri's *Enough of Dreams*, New York, 1929 (a translation of *Emigranti*, Milano, 1928), Luigi Villari's *Italian Life in Town and Country*, Roselli's chapter in Henry Pratt Fairchild's *Immigrant Backgrounds*, Park and Miller's *Old World Traits Transplanted* and a couple more of the same type.

Then I would have included Musmanno's *The Story of The Italians in America* (1965) as a general introduction. Before we go any further let me clear up a point, as Musmanno, who was a good friend of mine, is no longer with us — his death was a real loss for the Italians in America — and therefore he cannot answer his critics. I have especially in mind Professor De Conde who called Musmanno's book "filio-pietistic, naive and inadequate for any real understanding of the subject." That's rubbish. Musmanno, a man hardened to the prejudices of his time, a man who grew up in the prejudiced environment of the coal mining district of Western Pennsylvania, a member of the Pennsylvania Legislature for years, a Judge of the Supreme Court of Pennsylvania (the highest court in the State, not to be confused with the Supreme Court of New York State, which corresponds to the Court of Common Pleas in Pennsylvania, or to the Superior Court of Massachusetts), one of the judges at the Nuremberg trials, the author of three or four pocket books on labor conditions in his state, a much-traveled man, how can anyone call such a man naive? Please!

If there is a person who has failed to understand the problems of the Italian immigrant and of the Italian-Americans it is Professor De Conde who has misjudged the book and has failed to understand why Musmanno wrote it. Musmanno did not try to write a sociological treatise or even a history of the Italians in America, regardless of the book's title. He simply tried to give a panoramic view of Italian achievements in Italy and in America, so as to lift the morale of his people who have been suffering from a colossal inferiority complex for generations (a natural trait, unfortunately, which the *New York Times* foreign correspondent, C. L. Sulzberger, noted even among Italian politicians in Rome and other Italian cities). He tried to show that the Italians have never been behind any other ethnic group and for that matter that without Italy the Western World would not be what it is today. I do sincerely hope that someday some Italian-American candidate for a Ph.D. will look into Musmanno's life as a subject for serious investigation.

After Musmanno, I would include some books that reveal the tribulations of the immigrants, such as Panunzio's *Immigrant Cross-*

roads, Angelo Patri's *A school master in the great city*, Covello's *The Heart is the Teacher*, Mangione's *Mount Allegro* (Professor Mangione should stick to narrative and leave Italian immigration problems alone), Nat J. Ferber's *A New American, The Life Story of Salvatore A. Cotillo*, Charles Margiotti's autobiography, *A Tiger at the Bar*, *Christ in Concrete* by Pietro Di Donato, *Sons of Italy* by Pasquale D'Angelo, and other books by Italian-Americans, good or bad —some of them are really good and could have become best sellers if Italian-Americans had more respect for education and for educated people instead of aping ward politicians, crooners and prize fighters. And gangsters, so long as they make money and are not caught. And that's the truth.

Of course, there are many articles like those included in the anthologies by Cordasco and Bucchioni, *The Italians*, 1974, and Lydio F. Tomasi's *The Italian in America*, 1972.

I would decidedly leave out the books listed in Professor Iorizzo's bibliography for the Balch Institute, for, as I have said elsewhere, when you have read one, you have read them all. If you want one, keep *The Children of Columbus* by Erik Antitheatrof, an honest man who does not claim that the facts shown in his book are the fruit of his research. But watch out, because as a *Time* magazine reporter, he is bound to bear the influence of his magazine and include quite a few "facts" which are only tall tales. As a whole, however, the book is acceptable.

Of course, all those books and a few more which did not come to mind while writing, like Rev. Mangano's *Sons of Italy* or Pellegrini's *American by Choice* will never tell the full story. For that, one must rely on books in Italian, beginning with Amerigo Ruggiero's *Italiani in America*, at the very top of the list, or Dr. Martellone's *Una Little Italy Nell'Atene d'America*, the best, absolutely the best, study of an Italian-American community ever written, which should be followed as a pattern for studies of other communities by young Italian-Americans, or the books by Prezzolini (again, his books must be handled "con le molle") or Papa and Fontana, Adolfo Rossi, Amy Bernardy, Preziosi, and many many more. Needless to say, no book about the Italians in America can ever be written without a close study of the reports of Italian consuls in America, or without the consultation of *Eco d'Italia* and of a few of Italy's magazines, as well, of course, Italian-language publications in the United States. *Repetita juvant.*

As for the present generation on, I would not give a cent and a half, at 1976 purchasing power, for all the learned dissertations of ambitious youngsters of Italian descent, with or without a Ph.D., who must learn that a reputation as a scholar cannot be built overnight and that even in a country in which charlatans and buffoons often get away with murder, sooner or later the quacks will be exposed. Furthermore, I doubt whether one can draw any valid conclusions about psychological and moral and economic conditions among the Italians in America, or among any other so-called ethnic group, without extensive and highly expensive surveys. Among the Italians, such surveys are not even pipe dreams.

In conclusion, impressive bibliographies like that of De Conde, or shorter ones, like that of Iorizzo, are meaningless, confusing and misleading, except for the specialist who may be able to pick a title or two.

As I see it, a bibliography of the usual type, that is, just the name of the author, the title, number of pages and year of publication (in the case of articles, the name of the periodical, with year and month of publication) should be limited to narrow subjects, such as biographies, one particular event, or a particular topic, such as "the padrone system," the "bankers," the "saloon in Little Italy," "causes of emigration," and so on.

When a charge is made, it should be substantiated. If it would take too much space, then the best thing would be to say nothing, or add an appendix about those errors, fallacies, or what not.

When dealing with broad subjects, that is, when a book deals with more than one subject, the table of contents might be reprinted, unless, of course, the bibliographer analyzes the errors and fallacies.

When a book is hard to locate, a symbol should be added, so as to indicate in which large library it can befound, such as LC,N.Y.P.L., Harv., Berk., and so on.

When the bibliographer has not been able to locate it after a diligent search, a symbol, likewise, should be indicated.

Notwithstanding all this, however, I believe that a general adjective or noun, like naive or jackass, may be allowed, provided the author or bibliographer shows in the text or in footnotes that his or her derogatory term is justified by the evidence shown. But to say that a book is "filiopietistic" or "unreliable" or "lopsided" is not justified, unless one shows why. For instance, if I say that De Conde's book, *Half Bitter-Half Sweet* is lopsided, I must add that three fourths of the book are devoted to the diplomatic relations between Italy and the United States, which have been of practically no significance, with no ripple, except in 1891 and 1941, whereas only one fourth of the book deals with Italian immigration, which is a subject of epic proportion.

BIBLIOGRAPHICAL OUTLINE FOR A STUDY OF THE ITALIANS IN AMERICA

(From my own files on immigration, exclusive of files by city, state, profession, business or trade; also biographical files)

STATISTICS: Emigration (Italy) — Immigration (U.S.) destination — occupations — urban, rural, age, sex.

BACKGROUNDS: Italy — North and South — National characteristics — Economic and social conditions — Folkways.

AMERICAN EXPERIENCE: Accidents — Agriculture — Anarchists — Armed Forces — Assimilation — "Bankers" — Benefits and losses, to Italy and U.S. — Biographies and autobiographies — Boarders — Casa Italiana — Causes of emigration — Chambers of Commerce (It. in U.S.) — Charity — Children at work — Clandestines — Clothing workers — Columbus Day — Community activities — Consuls (It. in U.S.) — Cooperatives — Cost of emigrant to Italy — Crime (immigrant) — Cultural and civic activities — Customs and traditions (changes) — Dago — Decorations — Discrimination and prejudice — Drinking habits — Education — Ellis Island and Castle Garden — Exploitation of Immigrants — Fallacies (of immigration) — Fascism (in U.S.) — Festivals — Family — Fishing — Folklore — Fraternal organizations — Gangsters (admiration for) — Get-rich-quick schemes — Health and disease — Historical societies — Hospitals — Housing — Inferiority complex — Italian-American language — Italy and the immigrant — Justice and the immigrant — Labor and trade unions — Labor camps — Laborers — Lawyers — Little Italy — Living conditions — "Lotto" — Loyalty to America — Loyalty to Italy — Lynchings — Mentral illness — Mining — Monuments (It. in U.S.) — Names (changed) — Naturalization — Occupations — Opera — Organ grinders — Padrone system — Peddlers — Peonage — Philanthropy — Physicians — Politics — Press (immigrant) — Puppets and "pupi" — Radicals and liberals — Rag pickers — Recreation — Religion (Cath.) — Religion (Prot.) — Remittances to Italy — Saloons — Socialists — Societies (See Frat. Org.) — Sports — Street musicians — Teachers to immigrants — Theater (It. in U.S.) — Wages — Welfare — Woman (It. in U.S.).

Appendix B

THE ANTI-DEFAMATION LEAGUE OF B'NAI B'RITH AND THE ITALIANS IN AMERICA

Late in May, 1975, I received a telephone call from a friend in New York (I was then living in El Paso) who told me that the Anti-Defamation League of B'nai B'rith in cooperation with the Columbian Coalition of New York had shown a film on the Italians in New York with illustrations and facts which seemed to have been lifted from my books, especially my large volume, *Four Centuries of Italian-American History* (1952). Having been away from New York since the end of 1958, I had never heard of the Columbian Coalition. To this date, I don't know who its officers are, except for its executive director, Mr. Frank Bianco. A few days later, however, I learned that the film was a filmstrip, that is, a number of views or illustrations, accompanied by music and narration. I learned that much from a story in the Boston Post-Gazette for May 30, 1975, and from another New York friend. Four weeks later, while in New York on my way to Europe, I contacted the Coalition, that is, Mr. Bianco, who was kind enough to give me a copy of the script. The front page of the script reads as folllows:

FILMSTRIP DISCUSSION GUIDE
ITALIANS IN AMERICA
Prepared by Lawrence Castiglione
Dept. of Education, Queens College
Part I: The Untold Story   Part II: Children of Columbus
Written by Millard Lampell — Narrated by Frank Langella
Advisor
Prof. Richard Gambino
Queens College, New York City
Produced by
The Anti-Defamation League of B'nai B'rith
315 Lexington Avenue
New York, New York 10016
In cooperation with
The Columbian Coalition
1185 Sixth Avenue
New York, New York 10036

151

The *Filmstrip Discussion Guide* consists of 25 typewritten pages, or script, matching word for word the recorded narration on tape, a cassette, both film and tape for sale at $40.00 a set, as advertised in at least one newspaper. I purchased a set. To avoid any confusion, the script or narration, as well as the filmstrip, is divided in two parts, as noted on the front page of the Guide. I was interested only in the first part, in the so-called *Untold Story*, which is, as I shall demonstrate in the following chapter, a stupid lie, as there is nothing in that first part that I had not told some forty years before. I was not interested in the second part, as it deals with immigration questions, even though it contains a few facts also lifted from my book, but nothing of any importance. As in the case of Charles Bonaparte who, as Attorney General of the United States under Theodore Roosevelt, ordered the creation of the Federal Bureau of Investigation, a fact that was seized by Mr. John La Corte of Brooklyn and publicized with the cooperation of the late director of the F.B.I., Mr. J. Edgar Hoover. (See my book, *Italian-American History*, Vol. I, p. 494.) However, as I say on page 299 of my later book, *Four Centuries of Italian-American History*, Bonaparte "cannot be considered an Italian-American, as in the case of American-born children of Italian immigrants."

The *Filmstrip Discussion Guide* has on pages 21-23 a "Suggested Bibliography" or list of books, which are mostly connected with immigration problems, except for a few which are also listed in another bibliography of 15 titles given to me by Mr. Bianco. On September 17, 1975, however, a similar list, with five books checked in pencil, was mailed to me by Mr. Samuel H. Elfert, Director, Audio-Visual Department of the Anti-Defamation League. As stated in Mr. Elfert's letter, the list of 15 titles is the list which Mr. Gambino, the advisor "provided to our writer at the early stages of script preparation," a most extraordinary statement, indeed, because the script or *Discussion Guide* does not contain, at least in Part I, a single fact that cannot be found in any of the books listed in the bibliographies (actually three, but one includes titles included in the other two, with the exception of a book, *WOP*, by La Gumina, as noted below). For that matter, the script or *Guide* contains facts which cannot be found in any of the books listed in the three bibliographies, but can surely be found in my *Four Centuries*, as listed, one by one, in the following pages.

Here let me quote a few pertinent lines from Mr. Elfert's letter. After expressing his regret that he missed me when I was in New York, as he was on assignment overseas, and telling me that he was informed about my meeting with Mr. Bianco, Mr. Elfert wrote me: "As Mr. Bianco has already indicated, the research for this production was rather extensive and many, many sources were used by the writer.

As with other productions we have done here on Puerto Ricans, Mexican-Americans, Jews and Blacks, we have gone to the source of many scholarly works for historic information."

That's an asinine statement, especially since he uses the words, "historic information." First of all, because Mr. Elfert has not the faintest idea of what the sources for the history of the Italians in America are, since the sources, except for half a dozen famous men, are scattered in literally hundreds of books and articles which not even an expert, that is to say, a trained historian of long standing, could devour in a few years. To give an idea, my 1934 book, *The Italians In America Before The Civil War*, begins with two small pages of names, just names, of persons to whom I acknowledged my indebtness and expressed my gratitude for their courtesy in supplying me with the information I needed, and ends with a bibliography of 47 pages in small type. My Volume One of *Italian-American History* has a bibliography of six pages on musicians alone; Volume Two of the same work, which came out two years later, has a bibliography of 22 pages on Italian clergymen in the United States. Hundreds of titles, not just in the English language, but in Italian, Spanish, French, German, and other languages.

The simple, unadulterated truth is that before the publication of my book in 1934 not only there was not one single book that gave out or included the hundreds and hundreds of facts revealed by me for the first time in the annals of the Italians in America, except for a few facts shown in an Italian book written by Alfredo Bosi in 1920, as explained in full detail in the following chapter, but there was not one single book on any noted Italian in America, except for Da Ponte and Mazzei. But that's a long story that is told in the following chapter, THE STUPID LIE.

Who, or whom, is Mr. Elfert trying to fool, except himself? How can one say that the research connected with the preparation of the Anti-Defamation League project on the Italians in America required a rather extensive research and that many and many sources were used, when, obviously, such was not the case? How could three persons not familiar with Italian, Spanish and other languages, and with historical works in those languages could have covered hundreds and hundreds of volumes in several languages in a few days, or even weeks? How long did those researchers work at it? Can Mr. Elfert say how long and indicate the sources under oath in a court of law?

The fact is, as we shall presently see, that there is not one single name or event mentioned in Part I of the *Filmstrip Discussion Guide* that cannot be found in my *Four Centuries*. And how is it that after such extensive research, and after using many and many sources, the

Anti-Defamation League researchers were not able to uncover or bring to light one single tiny fact not mentioned by me some forty years before? And how can the Anti-Defamation League afford to say that the first part of that project on the Italians had not been told before? For the title of Part I is exactly that: *The Untold Story*. That's a lie, a dastard lie, and, above all, a stupid lie. But read the details in the following chapter. No wonder Mr. Gambino and the researchers did not include any of my books in their bibliographies. Can one imagine a bibliography on the Italians in America that does not mention my books? And to say that my books are listed and cited over and over again in many, would say most, of the very books listed in the three bibliographies prepared by the Anti-Defamation League! How stupid can one be? Does it not look, indeed, as if somebody, starting with Professor Gambino, was trying to cover up something? I leave that conclusion to the reader.

Having said that much, let us examine the evidence.

In order to compare the text in the filmstrip with the corresponding part in *Four Centuries*, the former is printed on the left, with the number of the entry, and the latter on the right, with the page number. I have omitted the fillings or padding, such as:

45. Elsewhere, there's more violent music in the air . . .

46. America's a powder keg. On the quiet country road . . .

47. At Philadelphia, the Continental Congress meets . . .

Also, I have omitted the first 25 entries because they deal either with men like Columbus, Vespucci and the Cabots, plus Galileo, Da Vinci and Michelangelo, such as 10, 11, 12, and 13, or because they are fillings, some with the only one word, "Music". Accordingly, I am starting with entry 26, or with Verrazzano. Furthermore, since the names are often mispelled, I am using the correct spelling.

Here we go:

26. Giovanni Da Verrazzano following in 1524. Crossing the coast of the Carolinas, heading north to enter New York harbor 85 years before Henry Hudson.

p. 60. Verrazzano in New York harbor 85 years before Hudson.

This headline is at the top of the page, all in capital letters, large. No other book has pointed out the fact that Verrazzano preceded Hudson by 85 years.

27. and 28. Marcos Da Nizza —	p. 66. Coronado's expedition
more than a hundred years before the Mayflower drops anchor . . . pushing on as far as what is now Nebraska.	made known for the first time the interior of the United States, from the border of Mexico to Nebraska.

My statement is wrong because Coronado only went as far as the middle of Kansas. Fra Marco, moreover, did not even reach the Kansas border as he went back before he got close to it. Obviously, somebody copied my mistake. Aside from all that, nobody, but nobody, had ever written about Fra Marco (Fra Marcos is wrong, because Fra is Italian and Marcos is Spanish. In Spanish it is Fray Marcos) before I wrote an article in *Atlantica*, November, 1930, pp. 112-114. Until then everybody referred to Fra Marco as a Spanish friar. To this day, the *Catholic Encyclopedia* calls the monk a Savoyard. See Chapter 15 in this volume. The Anti-Defamation filmstrip even copies a photograph I took of the rock with the inscription allegedly by Fra Marco. At that time, however, I did not know that the inscription is a fraud, as anybody could have ascertained by some elementary research, as I did not long ago. I challenge anybody to show a book by an Italian, or Italian-American, which even distantly alludes to Fra Marco. Anyway, Fra Marco entered Arizona in 1539; the Pilgrims landed in 1620.

30. A Venetian sailor, Cesare	p. 101. A Venetian landowner in
Alberto, jumps ship to settle in New Amsterdam.	Manhattan and Brooklyn in 1635.

The headline at the top of the page in large type cannot be missed. The name, anyway, is Alberti and not Alberto. At the most, one could say, Alberti or Alberto, as the name is at times spelled Alberto, but that is an error, because in Italian Alberto is a Christian or first name, and Alberti is always a surname. For that matter, Alberti is the name of numerous famous Italians, as one can easily ascertain by leafing through a popular or learned Italian encyclopedia. But can one expect Anti-Defamation League researchers, not familiar with the elements of research and without any knowledge of the Italian language, so far as the Italians in America are concerned, to know this very elementary fact? Have they ever heard of *Nuovissimo Melzi* or of *Brunacci*, the two most popular *dizionari generali di cultura* in Italy? I brought my own Brunacci from Italy when I came over in January 1916 and I bought the latest edition not long ago.

31. Francesco Bressani . . . to	p. 84. Father Giuseppe Bressani,
live among the Iroquois at	S.J. . . . captured by the
what will one day be Albany,	ferocious Iroquois . . .
New York . . .	the second Catholic
	priest to visit the present
	site of the City of Albany.

I devoted a full page (9 x 12) with two maps and a drawing by Onorio Ruotolo, who drew the frontispiece of my *Italians in America Before the Civil War*. Ruotolo's drawing of Father Bressani among the Indians was made to illustrate a pamphlet. I suppose the Anti-Defamation researchers went through the 73 volumes of the *Jesuit Relations* or found Bressani's name in the Talmud. Anyway, what strikes me is the similarity of the language used in the filmstrip guide and my own wording.

32 and 25. Tonti, pp. 85-90:

Tonti, of course, was well-known, although not as well as he was after I did my own extensive research. I devoted six large pages to Tonti with six photographs, including three snapshots I took at La Salle, Ill. and at Starved Rock, plus the facsimiles of two unpublished documents I got from the Bibliotèque Nationale in Paris which show beyond doubt that Tonti was born in Italy, a fact which is still questioned in the brief article on Tonti in the 1968 *World Book Encyclopedia*. I should mention that in earlier editions the sketch about Tonti was accurate, whereas the recent one is full of errors. Of course, one has only to look in the New York Public Library catalog, or in the Library of Congress subject catalog, to find a book about Tonti. That's not research, any high school boy can do that. Research is to examine the controversial points, like those in the 1968 *World Book* and get the facts straight. The filmstrip shows a basrelief of Tonti which is identical with the basrelief I printed on page 85 of *Four Centuries*. I obtained my photograph of that basrelief from the Chicago Historical Society. E. R. Murphy also prints the same basrelief in the frontispiece of his book on Tonti, giving credit to the Illinois State Historical Society. There is the possibility, of course, that the Anti-Defamation League got its photograph from the New York Public Library (that is, from the Murphy book) but why go through the extra expense when the illustration could be had from *Four Centuries* at no expense? Anyway, let the Anti-Defamation League produce the invoice and the check in payment for it. The purpose of such proof is to show weather or not the Anti-Defamation people used my book, which they do not quote or list in any of the three bibliographies they published.

36. A certain Grimaldi, with Oglethorpe at the founding of Georgia.	p. 109. Headline, at top of page. "With Oglethorpe at the Founding of Georgia. Below: His [Oglethorpe's] servant, was an Italian named Charles Grimaldi, a man without many scruples, for during the crossing to Georgia he drank all of the several dozens bottles of Cyprus wine which Oglethorpe had ordered especially for himself.

Here, the point is, why mention Grimaldi, just a servant, and not the other Italians like the Amatis brothers who came with Oglethorpe to introduce silk culture in Georgia as I mention on the same page? The filmstrip also shows two illustrations on pages 108 and 109 of my book, one of which I credit to the New York Public Library, and the other as "from an old print." What a coincidence! The first photograph is the title page of a book printed in 1741, which, however, was reprinted by the University of Georgia Press in 1960, with comments and introduction which did not appear in the first edition. One would suppose, therefore, that researchers would consult the later edition, with a title page different from that of the first edition. And why a view of Savannah about 1741? Again, invoice please!

37. A certain Bautista Antonelli, military architect in charge of building forts in Florida.	p. 76. Headline at top of page: Italian Military Architects in the Americas, with three illustrations.

Text: "As professor Diego Angulo Iniguez says in his study on 'Bautista Antonelli'." The Anti-Defamation League researchers must be experts in the history of South America or Central America, as well as in the history of Italians in Spain. Actually, I doubt whether that book on Antonelli can be found in any library in the United States, as I had to write to Spain to obtain a copy, which I still have. The book is, besides, in Spanish. Are the Anti-Defamation experts familiar with the Spanish language? And why would they consult, of all things, a book on architects? On the same page 76 I have the facsimile from Vol. VIII of the British Calendar of State Papers with the translation of a letter, in English, dated Dec. 12, 1787, mentioning Antonelli. Of course, the Anti-Defamation League researchers and experts on the Italians in America studied the *Calendar of State Papers* just to dig out one single name. And all that in a few days or weeks, at the most. In any event, not one of the books listed in the three bibliographies prepared by the Anti-Defamation people mentions Antonelli, just as they do not mention Grimaldi.

40. A surgeon in Philadelphia, a
    shipwright in New Haven.
    The Priolo family in South
    Carolina, the Palavinci's in
    Virginia.

Pp. 95-98. On those four pages I mention numerous Italians who came to America in colonial times, with facsimiles showing two men named Palavicine [Pallavicino] who owned land in Virginia in 1619-1620. None of those names is mentioned in the books listed in the Anti-Defamation bibliographies. Since those names were culled from literally dozens of books, did the Anti-Defamation researchers examine all those books? That's incredible! But let them prove it. (See also p. 106, Italian Huguenots in XVII Century America.)

41. Onorio Rassolini, armorer and   p. 110. Headline: Onorio Razzo-
    keeper of the stores for the   lini armourer of Maryland
    colony of Maryland.   1732-1747 and below,
                                                   "armourer and Keeper of
                                                   the Stores of Maryland".

The only book of those listed in Anti-Defamation bibliography that lists Razzolini is *Father Gatto,* who, I feel confident, would not hesitate to state under oath that he picked that name from my book. He could have picked it from Musmanno, who got it from me, but that's doubtful because Musmanno mentions in the following line Mayor Pacetti, not listed in *Gatto's.* The Anti-Defamation people would have to do quite a bit of research (an unthinkable research) to come across that name.

42. In New York, Giovanni Palma   p. 112. One John Palma gave a
    presents a concert . . .   concert in Philadelphia
    Signora Massanti gives a   [facsimile of a newspaper
    recital . . . Francis Alberti   ad on the right column]
    teaches Tom Jefferson to play   . . . Right in the next
    the violin.   paragraph, "According to
                                               Thomas Jefferson . . .
                                               Alberti came over . . .
                                               subsequently I took les-
                                               sons for several years."

p. 113. More interesting is the
appearance of "Signiora"
Mazzanti.

I do challenge B'nai B'rith to produce one history of American music
that mentions those three persons in two suceeding pages.

44. Mazzei: A truly republican
form of government cannot
exist except where all men,
from the very rich to the very
poor, are equal in their natural rights.

As I have shown in Chapter 21 on Mazzei, in this volume, and in Appendix C, A STUPID LIE, I discovered the Mazzei article with those
words, which I was the first to translate into English, except for Jefferson's translation which cannot be found, as of this writing. Every mon-
key has been copying from me, without giving due credit. My study of
Mazzei takes 53 large pages, the equal of 106 pages, with 40 facsimiles
never published before. Marraro's translation which many copycats use,
without giving him credit, followed mine by eight years, in the case
of my 1934 book, and seven years after my article which Marraro lists
in his bibliography. Of course, according to the inimitable Mr. Elfert,
that's extensive research by his three "experts". What a farce!

47-48. Among the signers . . .
William Paca.

Why doesn't the powerful B'nai B'rith prove that Paca was an Italian?
I am the only one who has produced the only evidence closest to the
truth. See Chapter 20 in this volume. Of course, I devoted two pages
to Paca in *Four Centuries*.

49. From Marblehead to Mobile
Bay, Italian-American
snatching up their muskets,
marching with the Conti-
nentals.

I didn't know that Mobile Bay was in one of the Thirteen Colonies. At
first, I thought that the B'nai B'rith experts had confused the Civil War
with the Revolution (I was thinking of Farragut) but then the Continentals were in the Revolution. If Mr. Elfert's experts had devoted a
few minutes of their extensive research to this point, they would have
learned that at the time of the Revolution Mobile Bay was in West
Florida, under the British, that in 1780 it was seized by the Spaniards,

et cetera et cetera. It so happened that the people of both East and West Florida preferred to remain neutral, as I learned during my research about the Italians in Florida in 1768. As for the Italian volunteers in Massachusetts, I don't think there were any Italians in those Puritan communities.

50. Mazzei, Bellini, Vincenzo Rossi fighting under Patrick Henry in the Virginia Militia.

p. 139. Among the first natives of Italy to bear arms against the British were Mazzei, Bellini and the gardener, Vincenzo Rossi, who joined Patrick Henry's force as we have noted on page 138. [misprint, should have been 130]

p. 130. When Patrick Henry with a small band of men marched against the English, Mazzei, Bellini and one of the gardeners Mazzei had broght to Virginia joined him, but the English withdrew and the Americans went home. In 1777 he tried again to join the Continental Army but Patrick Henry [who was then governor] forbade him to do so, as he could be more useful in other ways.

I do realize that my statement on page 139 was not exactly felicitous, but I do everything myself, from research to typing to proofreading and at times I get so tired that I can't see everything. But the statement on page 130 is more accurate. Anyway, if Mr. Elfert's experts had not copied my statement and had instead done their home work, they could have learned that none of the three Italians did any fighting, although all three took up arms. Since Garlick does not mention Rossi, the only other place the Anti-Defamation experts could have learned about the three volunteers would have been the Memoirs from page 209 to page 221. In that case they would have learned what did really happen. I repeat, there was no fighting. And no research by the Anti-Defamation experts.

| 50. Major Cosimo Medici galloping to battle with the North Carolina Light Dragoons. | p. 141. Major Cosimo Medici of the North Carolina Light Dragoons. |

The above is a headline over the entire page, with an illustration and a facsimile on page 140 and a little over one third of page 141. Had the filmstrip experts known about him, they could have copied some other item. Ergo . . .

| 50. 49 Sons of the Fonda family in the ranks | p. 136. In New York State, to mention one instance, we find at least 49 members of the Fonda family who at one time or another served in the War. |

| 50. Along with Pasquale De Angelis, Private in the Infantry — age 13. | p. 139. Pascal Charles Joseph De Angelis . . . He is said to have served from 1776 (when he was thirteen years of age!) to the end of the war. He died in 1839. (*New York Evening Post*, Sept. 14, 1839.) |

Of course, the script experts or researchers checked the *Post* of more than a century ago or the other works cited by me on page 139, two in French.

| 51. Paly Bonnaventura, dead at Yorktown. | p. 139. Paly Bonnaventura died at Yorktown in 1781. |

| 51. Col. Richard Taliaferro killed at the Battle of Guilford Hall. Lt. Bracco, dead at White Plains. | p. 136. Col. Richard Taliaferro . . . was killed at the Battle of Guilford Hall on March 15, 1781. [a few lines above on the same column] one lieutenant Bracco who was killed in action at White Plains on October 28, 1776. |

On the same page a photograph of the monument to Major Winston, Captain J. Franklin and Richard Taliaferro, which I obtained from the Guilford Courthouse National Military Park, Greensboro, N.C.

54. Allesandro (sic) Malespina (sic) sails at the head of a scientific expedition mapping the Pacific Coast from Mexico to Alaska.	p. 82. [Headline] Malaspina's voyage around the world. [below] Surveyed the entire Pacific Coast from Alaska to Mexico.

Entire page to Malaspina, with portrait and map. The portrait appears in the filmstrip. Since I got that portrait from a large book which I had to order from Italy (it was published in 1935) I wonder how the Anti-Defamation League learned where that portrait was to be found and since the book is in Italian . . .

61. Off the coast of Boston, Salvatore Catalono (sic) serves as Sailing Master of the U.S. frigate Constitution — "Old Ironside" establishing America's right to freedom of the seas.	p. 116-117. Catalano served as pilot on other American War vessels, including the two frigates, Constitution and Congress.

If there is one man who would have remained completely unknown except for my research it is Salvatore Catalano. It is a long story which got me a personal letter from President Roosevelt and a long article in *Il Progresso Italo-Americano*, New York daily, November 18, 1934. I challenge the Anti-Defamation League of B'nai B'rith to prove that it did not pick that story from either my book or from some recent book that stole it or picked it from my books. In other words, let them prove it that they learned about Catalano through their own research.

82. In Augusta, Georgia, John Phinizy has just been elected mayor.	p. 300. The first son of an Italian immigrant to become mayor of an American was in all probability John Phinizy, the son of Ferdinand Phinizy of Parma, who became mayor of Augusta, Ga., in 1837.

There is a long story about Phinizy's father (Ferdinand). I came across his name in his obituary in the *New York Post* in 1818 which led to some correspondence with one of his descendants, Dr. F. F. Calhoun, who sent me a thick volume of his with the full story of the Phinizy family. His photograph appears on page 309 of my *Four Centuries*, but see also page 138 (he came over with Rochambeau and saw action at Yorktown).

66. In New York, Antonio
     Meucci is inventing the first
     primitive version of the
     telephone, 26 years before . . .
     Bell.

On Meucci see my book, *Antonio Meucci*, New York, 1958, 268 pages. Should I say more?

72. Italian-Americans taking up
     arms for the North, forming
     the Garibaldi Guards.

I first learned about the Garibaldi Guard (singular) when scanning page by page the files of the New York weekly, *L'Eco d'Italia*. On pages 318-319 of *Four Centuries* one will find a brief account of the Guard, a facsimile of a recruitment ad in *Eco* for July 26, 1862, and a photograph of the Guard being reviewed by Lincoln. The illustration takes the entire half bottom page. After I wrote about the Guard (in 1934), Professor Marraro wrote an article in which he often cites my book, but still he got some of the facts mixed up, as in the case of the commandant, Col. Utassy, who was not Italian, but Hungarian. On pages 322 and 323 I have a full-page facsimile of an article from *Eco* about the Guard at Shenandoah, and a full-page photograph of the monument to the Guard (39th N. Y. Infantry) at Gettysburgh. Only 50 of the 850 soldiers in the Guard were Italians. Even a blind man could not have missed those three large illustrations. One of the illustrations was from the *Illustrated London News*. I should add that before I moved to Texas in 1958 I had many of the 130 (one hundred and thirty) large and thick volumes of the *Official Records of Union and Confederate Armies*, which I sold to a book dealer in New Brunswick, N.J. I went through every one of those 130 volumes. I suppose the ineffable Mr. Elfert will maintain that his experts also scanned every one of those 130 volumes.

74. From the long rollcall (sic)
    choose a few to stand for
    the many. Rear admiral
    Bancroft Gherardi under fire
    at Mobile Bay. Edward
    Ferraro (sic, should be
    Ferrero), the only general
    to take command of an all-
    black combat division.
    Brigadier-general Francesco
    Spinola, twice wounded at
    Wapping Heights, corporal
    Edward Venuti—killed at
    Gettysburg.

On pages 318-320, 324 and 325 of *Four Centuries* I list the names and
regiments of Italian officers in the Union Army, with a brief account
of Admiral Gherardi on pp. 324 and 325. To be exact, brief accounts
of Generals Ferrero, Spinola, Cesnola and Fardella, all natives of Italy
with the exception of Spinola, plus 9 colonels, 6 majors (including
Venuti and his death in action) 22 captains, 32 first lieutenants, 21
second lieutenants, 4 surgeons, 4 chaplains, 3 Medals of Honor, plus
four portraits of Spinola, Cesnola, Tinelli and Gherardi. I must have
spent weeks and weeks, from 1933 to 1952 to get all those names from
scores and scores of volumes and articles. In the case of Spinola, I
learned about him one day, by chance, when during my visit to the
bookstands on Fourth Avenue (now called Park Avenue South) I
picked up a little volume, one of those little black volumes (small in
number of pages, but the size was about 9x12, or just about) put out
by the Congress of the United States on the death of a member or
former member. As I have said elsewhere, Congressman Marcantonio,
a good friend of mine, borrowed it from me, but then he had a heart
attack and I never saw that booklet again. And that's how I happened
to write an article about Spinola in the April, 1930, issue of *Atlantica*
and that's how Italian-Americans first learned about him. After my
article and my book on the Civil War, every expert bragged and
bragged, passing off for their own research what had cost me weeks
and weeks of research and hundreds of dollars. As I have said in the
preceding pages, the experts of the Anti-Defamation League of B'nai
B'rith went through some 130 books to find the Italian names, assuming
that they could tell an Italian name from a Spanish name.

75. And their brothers of Italian-descent fighting for the South. Five hundred in Louisiana's European Brigade. In the Alabama Infantry, the Mississippi Cavalry. A colonel and two captains from Georgia's Phinizy family.

p. 326. In the confederate army and navy [headline at top of page] . . . The European Brigade from New Orleans alone included some 500 Italians . . . In Georgia, the Phinizy family contributed one colonel, two captains, one sergeant and one financial agent. In Alabama, Sylvester Festorazzi served as a captain in the infantry; in Mississippi Frank J. Arrighi served as a captain in the infantry and was wounded at Antietam, Chancellorsville and Spottsylvania.

76. One dead at Manassas

p. 326. One of whom died at Manassas [as already noted above, in preceding quotation from page 326].

I got those names from several sources, too numerous to mention.

81. In the wild West, Angelo "Charlie" Siringo, son of an Italian immigrant, starts herding longhorns at 14, chases rustlers into Mexico, leads the posse that captures Billy the Kid at Stinking Springs.

Pp. 169-170. Two facsimiles of title page and frontispiece on p. 168 and facsimile of two pages from the first edition of Siringo's *A Texas Cowboy*.

I did not know whether Siringo was Italian or Mexican, that is, of Spanish descent. I had to get hold of a copy of the first edition of his best-seller to learn that his father was born in Italy, as in later editions that fact is not mentioned, leaving the reader in doubt as to his father's birthplace.

85. Ambassador to Cypress.

Of course, the learned researchers meant Cyprus!

57. In Minnesota. Nathan
    Taliaferro, agent to the
    Chippewas.

I am placing this entry at the end of the list, and not in its numerical
order, because I was sure that there was no Indian agent named Nathan
Taliaferro. The only Indian agent I could recall was Lawrence Taliaferro, who was with Beltrami when they landed in Minnesota in April
1823, as I noted on page 95 of my book, *The Italians in America Before the Civil War* in 1934. My conclusion was that the Anti-Defamation League researchers confused Lawrence with Nicholas, but I had
to be absolutely sure that such was the case, and that caused me over
three days of search.

To give an idea, I first looked up all the encyclopedias and dictionaries of biography I could get hold of, but no luck. Then I checked,
one by one, all the references I could find in 13 volumes of the *William and Mary Quarterly* and *The Virginia Magazine History and
Biography*, where I learned that there had been several men named
Nathan Taliaferro, including one who was a lieutenant in the Continental Army and a member of the Society of the Cincinnati, but no
Indian agent. However, he was present at the surrender of Cornwallis
at Yorktown. Then I checked the 17 volumes of the *Minnesota Historical Society Collection*, which I had used forty years before, and
this time I was lucky, because on page 547 of Volume VI I found
the full list of all Indian agents from the first one to the end of the
century, eleven in all, including Lawrence Taliaferro, but no Nathan
Taliaferro. I hope Mr. Elfert has by now learned what constitutes
the elements of research.

Of course, it could be argued that even if the passages in the
Filmstrip Guide and in the tapes correspond to the passages in my
Four Centuries, there is the possibility that the researchers of the
Anti-Defamation League might have found those passages in books
by authors, or petty thieves, who copied them from my book, or books.
Such a conclusion, however, is not valid, first of all, because all those
books mention and in some cases cite my books, often so prominently
that no researcher, no matter how superficial, could have missed them.
Therefore, one would have been compelled to look up my books, as
any researcher worthy of the name would normally do, if for no other
reason out of curiosity alone. In the second, and more important,
place, the *Filmstrip Discussion Guide* and the tapes with the narration
by the actor contain many names that cannot be found in any of the
books listed in the Anti-Defamation League bibliographies. In other
words, those names had to be copied either from my books (*Four Cen-*

turies alone would have been sufficient) or after a very long and very expensive research in works in various languages aside from the fact that a researcher had to know where to look, not in the usual books or histories.

I have, accordingly, listed all the names in the filmstrip and tape in alphabetical order, so as to facilitate the search in other works, beginning with Verrazzano as already noted, with two figures, one at the left indicating the entry in the script, and another on the right indicating the page in *Four Centuries*. Here they are:

75—Alabama—326
42—Alberti—112
30—Alberto—101
37—Antonelli—76
50—Bellini—118 and 130
51—Bonaventura—139
51—Bracco—136
31—Bressani—84
67—Brumidi—231-233
61—Catalano—315-316
75—Cesnola—236-320-324
63—Da Ponte—183
50—De Angelis—139
74—Ferrero—318
50—Fonda—136
72—Garibaldi Guard—318-319
74—Gherardi—324-325
36—Grimaldi—109
75—Louisiana European
    Brigade—326
54—Malaspina—82
76—Manassas—326
28—Marco da Nizza—65
42—Mazzanti—113
43—Mazzei—129-135

57—Mazzuchelli—243, 248
50—Medici—140-141
59—Mengarini—249
66—Meucci—274-289
75—Mississippi—326
49—Paca—122-123
40—Pallavicino—95
42—Palma—112
62—Phinizy—300
75—Phinizy—326
40—Priuli—106
41—Razzolini—110
58—Ravalli—249
38—Paul Revere—not an Italian
50—Rossi—130
881—Siringo—168-169
74—Spinola—326
51—Taliaferro—136
57—Nicholas Taliaferro
    (see above)
42—Tonti—85-90
83—Tontitown—312
74—Venuti—318-320
56—Vigo—124-128
Total: 47 entries

Let us check now and see how many of the names listed in the *Filmstrip Discussion Guide* and mentioned in the narration, or tapes, can be found in the books listed in the bibliographies prepared by the Anti-Defamation League in connection with their filmstrip on the Italians in America. First, however, I must emphasize that the comparison is only with Part I, or what the Anti-Defamation League has stupidly and falsely labeled *The Untold Story*. In other words, only Part I, on the one end, and my books, *Four Centuries* and *The Italians in America Before the Civil War* on the other, as I made very very clear to Mr. Theodore Freedman, director of the Community Service of the Anti-Defamation League when he asked me, on the day I was returning to Texas on August 1, 1975, what or which were the books of mine which I said had been pilfered or used without my permission and without payment by the Anti-Defamation League.

Let us start with the five books checked by Mr. Elfert in the bibliography he sent me on September 17, 1975, that is, Lo Gatto (1), Gambino (2), De Conde (3), La Gumina (14), and Amfitheatrof (15).

The only names in the filmstrip or guide to be found in Father Lo Gatto's *The Italians in America* (a chronology) are, in chronological order, skipping Columbus, Vespucci and Verrazzano; 1539, Marco Da Nizza; 1639, Alberto; 1678, Tonti; 1736, Razzolini; 1773, Mazzei; 1774, Vigo; 1776, Paca; 1791, Malaspina; 1805, Da Ponte; 1833, Mazzuchelli; 1835, Meucci; 1837, Phinizy; 1846, Catalano; 1851, Mengarini; 1855, Brumidi; 1861, Cesnola; 1872, Tontitown; 1887, Spinola — in all, 17 names out of 47 (or 48, including Verrazzano). Where did the Anti-Defamation League find the other 29? Not in Lo Gatto's book for sure. I prefer to say nothing unpleasant about the good Father, since he was gracious enough to mark the year 1916 in his chronology as the year of my arrival in America, although he knows very well that he found some of his names in my books, as they could not be found in any other general book, as in the case of Phinizy.

As for Professor Gambino's book, *Blood of my Blood,* we need not waste any time on it, first of all because it does not contain any names of Italian settlers in colonial times, not even Mazzei or Vigo. As for the rest, I shall single out his asininities and imbecilities in a forthcoming bibliography of Italian immigration to the United States. Why, that *professore* is so ignorant about anything pertaining to Italy and the Italians that he places not only Tuscany, but even Rome, in Northern Italy! As for his ignorance of the Italian language, not to mention everything else about Italy (he himself admitted to a friend of mine that he knows very little Italian) enough to say that he translated the word "infamità," as used by Pirandello in a Sicilian story, as 'outrage," whereas every Italian kid in western Sicily (the area Gambino's parents came from) knows that it means "squealing" and that "infame" or more correctly "nfami," means stool pigeon or spy.

The third book in the Anti-Defamation bibliography is De Conde's *Half-Bitter, Half-Sweet.* I have already referred to this book in the Introduction and in the Bibliographical Essay, in this volume. Here I shall point out that he mentions only half a dozen names, excluding such names as Da Nizza, Razzolini, Bressani, Paca, Spinola, Catalano and so on. Obviously, De Conde is not an authority on the notable

Italians in American history listed in Part One of the script. Part II is something else, but it is beyond the province of the present exposé to go into that.

The fourth book in Mr. Elfert's bibliography, *An Album of the Italian-American*, is a book for young readers. Most certainly, Mr. La Gumina is no authority on the Italians in America. His book, anyway, has no historical or even sociological value, as it shows largely vignettes or pictures about immigrants and their children. Aside from that, it contains numerous errors of both fact and interpretation. For instance, no four million Italians emigrated to America between 1880 and 1914, because close to twenty percent had been in America before and had left one or more times. Some, as many as seven times. He mentions a few names of famous Italians, but he gets the facts wrong, as in the case of Vigo, who was not an adventurer, or of Mazzei who was not a political philosopher. Garibaldi was not an American citizen, and he remained in America only a few months. He did return to America in 1854, but that was on his way back from China to Italy. And so on. At any rate, it is ridiculous to include that book as a source. I should add that La Gumina's book was replaced by, or replaced, another book of his, *WOP* about discrimination against the Italians, another field in which the author is still groping in the dark.

The fifth book checked by Mr. Elfert is *The Children of Columbus*, by Erik Amfitheatrof,a member of the staff of *Time* magazine, a questionable credential. Yet the book is honest, with very few errors, most of them due to his association with *Time*. Mr. Amfitheatrof, the son of Russian father and Italian mother, who came to America not many years ago, knows nothing of the problems of the Italians at first hand, and most certainly did no research of any extent. He simply consulted a few books, mine for the history of the Italians in America, which he duly and honestly acknowledges and cites, and a few more which can be found in most libraries in America. He does not mention Marco Da Nizza, or Razzolini, or Antonelli, or Paca, or Taliaferro, or Mazzanti, or De Angelis; not even Vigo, or Catalano, or Phinizy. He cites my *Four Centuries*, which he calls "a basic reference work on Italian-American History" in one place, at the beginning of the work, and again in other places, as on page 334, where he says, "Again useful for the record of early Italian settlers in America was Schiavo's *Four Centuries.*" Obviously, Mr. Elfert's industrious researchers must have missed those citations and references to my books. In any event, no individual with a slight acquaintance with the subject would have included this book as one of the sources for the study of the Italians in America. To be frank about it, there is nothing in this book that cannot be found in other books, except for the fact that it is well written, much better written than the books by Italian-American professors.

Of the other ten books listed in Mr. Elfert's *Italian-American Studies* only three contain names of famous Italian-Americans, or just pioneers. The other seven deal with immigration since the 1880's, and therefore beyond the scope of the present investigation. They are: Nelli's book on the Italians in Chicago; Vecoli's unpublished thesis on th Italians in Chicago, which is not available, except through special permission, and so on (in that case, why not include some worthwhile thesis by other authors?); Cordasco's bibliography (just titles); Lo Preato's *Italian-Americans*, which deals with sociological questions; Covello's book on the background of Italian-American school children, now outdated, except for background studies; Glazer and Moynihan's *Beyond the Melting Pot*, which has nothing about Italians in American history; Tomasi's *The Italian in America*, a reprint of articles from the magazine *Charities*, later *The Survey*, with nothing about early settlers. That leaves two books by Rolle and one by Iorizzo and Mondello.

I have referred to Iorizzo and Mondello in Appendix A, and I need not repeat here what I have already said, except that they cannot be considered in any way as source material. Although they cite my books fourteen times (2 *Civil War*, 5 *Four Centuries*, 4 *Italian-American History*, Vol. I and 3 Vol. II) they do not mention Vigo, or Marco da Nizza, or Tonti, or the Waldenses, and practically all the rest of the names in the Anti-Defamation tape or narration. Even then they do not always get the facts straight, as in the New Smyrna rebellion. Bishop Rosati, to give another instance, was not a Neapolitan, but a Roman, for Sora, his birthplace, is in the province of Frosinone, even though in the past it was in the province of Caserta. Of course, such a mistake would be inconsequential if it were not made by two young men who have the gumption of writing about Italian immigration wtihout getting acquainted first with the geography of Italy. (Since Professor Iorizzo has included in one of his bibliographies the *Annuario Statistico Italiano Della Emigrazione Italiana dal 1875 al 1926*, I suggest that he look up the emigration figures from Lazio with those from Campania, on pages 120 and 126 — all of which has nothing to do with Bishop Rosati, but is certainly important when studying the causes of Italian emigration.)

We come finally to Professor Rolle's two books, *The Immigrant Upraised* (1968) and *The American Italian* (1972), the first of which deals largely with the Italians in the West, and the latter with Italians throughout the United States.

The first volume had a semblance of scholarship; I would even say that it was rather scholarly, although it does not contain much which required extensive research. As it is, it lists or mentions 10 names (or 11 if we include Lawrence Taliaferro, instead of Nicholas Taliaferro) out of the 47 names in the Anti-Defamation League script and tapes. Most certainly the Anti-Defamation researchers could not have found the other 36 in Rolle's *Immigrant Upraised*. Actually, Professor Rolle refers to or cites four of my books (Missouri, Civil War, *Guida*, which I wrote, anonymously, and *Four Centuries*) 30 times. To be precise, on pages 48, 49, 51, 63, 65, 69, 72, 73, 75, 159, 161, 167, 204, 250, 211, 214, 218, 244, 245, 254, 255, 259, 342 — with more than one citation on some pages. Thirty citations in a book that deals largely with the Italians in the West is quite a large number.

Professor Rolle, however, forgot that the shining badge of the scholar is to give credit in every instance and preferred to lump all the material he lifted from my books in a mention at the end of seven chapters. Thus we find on p. 7 (Chapter I) "Giovanni Schiavo's two volumes, *Four Centuries of Italian American History* (New York, 1952) and his *Italians in America Before the Civil War* (New York, 1934) are useful for enumerating the contributions of specific Italians although these books do not discuss social or adjustment problems; p. 14 (II) "For information about Italian explorers, see the two Schiavo volumes *Four Centuries . . .* and *Civil War*, as well as more modern works such as Pisani's *The Italian in America* and *The Italian-Americans* by Iorizzo and Mondello; p. 20 (III) "The role of Italians in the American colonies is covered generally in Schiavo's two volumes, *Four Centuries . . .* and *Civil War*, Pisani's *The Italian in America* and Iorizzo and Mondello's *The Italian-Americans*, as well as Marinacci's *They came from Italy . . .* Books useful for studying Vigo are Goggio's *Italians in American History* and Roselli's *Vigo*"; p. 26 (IV) "For this chapter on Italians and early culture, the two books by Schiavo are again useful. The Pisani book and the one by Iorizzo and Mondello, as well as The Federal Writers' Project, *The Italians of New York* should be consulted"; p. 36 (V) "Books on Italian travelers are Schiavo's *Four Centuries* as well as his . . . *Civil War*"; p. 45 (VI) "Books with information on Italian missionaries in America include Schiavo, *Four Centuries* and his . . . *Civil War* . . ."; p. 56 (VII) "Books helpful for understanding the period before mass emigration occurred include Schiavo's two volumes, *Four Centuries* and his . . . *Civil War*, and the Pisani book."

Professor Rolle must have been in a great hurry when he wrote his bibliographical notes, even though he starts the first seven chapters with my books (after Chapter VII he deals with mass immigration), or he must have written them long after he had forgotten where he got his information. For the fact is, that my books are the only source for a general treatment of those seven chapters, besides, of course, a few monographs on such individuals as Brumidi or De Cesnola. For instance:

At the beginning of Chapter Two Bibliography on p. 14 he says "as well as more modern works such as Pisani's . . . and . . . by Iorizzo and Mondello." That's simply ridiculous. For one thing, all the names and facts about Italian explorers in Pisani's book are lifted from my own books including Vol. II of my *Italian-American History* which Professor Rolle does not list at all, but Pisani does on page 264. Let Professor Rolle mention one single name in Pisani's chapter on "Beginnings" that is not in any of my books. As for the Iorizzo and Mondello book, that's for the birds. There is Goggio, but that's a 17-page pamphlet. More modern works? The professor surely must have been in a great hurry, otherwise I would be compelled to accuse him of bad faith.

At the top of Chapter Three Bibliography he adds, after my books, Pisani's, Mondello and Iorizzo and Marinacci. I have said all that I have to say for the time being about those three authors; as to Miss Marinacci, I have not seen her book or booklet. I only have read that it contains some, about six or so, biographies for young readers. And that's a source for the study of the Italians in the American colonies? To include Mariano's book is simply preposterous and irresponsible, for Mariano's book — a good book, incidentally — does not deal with pioneers. When the Mariano book came out, in 1921, neither he nor anybody else even dreamt that there had been any Italians in the colonies. For that matter, the title of the book, a doctoral dissertation, was at first *The Second Generation of Italians in New York City*. As for Goggio's pamphlet, it has one small page about Vigo, but that was months after the publication of my article on Vigo in *Atlantica*, for March, 1930. Professor Goggio contributed to the same magazine but on Italian educators beginning with the 19th century. Professor Rolle should double-check, or just check, his facts before making such statements, as his notes may cause serious researchers to waste precious time.

The mention of Iorizzo and Mondello's book in Chapter Four Bibliography is even more ridiculous, because the only book on Italian musicians is Vol. I of my *Italian-American History* which the head of the music department of the New York Public Library called "monumental work" (it is available also in microfilm), and as for artists, there is only my *Four Centuries*.

Coming to Chapter Six Bibliography, it is a pity that Professor Rolle had not seen, as late as 1972, Vol. II of my *Italian-American History* for which I received the congratulation of Pope Pius XII in a letter signed by the present Pope Paul VI and the high praise of the famous Jesuit historian, Father Tacchi Venturi. As *The Catholic Booklist* put it, "This will be the source-book for all future writing on the subject", and Professor Rolle did not even know about it, unless he had a good reason for omitting it, but as the French say, *tu l'a voulu*, or, "you asked for it." No grudge, but let us get the facts straight and let us stop pontificating.

As for Chapter seven, everything about it, or just about, is lifted from my books and my articles. To mention Pisani in connection with that chapter is simply utterly ridiculous. And now I am sick and tired of all of Professor Rolle's erudition, largely at my expense. What everybody will agree on, is the insuperable stupidity of whoever it was on the staff or board, or whatever, of the Anti-Defamation League that included in its bibliography a book that places on the very first line of the bibliographical notes of the first seven chapters of the book, my own works, not one of which is included in three Anti-Defamation bibliographies. That's stupid, in any language.

The only other book which mentions about twenty names included in the *Filmstrip Discussion Guide* is Judge Musmanno's *The Italians in America* which is listed in the final bibliography at the end of the *Guida*. Of course, Judge Musmanno, who was a good friend of mine and who received my permission to quote or refer to my books, took good advantage of my offer, and mentions many more names than one can find in the Anti-Defamation script or tapes. What I have said about him in Appendix A (*A Bibliographical Essay*) covers to some extent what it might be appropriate to say in this volume. However, the fact remains that in three pages (15, 23, and 253) he says, "Giovanni Schiavo advances . . ." and again "Giovanni Schiavo records the names of Italians who served . . ." and lists eight names ,including Phinizy; and again, "Giovanni Schiavo lists the following [mayors]:" twenty-three names follow. At the end, Musmanno lists four books of mine in the bibliography, but, to top it all, he begins his book by acknowledging on the very first line:

"I am grateful to Giovanni Schiavo for the valuable assistance I derived from his splendid work, *Four Centuries of Italian-American History*. The entire Italian community of America should be indebted to Mr. Schiavo for his dedicated and stupendous labors in digging out of old records, books, and documents much of the history of the Italian in early-day America."

In conclusion, the statement by Mr. Samuel H. Elfert, Director, Audio-Visual Department, Anti-Defamation League of B'nai B'rith, in his letter to me of September 17, 1975, to the effect that "the research for this production was rather extensive and many, many sources were used by the writer" is a figment of his imagination, whether due to his abysmal ignorance of the vastness of the subject, or to other factors.

The facts are:

1) Limiting ourselves to Part I of the *Filmstrip Discussion Guide*, the so-called "untold story," an even more stupid lie as demonstrated in the following chapter, there is not one single fact or single name, with the exception of one due to somebody's error or carelessness in copying, that cannot be found in my book, *Four Centuries of Italian-American History*.

2) Even granting for the sake of argument that the researchers got or would claim that they got their facts from other books which reprinted without my permission the facts mentioned in my book, the fact still remains that the Anti-Defamation script, Part I, of the *Filmstrip Discussion Guide*, contains names and facts that cannot be found in any other book on the Italians in America, except in my own book, or in obscure sources which would require years and years of research and thousands upon thousands of dollars to dig out, assuming that the researcher had a command of such languages as Italian, Spanish and French.

3) Assuming, for the sake of argument, that "the research was rather extensive and many, many sources were used," how is it that three researchers were not able to produce or uncover or unearth, one single fact, one single name, that cannot be found in my book or in any other book on the Italians in America? Personally, I have found many more facts and names since 1952, which are mentioned in the present volume for the first time.

4) Mr. Frank Bianco, Executive Director of the Columbia Coalition, told me that the Coalition paid the Anti-Defamation League the sum of $10,000. How much research could three individuals do on a pittance, considering the other costs, such as writer's fee, filming, the music, the art work, et cetera, et cetera?

Appendix C
THE STUPID LIE

A stupid lie! What else would one call a heading as "The Untold Story" the narration of events which I had disclosed over forty years before, namely, in my book, *The Italians in America Before The Civil War*, in 1934? Actually, even before that, as far back as 1928 and 1930. I am referring, of course, to the title of Part I of the filmstrip *The Italians in America* by the Anti-Defamation League of B'nai B'rith, as I have noted in the preceding chapter. The lie, really is more stupid than brazen, because even a high school boy could tell at once that the names and facts mentioned in that part I of the Anti-Defamation League filmstrip can be found in my 1934 book, as well in the enlarged work, *Four Centuries of Italian-American History*, which came out in 1952.

To be precise, before the appearance of my books, *The Italians in Chicago* (1928) and *The Italians in Missouri* (1929), plus my articles in *Atlantica magazine* (of which I was managing editor) in 1930 and 1931, there was nothing about the Italians in America, with the exception of Columbus, the Cabots, Vespucci, Verrazzano (even his exploration of New York Bay was doubted by some or many) and some fleeting allusion to Tonti. Of course, in the history of the Catholic Church in America one could find a few names, but only a drop in the bucket compared to what I unearthed and told in my 1100 pages of the second volume of my *Italian-American History*. Odell's *Annals of the New York Stage* had just begun, but I had already discovered the veritable mine of clippings and other material in the files of the music department of the New York Public Library, which then were in cabinets open to the public.

So much so, that when my book came out it was hailed with a welcome which I did not expect, with editorials in the two Italian-language dailies of New York City and banner headlines in Italian-American weeklies from Boston to Rochester and Detroit and Chicago and San Francisco. Why? Simply because no one, not even the best informed Italian journalists in the United States (not to say Italy) had an idea of what had remained hidden until I — and only I, single-handedly — revealed it. Let me give some samples in the original language, to avoid any possible misunderstanding:

Giovinezza, Boston monthly, September, 1934 — "Il giorno in cui

175

apparve per le stampe il libro *The Italians in America Before the Civil War* . . . dovrebbe essere celebrato ora e negli anni avvenire come uno dei più lieti e gloriosi nella vita della razza italiana negli Stati Uniti. Infatti abbiamo in questo volume un'opera di altissimo valore scientifico, che in modo inoppugnabile dimostra la parte importantissima che *sempre* gli italiani hanno avuto nella formazione e nella storia di questo Paese" — Vittorio Racca, noted economist, former professor at the University of Rome and the University of Basle, Switzerland, and then at the Institute of Human Relations at Yale University. The article was preceded by a brief introduction by the editor, Francesco Macaluso, who said, "Il libro di Giovanni Schiavo per la sua indiscutibile importanza e per la rigorosa documentazione . . ." ("The day of publication of *The Italians in America* . . . ought to be celebrated now and in the future as one of the happiest and most glorious in the life of the Italian race in the United States." Macaluso called attention to its "unquestionable importance and extremely accurate documentation."

Amerigo Ruggiero, the foremost correspondent of Italian newspapers in America, a resident of the United States for many years, and the author of *Italiani in America* (1937), the most valuable single book on Italian immigration to the United States to this very day, wrote a very long article (over two full columns) in *La Stampa*, a Turin daily (the second in Italy, next to the *Corriere della Sera*), in which, after mentioning countless names of Italians until then unknown to most readers, he said: "It is a thick volume of about 400 pages which cost the author years of intensive research in libraries and archives scattered throughout the vast north-American continent. One cannot read Giovanni Schiavo's book without feeling a sense of sadness. It is always Italian activity, Italian genius, Italian initiative that bring to other nations, other peoples, who, in return, fail to recognize their merit and belittle their value. Nevertheless, this book should be read by all cultivated Italians."

The two editorials by Carlo Falbo, editor of *Il Progresso*, "Gl'italiani in America,"" July 22, 1934, and "Un Libro da diffondere," September 16, 1934, cannot be summed up in a few lines. The title of the second editorial, "a book to make known" should suffice. Dr. Falbo, who had been editor of *Il Messaggero*, a Rome, Italy, daily newspaper, before he came to America, called attention in his July editorial to my chapter on Mazzei, to my note about Paine's *Common Sense* which simply repeated what Mazzei had been telling the American people for the preceding two years, and ends with the words, "This book will afford American historians not imbued with racial prejudices to give the Italians the place they deserve in American history. A dutiful, however late, recognition might make up for the errors, the forget-fulness and the injustices of the past."

The editorial in *Il Corriere d'America,* the other Italian daily newspaper, by Francesco Panciatichi was no less enthusiastic. Panciatichi had been editor of that newspaper, founded by Luigi Barzini, Sr., since 1921 (at first as managing editor) and a working journalist in the United States since 1904. He was also the New York correspondent of Mussolini's newspaper, *Il Popolo d'Italia,* of Milan.

I mention these facts in order to show that what I brought out in 1934 was almost totally unknown to cultivated Italians who knew what had been published about the Italians in America before I came along. Like Falbo, Panciatichi, who was a good friend of mine for years, lists some of the important names unearthed by me, and points out how the book was the "risultato di lunghi anni di pazienti, coscienziose ed appassionate indagini, uno studio profondo e, quel che più giova, seria-mente documentato, con un'esposizione sintetica, bene ordinata, chiara, obiettiva, e convincente . . . rivelano uomini e fatti ignorati o caduti nell'oblio (men and events either unknown or forgotten) . . ." The Istituto Italiano di Cultura of New York, which recently called my book "compilations" (possibly a slip of the pen), would do well to ponder those words.

Then there was Agostino De Biasi, the dean of the Italian jour-nalists in the United States from the turn of the century until he died in 1964, editor of *Il Progresso* for years until 1915 when he established *Il Carroccio,* the foremost magazine in a foreign language ever pub-lished in the United States and a mine of information for the history of the Italians in America, unfortunately ignored by the presumptuous Italian-American experts on immigration (not to mention the non-Italians). De Biasi promised a review which he never wrote because in those days he had a little trouble with Mussolini and his minister for popular culture, Piero Parini. He announced the publication with the words, "A Giovanni Schiavo dobbiamo un volume d'importanza capitale per la storia degli emigrati italiani" (To Giovanni Schiavo we owe a volume of paramount importance for the history of Italian im-migrants." Coming from De Biasi, that's more than a long editorial.

Other Italian-language newspapers throughout the country, too numerous to mention, followed suit. One of them, *La Stampa Unita* of Rochester, N. Y., devoted the entire page, with large types and ban-ner headlines; two, *La Tribuna Italiana d'America* of Detroit and *La Gazzetta del Massachusetts* of Boston, devoted almost a full page each.

The American press was no less generous. For instance:

"Mr. Schiavo, with the thoroughness of the scholar and the facility of the practiced journalist, has conveniently gathered within the covers of this single volume a wealth of biographical material hitherto almost totally ignored and accessible only to the research worker. It is a commendable effort and the result is a valuable book, informative and well written . . . Mr. Schiavo's sleuthing is fascinating indeed."

DINO FERRARI, *The New York Times Book Review.*

"This book represents a laudable effort to establish the contributions of Italians to the development of American society and culture in the period prior to the coming of the "new" immigration. Mr. Schiavo feels, rightly, that the majority of historians have been inclined to underestimate the influence of minority racial groups in the early years of American history, and he has attempted to prove that the Italians played a much larger role in this period than is generally assumed.

BOOKS, *New York Herald-Tribune*

"He undertakes in his scholarly volume to show that Italians from the days of Columbus have made enormous contributions to the development of America, which are not generally known or appreciated. . . . Schiavo's scholarly volume is extremely valuable reading for students of American history, and for Americans of Italian origin eager to know the role Italians have played in the making of America."

PERCY WINNER, *New York Journal*

"Italy plainly comes into her own in this book . . . As to contributions as a whole, the Italians, in proportion to their numbers, have perhaps contributed more to America than any other national group."

Boston Transcript

"The dispute of many years' standing between local Italians and some historians as to who really was the founder of the city of Buffalo is settled, apparently, by Giovanni Schiavo in his book . . . quoting numerous documents to bolster his contention."

Buffalo Evening News

"The names of Italians who helped to build our republic are rescued from oblivion in a brilliant volume by Giovanni Schiavo."

M. E. HENNESSY, *The Boston Globe*

"Contrary to popular belief, a large number of Italians settled in this country in the years following the Declaration of Independence, and their contribution to the early history of the United States was of substantial importance."

New York Sun

"A veritable encyclopeadia of American-Italian history . . . Giovanni Schiavo has produced one of the most historically valuable books issued in recent years."

The Commonweal

"Schiavo's book is extremely valuable reading for students of American history, and for Americans of Italian origin eager to know the role Italians played in the making of America."

New York Journal

"We are grateful to Mr. Schiavo for doing justice, in this record of the Italian contribution to American civilization, to the labors of the sons and daughters of Italy as missionaries and educators."

Catholic Missions

Among the personal letters, I would mention one from G. A. Borgese who said that my book was "a precious gift" and three notes or letters from H. L. Mencken, who wrote in the first one that he "had spent a couple of very pleasant hours last night reading it. It is full of unfamiliar and interesting stuff, and I am delighted to have it. I was especially pleased to see you tackling the Anglo-Saxon myth." Two days later, on August 18, 1934, he wrote me: "I have been going further into your book, and find it more and more interesting."

No less significant, if I may be allowed to say so, are the 165 subscriptions at $10.00 each paid several months before the publication of my book for a copy of the deluxe edition by the most prominent Americans of Italian birth or extraction, from His Eminence, Amleto Cicognani, the Apostolic Delegate to the United States and the Italian Ambassador to Washington, Augusto Rosso, to A. P. Giannini of San Francisco; Gatti Casazza, general manager of the Metropolitan Opera House; Rosa Ponselle; Giovanni Martinelli; Amedeo Obici, the founder of Planters Nut and Chocolate Company; Angelo Petri; Aroldo Palanca, the general manager of the Italian Line; F. A. Saroli, President of the Banca Commerciale Italiana Trust Co.; Pietro Yon, the famous organist of St. Patrick's Cathedral; Dr. Paterno, the leading builder of New York City in those days; Attilio Piccirilli, the famous sculptor; judges, politicians, et cetera, et cetera. Many of them subscribed because they knew me personally (most of them did because I had been managing editor of *Atlantica*) or because they had read some of my articles on early Italians, like Vigo, Spinola, Chino, and so on. I must add that my book was to be published, as it was, under the auspices of the Italian Historical Society, the only society by that name of any importance ever organized by Italians in the United States, with regular office at 113 West 42nd Street, diagonally opposite the New York Public Library. Before publication, however, the directors of the Society asked the opinion of an Italian-American instructor at Columbia University, to whom I showed my galley proofs. However, he did not feel that my book had any merit and gave a negative report. The Society concluded otherwise and sponsored the book, giving me, besides, $100 in cash. The president was Dr. Giuseppe Previtali, probably the most prominent Italian physician in the country, Dr. Cassola, and the board of directors included Duke Carafa D'Andria, Count Di Revel, and others of high social and intellectual standing. Harold Lord Varney, the executive director of the Society, a well-known journalist, most likely tipped the scales in my favor, probably because, a few months before, he had received a review copy of the book, *Italy and the Italians in Washington's Time*, with a yellow sticker on the inside cover reading "To: Mr. Varney from Giuseppe Prezzolini." Varney, who was a friend of mine, compared that book with my galley proofs and quickly drew his own conclusion, regardless of the opinion of the Columbia instructor (later full professor). I must also add that my book, together with four more volumes of mine, were reprinted by the Arno Press, a division of the *New York Times* in 1975. *A buon intenditor poche parole.*

At this point, is it not permissible to say that my book would not have been supported and would not have been welcomed the way it was, if it had not revealed facts which were not dreamt of even by seasoned historians?

Because of space limitations, I have to forego my plan to mention in detail the names of the Italian pioneers known to educated Italians and especially journalists who had been defending the Italian name in America for more than half a century. I shall, however, name the books and articles that contained a few names. They were: Alfredo Bosi's *Cinquant'anni di vita italiana in America*, New York, 1921, 531 pages; Branchi's *Primato degli italiani in America*, Bologna, 1925, 67 pages; five articles by Fiorello La Guardia in "*What Italians Have Done for New York*" in the *New York American* (August, 1927 — no mention of any pioneers); Goggio's article "Italy And The American War of Independence" in the *Romanic Review* (1929) and his pamphlet, *Italians in American History*, 1930, 17 pages; and the book *Italy and the Italians In Washington's Time* which was a flop, as I have noted elsewhere. The only chapter that dealt with the pioneers in that book, with the exception of Roselli's chapter on Vigo (see Chapter 22), Garlick's chapter on Mazzei (see Chapter 21), and Russo's chapter on Da Ponte, was Angelo Flavio Guidi's chapter, of doubtful value. Two years later Guidi enlarged his study and put out a fine book, which, however, dealt primarily with political relations between Italy and the United States.

The only writers who added a few names to what I had uncovered were Edoardo Marolla of Pence, Wis., who wrote three or four articles on Italian missionaries and one on General Ferrero in the magazine *Atlantica*, Bruno Roselli (two pamphlets on early Italians in New Orleans and Florida), and Branchi, who published some articles on the Italians in California in *Rassegna Commerciale*, the organ of the Italian Chamber of Commerce of San Francisco, Cal. of which he was then secretary. One of them appeared in the October, 1935, issue, not signed but I know that Branchi wrote it because he gave it to me. In 1956 Branchi wrote an article for the magazine *L'Universo*, the bimonthly organ of the *Istituto Geografico Militare* of Florence, Italy, for May-June. Branchi sent me a reprint with the annotation in ink on the first page "pagina 6" in which he quotes what I had said about Malaspina's expedition in my book, *The Italians in America Before the Civil War*. Coming from Branchi, that is one more proof that nobody had ever heard of Malaspina in the United States before I wrote a chapter about him. Branchi contributed two more articles (probably more) to *l'Universo* in 1955, one for March-April, "San Francisco Della Porta D'oro" (with illustrations and one map) and another for September- October, "Manhattan, Cuore di Nuova York," a description of the city, with no historical data. One will find the names of some obscure Italians in Pesaturo's books on the Italians in Rhode Island, in Schiro's book on the Italians in Utica, N. Y., and in Marraro's two or three articles on the Italians in New York and Philadelphia, mostly names already mentioned by me, as he follows in my footsteps and gives me credit in his article on the Italians in Philadelphia. Nothing of any importance. I think some interesting facts will be found in some unpublished thesis or dissertation, like the one on the Italians in California I read in manuscript form in the University of San Francisco, but I don't have the name at hand. The only other books is Rolle's *The Immigrant Upraised*, 1968, but with no names of any significance or worth quoting, except for those he found in my books, as noted in Appendix A of this volume.

To conclude, my books still remain the fundamental works of any historical importance on the early Italians in the United States, that is, *The Italians in Chicago, The Italians in Missouri,* my Civil War book, my study on Mazzei, my *Four Centuries,* and my two volumes of *Italian-American History.* The best proof that such is the case is attested in the little book *Negli Stati Uniti* by Luigi Villari, in the collection "Civiltà Italiana Nel Mondo" published in 1939 by the Dante Alighieri Society of Rome (20 small volumes). Villari was the highest Italian authority on the Italians in America, where he served for many years as a consul, at Philadelphia, New Orleans, and other cities. At the end of his small volume, Villari has a bibliography of 16 titles, including four articles of his, but at the very top of the list one will find, "G. Schiavo, *The Italians in America Before the Civil War,*" the only one that deals with early Italians in what is now the United States of America.

In recent years, I have gathered more material which I may publish in the near future, should I live that long. For instance, how is it that all the great researchers, including those of the Anti-Defamation League of B'nai B'rith, never heard of the Italian who founded a well-known city in Alaska?

I prefer not to dwell on Giuseppe Prezzolini's petty, envious and false remarks about my books (according to him no responsible review has called me a scholar) as I have already taken care of that in a long and well-documented reply in the Philadelphia weekly, *Il Popolo Italiano,* for March 20, 1963, also reported in *Stampa Italiana Nel Mondo,* of Rome, Italy, for March 26, 1963. I regret only that space limitations do not allow me to reprint the reviews and opinions of prominent men about other books of mine, such as that of Father Tacchi Venturi, the famous historian of the Catholic Church who called Volume II of my *Italian-American History* "opera egregia" or of the musicologist and head of the music department of the New York Public Library, C. S. Smith, who called Volume I of the same history "a monumental study." Or the opinion of Camillo Branchi of my study of Mazzei (the 1951 pamphlet, even though of 45 large pages). I suggest that Signor Prezzolini, who is still active at 94, writing as lucidly and as intelligently as when he was much younger (however, from his slanted, peevish, personal angle) consult or has some of his American friends send him a Xerox copy of the reviews of my 1934 book in *The Book Review Digest for 1935,* which he may have seen and preferred not to mention, still smarting from the colossal failure of the book, *Italy and the Italians in Washington Time* promoted and edited by him, followed by the raving reviews of my book a year later.

INDEX

ABOUT

GIOVANNI SCHIAVO is considered one of the pioneers of Italian American studies. He dedicated his life to highlighting Italian contributions to the United States of America. Schiavo has published numerous volumes on Italian American history including *Italian-American History: Volume I: Italian-American History* & *Volume II: The Italian Contribution to the Catholic Church in America*, *Four Centuries of Italian-American History*, *The Italians in America Before the Civil War*, *The Italians in America Before the Revolution*, *Antonio Meucci: Inventor of the Telephone*, *Italians in Missouri*, and *The Italians in Chicago*.

STEPHEN J. CERULLI is a Ph.D. candidate in modern history at Fordham University and a Lecturer at Hostos Community College, The City University of New York. He holds an M.A., in Liberal Studies with a concentration in American Studies, from the Graduate Center, CUNY, and a B.A., in History, from the University of Connecticut. He specializes in the history and culture of Italian America and is a researcher at the John D. Calandra Italian American Institute, Queens College, CUNY. He has been published in and invited to speak on: The Italian American Podcast, *La Voce di New York*, Grown Up Italian, *Ovunque Siamo*, and the Italian Enclaves Historical Society, on topics ranging from Italian American studies, Italian American identity, and Italian American history.

www.ingramcontent.com/pod-product-compliance
Lightning Source LLC
Chambersburg PA
CBHW031952010726
47493CB00007B/2176